The Move to COMMUNITY POLICING

NATIONAL UNIVERSITY
LIBRARY   SAN DIEGO

The Move to COMMUNITY POLICING

Making Change Happen

MERRY MORASH   EDITORS
Michigan State University **J. KEVIN FORD**
                          Michigan State University

Sage Publications
International Educational and Professional Publisher
Thousand Oaks ▪ London ▪ New Delhi

For information:

Sage Publications, Inc.
2455 Teller Road
Thousand Oaks, California 91320
E-mail: order@sagepub.com

Sage Publications Ltd.
6 Bonhill Street
London EC2A 4PU
United Kingdom

Sage Publications India Pvt. Ltd.
M-32 Market
Greater Kailash I
New Delhi 110 048 India

Printed in the United States of America

Library of Congress Cataloging-in-Publication Data

Main entry under title:
The move to community policing: Making change happen / editors, Merry Morash, J. Kevin Ford.
     p. cm.
Includes bibliographical references and index.
  ISBN 0-7619-2472-8 (cloth: alk. paper) — ISBN 0-7619-2473-6 (pbk.: alk. paper)
  1. Community policing. 2. Organizational change. 3. Police administration. 4. Police training. I. Morash, Merry, 1946- II. Ford, J. Kevin (John Kevin)
  HV7936.C83 M69 2002
  363.2'3—dc21   2001004075

01 02 03 04 05 10 9 8 7 6 5 4 3 2 1

Acquiring Editor:	Jerry Westby
Editorial Assistant:	Vonessa Vondera
Production Editor:	Diana E. Axelsen
Typesetter:	Marion Warren
Cover Designer:	Michelle Lee

Contents

PART II   Changing the Police Culture

PART III Creating Partnerships

PART IV *Dealing With Ongoing Challenges*

Preface

Since 1996, the Michigan State University (MSU) School of Criminal Justice has embarked on a plan to work intensely and over an extended time with police departments to address the complexities of making community-oriented policing a reality. The definition of community policing that has guided the work emphasizes that this form of policing involves customer-based organizational transformation, unlimited partnerships, and an information-based, unified effort to solve problems.

The work has been funded through a special grant from the Office of Community Oriented Policing Services (COPS) in the U.S. Department of Justice. The grants led to the creation of the Michigan Regional Community Policing Institute (RCPI), which has focused on organizational change to support community policing. These efforts have been organized around a creative mix of faculty from several academic disciplines and organizational change specialists who work at the School of Criminal Justice with police agencies. An explicit objective of the RCPI has been to field-test models for carrying out problem solving or action-oriented research to enable police departments to transform towards the goals of community-oriented policing. These research and direct assistance efforts have been defined broadly to include feedback to police and community regarding organizational context, organizational structure, and police-community relationships that might impede or support community-oriented policing.

The four years of support as an RCPI occurred in a statewide context that is unique because of the long history of the MSU School of Criminal Justice in working directly with police agencies to promote the adoption of what was initially known as *neighborhood foot patrol.* Beginning in 1982, Professor Robert Trojanowicz, with funding from the Mott Foundation, established the National Center for Community Policing. He assumed leadership of a decade-long project to promote neighborhood foot patrols and other progressive community-policing techniques. Police departments throughout the United States, and in some cases from other countries, were exposed to the concepts, the approach, and the models for implementation of this new form of policing. Numerous conferences, workshops, and training programs, along with extensive technical assistance—much of it provided through a telephone hot line or through site visits by Dr. Trojanowicz and others employed by the project—disseminated information. A series of publications provided detailed information and summarized various studies conducted as part of the Mott Foundation–supported program.

The seminal work that shaped Trojanowicz's ideas about neighborhood foot patrol was a study in Flint, Michigan. Flint, an industrial "auto city" in economic decline during the two decades before he undertook his research, faced numerous social problems, including high unemployment and correspondingly high crime rates. The emphasis on foot patrol was intended to get officers out of their patrol cars and walking in both residential and business areas so that they could communicate with and be held accountable by citizens, and so that they could engage in crime prevention and alleviating fear of crime. Over time, Michigan police agencies other than Flint were heavily represented among those with which Trojanowicz and his colleagues worked, and police in Michigan made up several of the cadre of speakers, trainers, and providers of technical assistance who worked on the Mott Foundation grant. Overlapping with the last years of the Mott Foundation grant, the MSU School of Criminal Justice embarked on a decade of growth in externally funded initiatives to provide outreach to criminal justice agencies and practitioners. Consistent with the MSU land grant mission, School of Criminal Justice faculty had been active in outreach, defined at the university as the application of research to design and implement initiatives, and the extension of education, training, and research into a myriad of settings outside of the university. At various points, between one and three personnel had been hired to provide training and technical assistance. However, between 1990 and 2000, the number of personnel involved in outreach grew substantially to include such programs as the Michigan Victim Assistance Academy (which provided a week of intensive training to people who work with crime victims), Internet-delivered master's degree programs with security management and international crime-control emphases, and the Michigan Training Center for DARE. (Drug Abuse Resistance Education) officers. It has also included the Michigan RCPI.

This book, then, is a culmination of years of efforts to facilitate the transformation of police agencies to community-oriented policing. Over time, the formal processes of assisting chiefs, sheriffs, and police agencies in general has led to the development of strategies for enhancing the move to community policing. The authors in this book have codified a number of these strategies for making change happen in police organizations. We believe that this book can be used in a number of undergraduate and graduate courses on contemporary issues in policing. Leadership academies and specialized educational programs for police should also find this selection of readings valuable for generating discussion and identifying lessons learned for making change happen in police organizations. More generally, police chiefs and other police leaders should find the emphasis on making change happen useful in their own attempt to transform their agency to a community-oriented policing philosophy. In each chapter, there are specific suggestions on how to implement the various aspects of community policing in a systematic way. The book has been developed to also inform research-oriented academics in the United States and internationally. Throughout the book, research needs in the area of transformational change and community policing are identified. Given that police and citizens throughout the world are struggling to reform or develop community-oriented approaches to policing, the exposure to research and examples in this book will, we hope, provide direction for exploring, planning, implementing, monitoring, and institutionalizing the move to community policing.

Acknowledgments

We want to acknowledge the support of the Office of Community Oriented Policing Services, U.S. Department of Justice, for our efforts to facilitate the organizational transformation of police agencies to the community-policing approach. We also want to acknowledge the efforts of the over 30 police agencies who have partnered with the Michigan RCPI over the last four years. We have learned much about the opportunities and the challenges of making change happen in police agencies from this partnership.

CHAPTER 1

Transforming Police Organizations

J. Kevin Ford
Merry Morash

*T*he movement toward community-oriented policing signals a major change in how police agencies operate. The overall philosophy of community policing focuses on a taking a customer-based approach to policing. This customer-based approach leads to the development of partnerships with the community to better meet community needs and thus enhance police effectiveness. Partnerships also include efforts to better integrate the internal functions of police organizations. Underlying the move to community-oriented policing is the recognition on the part of police agencies that they need continuously to learn about and improve their policing efforts. This requires that police agencies work with the community to develop and implement unified, information-based efforts to solve problems in the community rather than only to react to events or incidents.

Although much has been written about the overall philosophy and general principles of community policing, fewer efforts have been directed to understanding the transformational processes underlying this effort to change. This type of transformational change is a very complex, long-term process with many opportunities for improving the delivery of police services. The move to community policing can lead to greater citizen input to help identify priorities. The move to

teams with geographic responsibilities can lead to stronger bonds between officers, supervisors, and the larger community. The focus on
prevention activities can improve police standing in the community.
Officers and supervisory personnel can begin to feel empowered to take
more control of their activities and to be more of a helper than simply a
defender. This enhanced level of empowerment can lead to lower burn-
out and stress on the part of the officer.

There are also many threats posed when attempting to transform a
police agency that can inhibit the implementation of a community policing philosophy. Many police chiefs and sheriffs have fully embraced
the concept and the movement of community policing, but are not sure
how to explore and plan for a transformational change. In addition, the
implementation process is often fraught with problems and challenges.
For example, police at supervisory levels can be lukewarm to the
change. Unions can, at times, be opposed to changes desired by police
executives because it is not clear what the benefits are for the officers
themselves. Within the rank and file, "community police officers" can
be criticized for failing to do "real" police work and for being rewarded
with flexible schedules and overtime pay. The community itself is often not easy to partner with, in some cases because it has much divergence in opinions, and in other cases because the community is unor-
ganized or uninterested in a linkage to the local police department.
Community policing is easier to think about than actually implement.

STAGE MODEL OF CHANGE

Community policing involves a significant change as the organization
begins to adopt procedures consistent with the new approach to work.
We have found that the changes follow a series of definable stages. The
following model serves as a framework for defining the change process
and for helping police organizations navigate through what can be a tu-
multuous period. The model consists of six stages: exploration, commitment, planning, implementation, monitoring and revision, and
institutionalization (see Ford, Boles, Plamondon, & White, 1999).

Exploration and Commitment

Exploration is the first step of any change effort. It occurs as a result of need or curiosity, and requires that organizational leaders ac-

tively investigate alternative approaches to the current system. Within this stage are three subcomponents: interest, awareness, and a decision point. Interest is the motivation or drive that fuels the exploration effort. It is the first point at which a leader recognizes that alternatives are available and may be worth pursuing. Awareness is the point at which a leader is conscious of the various approaches available and has enough information to make an informed decision regarding the viability of various alternatives. A decision point concludes the exploration stage and requires the leader to weigh the available information. The individual must make a choice either to invest additional time and resources learning about the change process or to maintain the *status quo.*

In the commitment stage, the leader makes the decision to pursue change and presents the idea to the organization's management team. This group evaluates the costs and benefits of pursuing an alternative approach and then makes the decision on whether or not to proceed. Commitment typically involves preplanning, a secondary decision point, and developing a sense of urgency. Preplanning is a rigorous phase in which the management team gathers a comprehensive collection of information on the proposed change effort (i.e., community policing). Unlike in the exploration stage, this information gathering is intensive and is designed to be a thorough evaluation of all available information. The group then makes a formal decision on whether or not to commit to the change process. If the decision is to move forward, then the management team presents their ideas to the entire organization and begins to build momentum for the change effort. This momentum is what we refer to as a sense of urgency. The organization is given a basic description of the intended change and provided with a compelling reason or motivation for moving forward.

Planning and Implementation

Planning is an organization-wide effort to articulate clearly the goals of the change effort and to develop a strategy for achieving those objectives. It is important that all departments, units, or subdivisions are represented in this process. Typically, a guidance team is formed to help facilitate the change process. Planning involves identifying the vision and goals for the organization, developing indicators of success, designing action plans, and collecting baseline data. Identifying the vision and goals is the phase in which top management articulates the main purpose of the change effort. The vision should be a concise description of the future state of the organization. The goals should be difficult but achievable objectives tied to specific action plans and aligned with the organization's new vision. From these goals, the organization can then identify indicators of success. These indicators are the observable and quantifiable signs that will be used to evaluate the change effort. The next phase of planning involves the development of specific action plans for achieving organizational goals. This step is to ensure that transformational change is conducted in a systematic and methodical manner. Finally, the organization should collect baseline data. This process involves measuring the indicators of success prior to action plan implementation to provide a baseline for future evaluation.

The implementation stage is perhaps the most visible component of the change process, and it involves the implementation of action plans, an adjustment phase, and the reconcentration of effort. The initial step is to implement the action plans that have been developed. During this implementation process, it becomes clear that some efforts are more effective than others are. This feedback should be used to adjust action plans and refine implementation efforts. In addition, it is important for organizational leaders to concentrate efforts and maintain a sense of urgency despite setbacks and adjustments. Leaders need to invigorate organizational members, maintain positive morale, and continue to make the change effort a top priority.

Monitoring and Institutionalization

Monitoring and revising are formalized systems for evaluating the change effort and revisiting the planning stage of the change process. This stage is used to quantify progress, identify gaps, develop new action plans, and revise organizational goals. Progress is assessed by comparing the indicators of success with baseline measures and evaluating them in light of organizational goals. Gap analysis is a two-part process of identifying first where deficits exist between desired goals and the current state of the organization and then the root cause of those deficiencies. If gaps are caused by unrealistic expectations, future goals should be modified to be more attainable. However, if gaps are caused by a flawed action plan or by improper implementation, the *process* used to enact change should be revised. Depending upon the results of this analysis, action plans can be modified to better achieve lasting change, new goals can be established based on those plans, and new indicators of success can be identified.

Institutionalization is the final stage of the change process and occurs when the procedures, policies, and systems that emerged as a result of the change effort formally replace the old methods of performing. This stage involves system alignment, solidification of new behaviors, and a transfer of knowledge. Alignment occurs when the organizational structure (e.g., roles and responsibilities, accountability, and communication patterns), operating systems (e.g., budget and time allocation), and human resource systems (e.g., rewards, selection criteria, and training) are consistent with the vision for the change effort. Solidification occurs when old policies and practices are replaced with new systems and methods of operation and those new behaviors become standard procedure. Finally, change is institutionalized when new employees are trained in the organization's new approaches to work and knowledge is systematically transferred from incumbent employees to new employees.

The stage model of change highlights the intensive, long-term approach that must be taken to move an organization from the exploratory and planning stages to the institutionalization of community policing in the police agency. To proceed through these stages, police organizations must have a clear understanding of the specific elements that need to change relevant to how the police agency operates on a day-to-day basis. The combination of these key elements provides the building blocks for a change to community policing.

This book focuses on the experiences of a number of police leaders, researchers and practitioners who have been involved in community policing initiatives that have attempted to transform organizations. Thus, the focus of this book is on systemwide attempts at transformation rather than on viewing community policing as a special program within a larger organizational system. Based on direct experience and informed research, strategies to move police organizations toward the goals of community policing are identified and described. The notion of organizational change as the centerpiece of the move to community policing highlights the need to shape multiple facets of the police organization (e.g., vision, mission, supervisory practices, and reward systems) to support community policing and allow it to develop as a new form of policing. It also includes the *community* aspects of community policing, with efforts to create ongoing cooperative ties of police agencies and their personnel to selected aspects of community, including public schools, victim advocates and service providers, neighborhood associations, and businesses and corporations.

ORGANIZATION OF THE BOOK

This book is divided into four sections that frame the key issues or elements in this transformational process: (a) developing data-driven problem solving and decision systems, (b) changing the police culture, (c) creating effective partnerships, and (d) dealing with the ongoing challenges of community policing. Each section contains a number of chapters that provide strategies for addressing each area of concern. These strategies improve the chances that the transformation to community policing will be successful.

Developing Data-Driven Approaches

The first section focuses on attempts to develop more data-driven systems to help police organizations take a more customer-based approach. The move to community policing emphasizes the need to enhance the type, quantity, and quality of the data entering the police agency. This information can help the organization to develop priorities and to drive action to meet the needs of the community. In addition, a data-driven approach can help the organization monitor itself more closely to determine if the organization is meetings its goals and objectives with the change to community policing. In this way, police agencies can not only take a more customer-based approach, but can also develop systems for continuously learning and improving. The three chapters in this section show how internal and external survey and data-collection processes can aid in the move to community policing.

In "Using Assessment Tools to Jump-Start the Move to Community Policing" (Chapter 2), Cori Davis and J. Kevin Ford build on their experience in bringing a theoretical perspective and research tools from organizational psychology to the task of assisting police departments in the shift from traditional to community policing. They describe the use of techniques to generate data that can help to jump-start the move to community policing. Facilitated assessments and survey feedback approaches are described, and it is shown how the data from these techniques can be a catalyst for motivating organizations to improve overall performance. The chapter includes a case study of the application of these techniques in a police department.

For Chapter 3, "Citizen Input and Police Service," Michael D. Reisig describes the use of community surveys as a way of incorporating citizen input into the planning process of police organizations. In particular, he emphasizes the importance of moving beyond traditional survey practices and toward using community surveys in conjunction with other forms of information, such as the encounter-level survey, to focus, develop, and improve police strategies. Examples of how this new system can help produce positive changes in police practices are described.

In "Using Multiple Methods in Community Crime Prevention and Community-Policing Research" (Chapter 4), Andrew L. Giacomazzi and Edmund F. McGarrel describe a two-year evaluation of Project ROAR (Reclaiming Our Area Residences), a collaborative problem-solving program in Spokane, Washington, public housing. The approach shows how evaluation research can play a role as a key input into the shift toward community policing. They argue for the use of multiple methods to provide both process and outcome evaluation of community policing and other community crime-prevention programs. In addition, they show the benefits of a research design that combines qualitative methods (focus groups and observation), community surveys, available crime data, and a social and physical inventory of neighborhoods to monitor and improve the community-policing initiative.

Changing the Police Culture

The failure rate of most planned change efforts, including the move to community policing, is quite high (French and Bell, 1999). The most frequently cited reason for failure is the neglect of the organization's culture (Cameron & Quinn, 1999). This failure to focus attention on and to expend energy in changing the culture has often doomed the kinds of organizational changes that were planned, implemented, and monitored. Rather than institutionalizing a new approach to policing, many community policing efforts end with piecemeal changes that never live up to their potential for making transformational change happen. The three chapters in the section on changing police culture focus on the various levels within the organization that can affect the change effort to community policing—from officers and sergeants to the midlevel management and top management. Unless efforts are made to change the "way we do business around here" at all levels of the organization, efforts at community policing will not succeed.

Based on observations of police-citizen encounters in Richmond, Virginia, Stephen D. Mastrofski, James J. Willis, and Jeffrey B. Snipes

examine the gap between a police leadership's ideal for community policing and the reality of patrol officer behavior. Their chapter, "Styles of
Patrol in a Community-Policing Context" (Chapter 5), questions the
extent to which the ideals of community policing will result in diversity
in the structure of police organizations. They also emphasize the need
for the new structures to be linked with greater changes in the styles of
patrol officers and sergeants. The authors illustrate the need for action
research as an ongoing input into attempts at reforming policing.

Mark E. Alley, Elizabeth M. Bonello and Joseph A. Schafer contribute Chapter 6, "Dual Responsibilities: A Model for Immersing
Midlevel Managers in Community Policing." They begin with an explanation of the changing job responsibilities for lieutenants and captains that result from the move to community policing. Midlevel supervisors must still manage, but they also must provide leadership to
their subordinates around the change effort. A case example is provided
of how midlevel supervisors seek, obtain, and use information to carry
out their leadership role in problem solving and other aspects of supervision in a department engaged in community policing.

In Chapter 7, "Organizational Change and Development: Fundamental Principles, Core Dilemmas, and Leadership Challenges in the
Move Toward a Community Policing Strategy," J. Kevin Ford sets forth
the key aspects of organizational development and the implications for
transforming police departments. He points to the pitfalls of initiating
a change effort, as well as to the importance of decentralized control at
the earliest stage of transformation. Police leadership must confront
the dilemmas of transformation by taking specific steps to create a
sense of urgency for the change, a powerful guidance team, and opportunities for innovation over both the short and long run.

Creating Partnerships for Community Policing

Various stakeholders are influenced by and can influence the direction of the change to community policing. Some stakeholder groups,
such as police unions, are internal to the organization, whereas other
stakeholders, such as schools, are external to the police organization. A
key challenge in the move to community policing is how to create and
maintain effective partnerships among the stakeholder groups
throughout the change process. The four chapters in this section emphasize both different internal and external types of partnerships with
groups such as unions and schools and different strategies for enhancing the creation and maintenance of partnerships. A key element of

creating a successful partnership is to empower police personnel to work with various stakeholder groups in a different way than occurs with traditional policing practices.

The first chapter in this section, "Focus on Internal Partnerships," by Michael J. Polzin and Julie L. Brockman (Chapter 8), contends that a considerable amount of union resistance to community policing can be abated by a concerted effort to address both internal and external stakeholder needs in the move to community policing. They focus on the need to forge a strong union-management partnership that supports the development of community-oriented policing. Polzin and Brockman highlight the key issues in building and sustaining internal partnerships and provide recommendations for forging effective partnerships.

Merry Morash and Amanda L. Robinson provide an analysis of the points of congruence and incongruence between community policing and domestic violence advocacy in Chapter 9, "The Nexus of Community Policing and Domestic Violence." They describe the historical issues related to police response to such violence, and review efforts to develop a cooperative and effective nexus of community policing and domestic violence. They provide specific examples of community policing strategies to combat partner violence, and offer several recommendations to victim advocates, concerned citizens, and law enforcement officials for how to build a partnership that enables an improved response to partner violence.

In "Action Research for Community-Oriented Policing and Comprehensive School Safety Planning" (Chapter 10), Audrey Z. Martini and her colleagues report on differences in stakeholders' perceptions of the information, training, and technical assistance needed to ensure safety in public schools. This information was collected during county-level summits of stakeholders in improving school safety. The summits were organized by the Michigan Regional Community Policing Institute to provide an information base that police and communities can use to shape their partnerships and address school safety at a local level.

For Chapter 11, "Social Capital, Collective Action, and Community Policing," Mark E. Correia examines why community participation in the efforts to form a police-community partnership are typically low. He presents stories of success and failure, and identifies the differences between areas with high and low participation: In addition, he presents a model predicting collective action. For example, communities with strong informal social networks are better positioned to solve complex community problems without outside assistance. Strategies for enhancing participation are also presented.

Dealing With Ongoing Challenges in the Shift to Community Policing

Transformational change efforts, such as the move to community policing, require much planning early in the process and much nurturing during implementation. Despite careful planning and implementation strategies, most change efforts result in both intended and unintended consequences that must be dealt with in an effective way. Stakeholder groups look to how the police organization responds to these challenges as a key indicator of how serious the organization is in making the transformational change a reality. How well police organizations respond and adapt to these changing priorities, issues, and challenges will, therefore, have a major impact on how likely the change to community policing will become institutionalized in the organization. The three chapters in this section focus on the challenges and opportunities facing police organizations today and in the future as they undergo the change to community policing.

In Chapter 12, Joseph A. Schafer provides a detailed review of the literature on organizational and individual influences that present barriers to the shift toward community policing. In this chapter on "The Challenge of Effective Organizational Change: Lessons Learned in Community-Policing Implementation," Schafer presents the experiences of a midsize police department in confronting several of these barriers and identifies those that were most difficult to overcome. The implications of these findings for planning, implementing, monitoring, and institutionalizing community policing are highlighted.

David L. Carter's "Reflections on the Move to Community Policing" (Chapter 13) considers the areas that are often superficially addressed in the move to community policing. In addition, he revisits some milestones of policing practices that have tended to be forgotten along the way but that have important implications for the effective delivery of police services.

In the final chapter, Morash and Ford, with Jane P. White and Jerome G. Boles, synthesize the material covered in this book. In particular, "Directing the Future of Community Policing Initiatives" highlights the importance of action research in identifying key issues to address to help drive the process toward transformational change. The chapter revisits the conceptualization of community policing and describes common challenges in shifting to a community-policing model. They then identify a series of decision points that must be considered in any attempt to adopt a community-policing philosophy in order to guide future research and practice in this field.

REFERENCES

Cameron, K. S., & Quinn, R. E. (1999). *Diagnosing and changing organizational culture.* Reading MA: Addison-Wesley.

Ford, J. K., Boles, J. G., Plamondon, K. E., & White, J. P. (1999). Transformational leadership and community policing: A road map for change. *Police Chief,* 66(12), 14, 16,18–22.

French, W. L., & Bell, C. H. (1999). *Organizational development: Behavioral science interventions for organization improvement* (6th ed.). Upper Saddle River, NJ: Prentice Hall.

Part I

Developing Data-Driven Systems

CHAPTER 2

Using Assessment Tools to Jump-Start the Move to Community Policing

Cori A. Davis

J. Kevin Ford

*C*ommunity policing involves a significant change in the way a department operates. The change process follows a series of definable stages, from initial exploration to commitment, planning, and implementation, with the goal of institutionalizing the move to community policing (see Ford, Boles, Plamondon, & White, 1999). Exploration occurs when leaders actively investigate alternative approaches to policing. Commitment occurs when the leader and the management team make the decision to change and begin the process of presenting their ideas to the entire organization to build momentum for the change effort. Planning is the organization-wide effort to articulate the goals of the change effort and to develop a strategy for achieving those objectives. The implementation stage is the visible component of the change process, and involves the concentration of efforts to make the plan a reality. Monitoring and revising is a formalized system for evaluating the change effort, identifying gaps, and revising action plans and goals. Finally, institutionalization occurs when the procedures, policies, and systems that emerged as a result of the change effort formally replace the old methods or "way things were done around here."

15

This model highlights the intensive, long-term approach that leaders must take to move a police agency from an exploratory stage to the institutionalization of community policing. What we have observed is that many well-intentioned efforts to move to community policing can become bogged down during the transition from committing to the ideas of community policing as the appropriate strategy to the nuts and bolts of planning and implementing for the change process itself. In particular, we have seen many cases where the police chief and top management, who are shouldering the responsibility for change, make decisions without having done the research within their own department and community necessary to understand the issues that must be considered in the change effort. Often, this leads to a misunderstanding of what successful implementation should look like, which can lead to frustration and misdirected attempts to change.

This chapter highlights two data-gathering methods—facilitated assessments and community policing organizational surveys—that we have used to obtain information to jump-start the change effort and drive the planning and implementation process. The chapter begins with a discussion of methods for effective qualitative and quantitative data collection and feedback processes. The second part of the chapter describes the method of facilitated assessment and presents data from one police agency that conducted a facilitated assessment. The case example shows the value in using facilitated assessments to identify clearly the goals of the move to community policing and the barriers that need to be overcome or considered during the planning and implementation process. The third section discusses the use of a community-policing organizational survey to identify key areas to be addressed by the change effort. A case example of survey results from a police agency is presented to illustrate the types of issues that can be identified as concerns across officers, sergeants, and upper-level managers. The chapter concludes with a discussion of the benefits of combining qualitative and quantitative data-collection strategies and of how the data gathered from these techniques were used to jump-start the planning and decision-making process.

DATA GATHERING AS A PROCESS

Most police departments are quite familiar with collecting and using data on a daily basis. For instance, citizen complaints are examined and categorized so that strategies can be devised to address common concerns. Or, more formal neighborhood surveys are conducted to gather information and ideas from citizens to drive police actions and solve key problems. Police departments are also accustomed to reviewing crime data to understand what types of crimes occur most frequently in particular areas. Top managers often want data on police activities to evaluate officer performance. Because police agencies routinely collect data, formally or informally, it is surprising that change efforts often lack the collection of high-quality data to guide the strategic planning and implementation process.

A Data-Driven Model

The learning process for any change effort must begin with the collection of data. The information generated could include charting of police activities, results from attitude surveys, everyday perceptions, normative beliefs or assumptions, and countless other types of information. All of these types of data can lend insight into organizational operations, underlying processes, and future vision and goals. Data represent the point of departure in the learning process—the more focused and targeted the data, the more focused and targeted the learning.

However, data are not knowledge. Data must be interpreted. The interpretation of data leads to hypotheses and theories that might account for the patterns or trends observed. The data can also be used to drive a discussion of what the data "really" mean. When it is possible to make sense of the data, knowledge about organizational operations has been generated.

To achieve learning and effective change, the knowledge must be shared and a consensus must be reached among people across organizational levels (e.g., leaders, sergeants, officers, and civilians) and functions (e.g., detectives, patrol, and records) about the meaning of the data. Then, action is required if this collective power is to be tapped. Actions might include experiments or pilot tests, policy changes, redeployment of resources, or other tangible moves. These actions will then require new rounds of data collection, analysis, and interpretation to monitor and adapt to changing realities. Therefore, continuous learning and long-lasting change can be achieved through a never-ending cycle of action steps guided by knowledge and rooted in action.

Characteristics of Effective Data

To be effective, data-gathering strategies must be tied to a specific purpose. Defining the purpose with regard to community policing involves identifying what success will look like when community policing becomes institutionalized. It is critical that this occurs early in the change process, because the goals and direction for the change effort stem from the department's definition of success. This type of data can help drive the development of new vision and values for the police agency. It also provides benchmarks for planning and implementation on which teams can focus their efforts.

Also critical early in the planning and implementation process is to collect data from the individuals most affected by the change—that is, the police personnel. If collected early in the process, this type of data can uncover perceptions that indicate areas of support or possible barriers to be overcome when planning and implementing change. Methodologies for gathering the data needed to guide the change effort can be categorized into either qualitative or quantitative techniques (Neuman & Wiegand, 2000).

Strategies for Collecting
Qualitative Data

Qualitative data relevant to organizational change are typically gathered through open-ended responses or focus group discussion. The qualitative researcher analyzes the data gathered to identify themes, concepts or similar features (Neuman & Wiegand, 2000). These common themes can then be examined by organizational members for consensus building and action planning. Common examples of qualitative data are one-on-one interviews, small focus groups, and large groups consisting of multiple stakeholders. We focus on large groups, because we feel that they have two major advantages over interviews and small groups in a community policing effort. First, large groups allow for participation by a number of representatives from various areas. For instance, large groups can consist of various stakeholders including officers, sergeants, command staff, civilians, and community members. Second, getting all of these representatives in the same room can lead to discussions that might not occur in other settings (Homan & Devane, 1999). For instance, this might be an opportunity for officers to speak candidly about their opinions with command staff, whereas during a normal working day, the officer might not approach a command staff member with his or her concerns.

One challenge in facilitating large groups is keeping individuals on task while thinking creatively. Asking pointed questions for group members to answer or discuss can force everyone to think about an issue. However, questions should be specific enough to give direction about the types of responses desired, but not so specific as to stifle new ideas (see, for example, Schein, 1999). For instance, alternative questions pertaining to partnerships in community policing include the following:

1. What kind of partnerships should the department form?

2. Partnerships with which of the following agencies would be most beneficial for this department: schools, NAACP, or landlord associations?

3. What types of nonpolice partnerships should officers form in order to establish a working relationship with community members?

The first example is too vague to be productive. For instance, should the group members be focusing on whom to partner with, on what characteristics define a successful partnership, or on what partnerships they think community members would like to see? The second example restricts members to considering only the partnerships presented in the question. Finally, the third option is specific with regard to what types of partnerships should be considered and what purpose the partnerships should serve; however, it is not so specific as to restrict ideas about what non–police agencies should be considered.

Another method of encouraging a systematic approach to data gathering is force field analysis (French & Bell, 1999). Force field analysis involves evaluating the gap between how the department currently functions and how it wants to be functioning. Then, the driving and restraining forces surrounding change can be explored to determine what needs to be influenced to reduce the gap. The steps for conducting a force field analysis are as follows:

• Decide upon a problematic issue that needs improvement. Describe how the issue is currently addressed and why current methods of addressing the issue need to be changed.

• Describe what the desired state of things would look like. Where do you want to be?

- Identify the forces that are driving change toward the desired state of things and restraining change from happening.

- Examine which of these forces are strong and weak. Which forces are susceptible to influence and which are not? Which forces are under your control and which are not? What can be done to change the restraining forces into driving forces?

Asking pointed questions and force field analysis are both good methods for getting groups thinking about issues of interest. Both of these exercises are first done individually, with each person jotting down his or her thoughts on paper to share with the group later. Once everyone has had an opportunity to think about the questions, their thoughts need to be synthesized. One way of accumulating information from a large group is facilitating a brainstorming session. Brainstorming is a process for collecting ideas that follows a strict set of rules. These rules are intended to encourage everyone to offer ideas and build upon each other's thoughts without fear of evaluation (Scholtes, Joiner, & Streibel, 1996). The facilitator should record all of the members' ideas and comments where everyone can see them. If anonymity is preferred, a formalized version of brainstorming can be performed on paper. Individuals can record their ideas on small pieces of paper, and the facilitator can then combine and copy the ideas where everyone can see them.

After all of the ideas are recorded, they will need to be summarized and prioritized. Multivoting and the nominal group technique are two methods for prioritizing information. Multivoting should be used when voting on the most important or popular items, or when prioritizing items gathered from brainstorming sessions. The process for multivoting is as follows (Scholtes et al., 1996):

1. Assign a number to each item on the list.

2. Combine any items that the group agrees are very similar.

3. Renumber the items to account for combining items.

4. Have members choose items they would like to discuss or address. Members can either write the item numbers down on a sheet of paper, or they can place a mark on the board or flipchart next to the items. Allow each member multiple votes. One guideline is to give members the number of choices equal to at least one third of the total number of items on the list. For example, if the list had 30 items, then each member should be allotted at

least 10 votes. Members should be allowed to use multiple votes for single items. For instance, they can put all 10 of their votes on a single item if they believe it to be the only truly important item on the list.

5. Count the number of votes for each item. Either member can raise their hands as the item numbers are called out, or, if there is a desire for anonymity, the vote can be conducted by ballot. If members marked their choices, then count the number of marks next to each item.

6. Eliminate the items with the fewest votes.

7. Repeat the voting process until only a few items remain. If the group members have trouble narrowing the list down through voting, they should discuss which items should receive top priority.

Strategies for Collecting Quantitative Data

Qualitative methods provide a depth of information that is important for guiding a change effort. Quantitative data gathering lends itself to summarizing a large number of responses. Surveying, for instance, can integrate the experiences and perceptions of all employees or customers (Bowers & Franklin, 1972; Kraut & Saari, 1999). Quantitative data can become a useful tool when it is logically organized and fed back to the organization. Surveys, specifically, offer a systematic and objective means of collecting data that can be used to take deliberate steps to improve organizational effectiveness (Kraut, 1996). We discuss four steps to creating and using surveys: creating the framework, developing the items, distributing the survey, and reporting the results.

Creating the Framework. Creating a framework for a survey involves determining the purpose of the survey (Burke, Coruzzi, & Church, 1996). Organizational surveys traditionally include a similar set of topics, including the organization's leadership style and arrangement of supervisory positions, the rewards system (financial and nonfinancial), the sequence and flow of work, the frequency of interpersonal contact or cooperation, the physical work environment, and the barriers to communication (Dunham & Smith, 1979). Survey instruments may also assess personal and organizational goals, social and interpersonal interactions, supervisor and subordinate relationships, and technical and social demands of the job or organization. The most common types of satisfaction surveys deal with supervision, pay, working conditions, job pressure, and organizational commitment. These topics are important because they all have significant implications for the functioning of an organization. They are, in essence, leverage points. A small change in one of these components can have significant effects on other aspects of the organization. For example, exploring the impact of a new policy or procedure may require consideration of the effects that supervision and rewards have on the new policy.

Developing the Items. After the framework is determined, items need to be developed to elicit the answers sought. Item development requires consideration of what questions should be asked and what those items should look like. Focus groups or interviews can be conducted to ask individuals about organization-specific questions that are relevant to the desired framework (Jones & Bearley, 1995). After determining what questions need to be asked, it is important to consider the format of the questions. Survey questions should be straightforward and objectively worded. In addition, the amount of time individuals dedicate to filling out the survey will likely be short, so questions should be brief and to the point, and the total number of survey questions should be kept to a minimum. Vocabulary should be appropriate to the organization and should be readily understood by respondents. The response format should be very simple, clearly stated, and easily understandable. A common format for organizational surveys is a 1 to 5 or 1 to 7 (*strongly disagree* to *strongly agree*) Likert rating scale.

Distributing the Survey. After developing the items, decisions need to be made about when and whom to survey. There are no set rules or procedures as to when surveys should be distributed. Providing time at work to complete the survey and administering and collecting the surveys in groups increases the return rate, and can lessen the chance that surveys will be forgotten or lost. The administration procedures should also take into account the purpose of the survey, the sensitivity of the information being collected, and the norms of the organization. If the information is particularly sensitive, it may be advisable to have a neutral individual (e.g., an external person or fellow employee) administer and collect the information to ensure confidentiality. The issue of who is surveyed also needs to be considered. Some researchers recommend a canvassing approach, in which a subset of personnel is surveyed (Dunham & Smith, 1979). It is often advisable, particularly when survey research is conducted as part of an organizational change effort, to obtain the perceptions of all employees (Kraut & Saari, 1999).

Reporting the Results. The importance of the feedback component of the organizational survey is probably the most underestimated part of the survey process (Hinrichs, 1996). Often, organizations or researchers will conduct surveys, but pay little or no attention to how the information collected will be fed back to the organization. The power of the survey data however, is in providing information relevant to crucial components of an organization. The information is useless if it is not disseminated; but, if shared, it can serve as a catalyst for motivating employees and facilitating change (Jones & Bearley, 1995). By obtaining input from all customers or employees and presenting the objective results back to the organization, everyone has an opportunity to identify the key problem areas to be targeted for change.

The importance of an effective feedback component has been demonstrated. Cohen and Turney (1978), for example, conducted a study investigating the effects of information penetration, the extent to which survey feedback reached frontline personnel, on an organizational change effort with the U.S. Army. Due to the hierarchical nature of the military, Cohen and Turney were concerned that feedback would not reach frontline personnel, who were the individuals most affected by the information. To combat this potential problem, they took extra steps to ensure that all levels of the organization were included in the feedback and problem-solving process. Specifically, they held feedback meetings with upper management as well as with frontline employees to ensure that the information penetrated throughout the entire organization and that all personnel were involved in the process. Results indicated a positive change in soldier perceptions and performance following the change effort. Cohen and Turney concluded that organizational programs that involve all relevant personnel in survey feedback, participative problem solving, and job enrichment techniques result in positive outcomes for the employees and organization. This interlocking approach of cascading feedback from top to lower levels in the organization has been found to be a powerful tool for creating and supporting change within an organization in a number of field studies (French & Bell, 1999). The bottom line is that the greater the level of involvement of all members of the organization, the greater the resulting change.

In sum, both qualitative and quantitative data-collection strategies are important components for aiding the move to community policing. Clearly, there is a need for high-quality information to guide the planning and implementation process, particularly in the beginning when no one is sure what direction to take. Specifically, tools are needed to identify the goals of the move to community policing, assess the current status of community policing as it is being implemented in the department, and explore ways in which community policing might evolve in the coming years to better meet the unique needs of the community. We talk next about two tools that can be used to jump-start community-policing efforts that are lagging or stagnant, or just getting started. Those tools are facilitated assessments and community-policing organizational surveys.

FACILITATED ASSESSMENT

A facilitated assessment is a qualitative method to identify critical issues in a change effort. It is a process by which a trained facilitator leads a diverse group of individuals (both within and outside the organization) with interest in policing to discuss the move to community policing (White & Bloss, 1997). Facilitated assessments can help to orient department members about the philosophy of community policing, as well as to get their opinions about organizational drivers and restraining forces surrounding change. The final goal of the facilitated assessment is to form a preliminary action plan to guide the planning and implementation process. Assessment sessions can last anywhere from two to three hours, and can vary in depth depending on each department's level of prior familiarization with and attempts at implementation of community policing ideals.

The following is an example of how a facilitated assessment was conducted in a medium-size police department (Boles, 1999b). Elements of community policing, such as dedicated community-policing officers, were already in place in the department. A new police chief and his top staff had explored community policing, and were committed to the transformation of their total organization to it. During the assessment, members of this department wanted to focus on ways in which community policing might evolve in the coming years to better meet the unique needs of the community. The facilitated assessment consisted of (a) an open discussion of issues, (b) a more structured self-assessment of the organizational goals and driving and restraining forces, and (c) the development of a preliminary action plan.

Open Discussion

The session included 14 department members: the chief, the deputy chief, two lieutenants, four sergeants, five officers, and one nonsworn employee. The session began with an open-ended discussion of the three core issues of community policing, with a facilitator first providing an overview of those elements: a customer-based organizational transformation, multiple community partnerships, and a unified, data-driven problem-solving approach.

During this part of the discussion, participants were asked to talk about how each element had been developed in the department and how each might be modified to make community policing more effective in the department. Because of the informal format, participants were encouraged to contribute their opinions and to be honest in their evaluations. The facilitator stressed that, to learn from what has gone in the past and improve in it for the future, everyone should get their thoughts on the table. Many positive and negative comments were made concerning each of the core issues. Examples for each of the three areas are presented below.

Customer-Based Approach to Organizational Change. The discussion highlighted a number of things happening in the department to transform it to a more customer-focused organization. Most of the comments focused on newly defined roles and responsibilities. For example, there were attempts made to change the way decisions were made in the department so that responsibility was transferred down the ranks to sergeants and officers. Sergeants and officers expressed that they had been given more autonomy to develop and implement their own ideas for problem solving. Some commented that sergeants were better able to develop their own employees knowing that they had administrative support in implementing their own ideas. However, others expressed the difficulty in understanding how to use this new opportunity.

Most agreed that two opposing orientations to police work existed in the department. There were officers and sergeants (many of them younger and newer to the department) who were receptive to taking more ownership of community needs and problems. However, there were many who were more comfortable with the traditional "numbers" orientation to evaluating success. This resulted in a struggle for some officers, who felt pressured to be responsive to community needs *and* to produce numbers. Many believed that a change in the evaluation process would help foster appropriate accountability. For instance, if supervisors were encouraged to reduce the pressure to produce numbers when they know that significant community activities are taking place, officers would feel supported for engaging in community-policing activities. The new approach to evaluation being offered was an interactive discussion between the supervisors and officers, as opposed to the typical rating forms. The evaluation discussions were expected to result in specific goals for each officer, including community-policing activities.

Another topic brought to the surface involved increased officer involvement with neighborhood associations. It was mentioned that officers had initiated the development of several new associations, which had not historically been done. However, some patrol officers responded to this shift with resentment, seeing neighborhood involvement as a low priority, especially when they are already experiencing stressful call loads.

Last, it was discussed that communication would be critical at all levels. There were sentiments that some would use community policing to accomplish its intended goals, but that others would use it as a crutch. Similarly, it was stated that a shift toward a customer-based approach should not be intended to eliminate traditional law enforcement roles. Communication, therefore, should avoid promoting community policing as an either/or proposition.

Multiple Community Partnerships. With regard to community partnerships, participants indicated that noteworthy partnerships were developed with schools and some neighborhood groups. Officers were frequently present in schools and involved in many school-related programs. In addition, the chief had worked to establish positive relationships with critical groups, like the NAACP and the Human Relations Commission. The group also agreed that collaborative relationships with other law enforcement agencies were very positive.

Data-Driven Problem Solving. The department was exploring the use of geographic information systems that would display data graphically. It was believed that this technology could help both officers and community members identify emerging trends and affect problem-solving strategies. Technological advances were also expected to help officers on 12-hour shifts communicate more efficiently across shifts and work units—something that had been a significant problem in the past. Conversations about this new reliance on data and technology led to the conclusion that the relationship between the records division and patrol officers would become more meaningful. Whereas it was once primarily the community officers who used records for problem-solving analysis, soon other officers would need to do so.

The group mentioned one impediment to problem solving: The community often wanted an immediate response rather than a thoughtful, deliberative one. The department members recognized that short-term responses often did little to affect root causes, but instead moved the problem from one place to another. Members determined that a realization by the community of the value of long-term strategies for improving conditions in a lasting way was needed.

Structured Self-Assessment

Based on the above responses during the open discussion, the facilitator then lead the group through a structured self-assessment exercise. Essentially, the exercise focused on three questions:

- Victory: If you are successful, how will things be different two years from now?

- Driving Forces: What will help you get there?

- Obstacles: What may stand in your way?

Victory. Participants were individually asked to identify the indicators that would demonstrate that the move to community policing was successful. Then, through a formal brainstorming technique, each individual was asked to provide one indicator of success or what a victory would look like in two years. Each individual in the group provided at least one idea.

The brainstorming session led to a large number of suggestions of what a victory would look like. These suggestions can then become drivers of the planning and implementation process. If the department is successful in the transformation to community policing, the group said that the following things should occur:

- A majority of the citizens will know the names of the officers assigned to their area.

- Citizens will actively identify and prioritize problems, and work with officers to resolve them.

- The entire department will feel that community-policing approaches contribute to solving problems.

- All section officers will have a neighborhood watch group of their own.

- Officers will routinely take time to pull up timely data and use it in problem solving.

- Citizens will have access to crime information in the neighborhoods.

- A standardized, accurate evaluation process will be in place that lets officers know how they are doing in relation to personal and departmental goals. This process will enable the individual officers to take responsibility for their success in the department by recognizing what needs to happen and making changes.

- Every employee will be able to identify two or three community partnerships that are important to successful police work.

- Community policing will be integrated into the entire department, which will be indicated by the elimination of the need for special inducements to get officers to participate in community-policing activities.

- Internally, the current culture of mild resistance to community policing will be gone.

Driving Forces/Assets. The facilitator noted that each organization brings to a change effort things that will likely aid in the accomplishment of the victory. The following things were mentioned as organizational drivers:

- Infusion of new employees.

- The youth of the department.

- More and more people countering "subterfuge."

- A generally favorable political horizon.

- The right fit: People want to be community-policing officers because they believe in it.

- A good foundation for community policing.

- The community's acceptance of and support for community policing.

- The department working to maintain that support.

- An individualized approach: recognizing that each neighborhood/area has different needs.

- Education and information are available.

- The collection and distribution of information.

Obstacles. The facilitator also noted that each organization comes to a change effort with barriers that were likely to hinder accomplishment of the victory. These barriers have to be acknowledged and addressed during the planning and implementation process for the change effort to have a chance to succeed. In fact, the key issue for planning is how to change a possible barrier into a driver for change. In this group, the following obstacles were identified:

- Decreased resources as the economy worsens.

- "Subterfuge" within the department.

- The political process.

- Some of the neighborhoods most in need are also the most transient. Just when a relationship is established, people move.

- A "do it for us" attitude in some neighborhoods.

- Obtaining partnerships with agencies.

- A lack of new ideas to reach a new level of implementation.

- A lack of education and information.

- The high cost of systems to collect and disseminate information.

Developing an Action Plan

For the final step, participants were asked to identify the important things that need to be done to achieve the victory as defined. This part of the facilitation tied together the issues of victory, assets, and obstacles. This information was collected on poster board, and was placed around the room so all members could review the lists. They were then asked, "Considering the assets and obstacles, what do you as a department need to do to achieve the victory?" An informal brainstorming discussion ensued, followed by attempts to categorize the information into manageable pieces to drive action. Responses for this department were grouped into eight clusters:

- Establish a planning process that clearly defines the goals and outcomes sought and engages a broader stakeholder base both internally and externally.
- Stabilize the effort to broaden community policing approaches by ensuring adequate political and financial support.
- Establish and maintain clear communication mechanisms within the department and in the community at large.
- Improve internal education processes to optimize opportunities to orient officers to the practical value of community policing principles.
- Ensure the recruitment of diverse, highly motivated individuals with a personal commitment to community-policing approaches.
- Reinforce the department's commitment to community-policing principles in employee evaluation procedures.
- Improve the capacity and performance of problem-solving efforts within the department.
- Build trust in the community through expanding partnerships, both internally and externally.

The group was finally asked to identify the catalytic steps of this process (the steps that, if accomplished, would most help bring the others along), and the group rated four of the eight items (the first four listed above) as being equally important. A framework for an action plan was built for each of the four catalytic steps. For example, Table 2.1 shows the framework for the first goal of clearly defining the objectives and outcomes sought in the change effort. The framework specifies the components of each objective, and provides space to record who is responsible for working toward the goal and the expected timeframe for accomplishing it.

TABLE 2.1 Framework for Catalytic Goal 1

Catalytic Goal 1: Establish a planning process that clearly defines the goals and outcomes sought and engages a broader stakeholder base both internally and externally.

Like many departments, this one struggles with the need for both a top-down mandate and a broad buy-in from all levels of the organization and all parts of the community. The participants in this discussion validated both needs and concurred that it is appropriate for the administration to articulate a clear vision of the desired model for broadening community policing approaches, so long as there is a long-term effort to gather internal and external customers in validating and refining the plan for implementation. The vision, goals, and outcomes need early articulation so that there are criteria for measuring success from the outset

Action/Strategy	Who	When
Formulate a clear vision of the desired model of implementation, including goals and desired outcomes. Set tentative timeline from planning and implementation.	Administration	
Identify and recruit internal and external stakeholders to participate in plan validation and refinement. This may be done as two separate processes for one combined effort.		
Convene planning groups through introductory sessions on the vision. Charge internal/external planning groups with plan development tasks. The authority of participants to develop/revise the plan and to oversee implementation should be clearly defined at the outset.		
Develop implementation plan clearly within the organization and to the community at large.	Planning groups	
Communicate the plan clearly within the organization and to the community at large.		
Transition all or some of planning participants to an oversight/implementation function, bringing on new stakeholders as viable and necessary.		
Evaluate success against initial criteria on a regular basis.		

SOURCE: *Report on Departmental Planning Session: June 23, 1999*, by J. G. Boles, 1999, Lansing, MI: Michigan State University, School of Criminal Justice, Regional Community Policing Institute. Permission to reproduce this table is granted by the Michigan Regional Community Policing Institute, Michigan State University, East Lansing, MI 48824.

COMMUNITY-POLICING ORGANIZATIONAL SURVEY

Initial involvement with police agencies interested in moving to community policing showed that there were few attempts to gather data systematically from the people—the police personnel—most directly affected by the change to community policing. Discussions with leaders often revealed that chiefs had some vague notions that most people were supportive of the idea of community policing, with some fears that there were pockets of resistance. When probed, it became clear to us that those perceptions by leaders were based on informal discussions and observations, rather than any systematic attempt to understand officer perceptions.

Based on that realization, a community-policing organizational survey was developed to focus on officer perceptions of key issues relevant to the move to community-oriented policing (Plamondon & Ford, 1999). The development of the survey, began with a theoretical framework that identified the various systems that might influence or be affected by the move to community policing. The survey focuses on three areas. One group of items focuses on systems that may support or hinder the implementation of community-oriented policing (assets and liabilities). These systems include the strategic direction of the department, management and supervisory support, resource allocation, and material support. Another group of items focuses on existing processes likely to affect the move to community policing, such as forming police partnerships with other agencies, engaging in problem-solving activities, and empowering department personnel to enact change (actions). The final group of items focuses on key organizational and individual outcomes relevant to the move to community-oriented policing. These items focus on such issues as perceptions of the overall community orientation of the department and individual perceptions of the commitment to the concept of community policing, as well as on the frequency of community-policing activities.

As a result of this framework, a survey featuring 119 questions across 20 different dimensions was developed. The dimensions and sample items from the survey are provided in Table 2.2 (Plamondon & Ford, 1999). Key demographic information was also collected to allow for comparison across different groups of respondents. This survey can be useful in three ways. First, because the move to community policing can generate both positive and negative responses on the part of police officers, it is important to capture these perceptions early in the change

TABLE 2.2 Organizational Survey Dimensions and Sample Items

Dimension	Example Items
Strategic Direction	The department has a clearly defined set of expectations for officers participating in community policing.
Top Management	Top management displays a commitment to community-policing ideals.
Managing Change	The department takes steps to remove barriers which prohibit implementing effective community policing activities.
Union	Union objectives and goals are consistent with the objectives and goals of community policing.
Rewards	Community-oriented activities are reflected in performance appraisals.
First-line supervision	Supervisors are willing to adapt their supervisory style in response to changes resulting from the move to community policing.
Support mechanisms	The department has reallocated resources (e.g. overtime, financial resources) to implement community policing.
Partnerships	Officers in this department regularly form partnerships with other non-police agencies (social services, housing, etc.) in the course of performing community-policing activities.
Problem-solving	Officers take preventative actions by focusing on conditions or root causes that lead to crime or affect citizens' quality of life.
Empowerment	First line officers are provided with sufficient autonomy to implement problem-solving strategies.
Climate for community policing	Police personnel within the department accept community-oriented policing as a valid strategy of policing.
Risk-taking and innovation	Officers take calculated risks when engaged in problem-solving activities.
Community ownership	Officers demonstrate a sense of ownership over the communities to which they are assigned.
Community orientation	Officers actively seek input from members of the community regarding neighborhood problems.
Commitment to community policing	I am committed to the idea of community-oriented policing.
Effectiveness	The department effectively maintains law and order within the community.
Role clarity	I prefer to have clearly defined goals and objectives for my job.

(Continued)

TABLE 2.2 Continued

Dimension	Example Items
Views of the department	I talk up this department to my friends as a great department to work for.
Views of the community	The typical community member is sincerely concerned about the problems of others.
Job satisfaction	All things considered, I am satisfied with my job.

SOURCE: *Organizational Assessment Instrument: Development, Implementation, and Findings*, by K. E. Plamondon and J. K. Ford, 1999, Lansing, MI: Michigan State University, School of Criminal Justice, Regional Community Policing Institute. Permission to reproduce this table is granted by the Michigan Regional Community Policing Institute, Michigan State University, East Lansing, MI 48824.

process. The results of the survey can be examined to uncover areas of concern that must be considered when developing and implementing community-oriented policing initiatives. Second, the survey of officer perceptions provides a baseline measure of the key issues and concerns regarding the implementation of community policing. The baseline data allow for an assessment of changes over time. Finally, the survey results can be analyzed for differences in perceptions between officers, sergeants, and management. Disseminating these results to the entire department can open a dialogue between management and officers regarding the move to community policing. Thus, responses can lead to a problem-solving approach between officers and management as the strategic planning and implementation processes are pursued.

Survey Results: A Case Example

For the department we have been discussing, all members of the department completed the survey. The survey results were generally positive in tone. Officers indicated a strong commitment to the department and to community policing. However, they also indicated a need for clearer strategic direction, better management of the change effort, and a removal of system barriers, such as union incompatibilities and resource constraints. Although most employees expressed support for community policing, many did not feel that the department facilitated community-oriented activities. Many cited insufficient personnel and training to implement community policing as the main indicators of the department's lack of support. In addition, most reported that community-policing activities were not rewarded. The survey results also indicated that despite being committed to community policing, officers were engaging in very few community-policing activities. Officers had little involvement in youth programs, rarely participated in problem-solving activities, and had few partnerships with other government agencies. Despite these issues, officers indicated being satisfied with their jobs and perceived the department as being effective in fighting crime.

Additional analyses were performed to compare the ratings between officers and sergeants across the 20 dimensions (see Figure 2.1). Interestingly, it was found that officers had more positive responses on many of the organizational survey dimensions than did sergeants. For instance, officers expressed having much higher job satisfaction, organizational commitment, and commitment to community policing. However, officers did have slightly more negative responses than sergeants did with regard to the use of partnerships (see Plamondon, 1999).

Organizational Survey Feedback Process

The feedback process should be a time for learning and development. For data to be useful, they must be interpreted. For learning and interpretation to occur, it is imperative that the survey researcher or survey feedback facilitator educate members of the organization to provide them with the skills needed to understand and interpret the survey results in an accurate and meaningful way.

Members of this department participated in a facilitated discussion regarding the results of the organizational survey. The group consisted of a representative sample of officers, sergeants, management, and support staff. The primary purpose of this session was to validate and clarify the data contained in the survey to turn it into information that could be used in the department's community-policing initiatives. The session also provided direct feedback to department members regarding the results of the survey. Finally, participants were encouraged to communicate the survey results to their coworkers throughout the department as consistent with the participatory nature of the survey process (Boles, 1999a).

Participants were randomly placed into small work groups and assigned specific categories of the survey. The task for the groups was to review the assigned categories and develop two statements that summarized the data reflected in each. Participants were also encouraged to discuss why responses may have been recorded on a given item. The

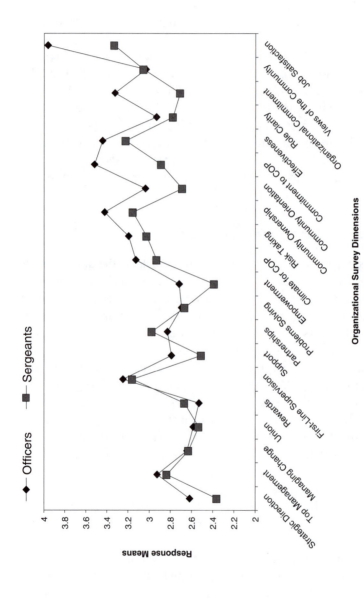

FIGURE 2.1. Organizational Survey Results by Rank. Reprinted from *Organizational Survey Feedback Report*, by K. E. Plamondon, 1999, Lansing, MI: Michigan State University, School of Criminal Justice, Regional Community Policing Institute. Permission to reproduce this figure is granted by the Michigan Regional Community Policing Institute, Michigan State University, East Lansing, MI 48824.

work groups took approximately 30 minutes to complete this assignment. Members from each work group then presented their results to the entire group for review and comment. Participants were encouraged to share any insights they had concerning given dimensions or responses.

Overall, the work groups verified that the majority of the data within the organizational survey was an accurate reflection of the perceptions, attitudes, and behaviors of the department personnel. In addition, the session participants expanded upon many of the results. Until such a feedback process is offered, it is often difficult to appreciate the magnitude of the information revealed from an assessment tool such as an organizational survey. Even in cases where the information is negative or less than prescriptive, the simple act of providing the survey results to department members often symbolizes significant movement and commitment on the part of the administration. Sharing information and gaining employee input advances the continual process of enhancing community policing within a department.

IMPLICATIONS FOR PLANNING AND IMPLEMENTING A CHANGE EFFORT

Benefits of Using Both Assessment Tools

As our case example revealed, some common themes emerged from both the facilitated assessment and community-policing organizational survey. Issues such as the lack of recognition for performing community-policing activities and the lack of sufficient community policing training were common themes. However, each data-collection technique also revealed unique information.

The facilitated assessment uncovered such issues as communication problems and the possible benefits of a youthful workforce. Such topics were not assessed in the survey. This highlights the importance of using qualitative methods to tap into subject matter that more quantitatively oriented methods might miss. In addition, the facilitated assessment was aimed not only at answering specific questions, but also at exploring solutions for the issues discussed. For instance, this department discussed the specific types of partnerships and technologies needed to accomplish their goals. This group even went one step further and developed a preliminary action plan to address some of the department's weak areas.

Just as the facilitated assessment offered unique information, so the community-policing organizational survey also served to provide distinct contributions. First, the organizational survey measures responses to topics that failed to emerge during the facilitated assessment. For instance, sensitive issues such as top-management support were rated quite low on the survey, but were not raised during the brainstorming sessions of the facilitated assessment. It could be that individuals are more comfortable sharing that type of feedback in an anonymous setting, or perhaps the individuals who participated in the facilitated assessment were not aware that others in the department had these negative perceptions.

The survey also provided an objective measure of the relative importance of issues. For instance, it was brought up on multiple occasions during the facilitated assessment that there was some resistance to community policing by the officers. Officer attitudes were thought to be an important factor to focus on. However, the survey indicated that most officers agreed with the community-policing philosophy and were committed to community policing. In addition, the survey results showed that a subset of sergeants had a more negative reaction to the concept of community policing. Rather than officer resistance, the findings point to the need to target sergeants as a key lever for making the change effort succeed.

The discrepancy between survey and facilitated assessment data also showed how survey results can be used to discover the root causes of surface-level problems. Participants in the facilitated assessment mentioned that new officers were resentful of having to perform community-policing activities. Perhaps more telling, however, were the low response means on the items assessing officer perceptions of direction and guidance in performing community-policing activities. It may be that officers do not like performing community-policing activities because they have no guidance for doing so, not because they necessarily dislike these activities. Without the inclusion of the survey data, it would have seemed reasonable to focus attention on changing officer attitudes. However, based on the survey data, it might be more productive to focus on defining processes and guidelines around performing community-policing activities.

Finally, the survey provided an assessment of the differences in response levels between ranks. As discussed, sergeants expressed more negative views with regard to many of the survey dimensions. This information was invaluable to this particular organization, because they determined that more attention should be directed toward gaining buy-in from the supervisors.

In sum, no one instrument can capture all of the important nuances within a department. However, qualitative and quantitative data-collection techniques can complement each other, and, if used early in the process, can provide information to drive effective decision making.

Impact of Assessment Tool Data

The facilitated-assessment and organizational-survey processes can provide police agencies with high-quality data to drive decision making that is often lacking when starting a change effort or when trying to keep the momentum going. The facilitated assessment helped the department considered in our case study to begin examining the major issues and concerns surrounding the community-policing initiative. Combined with the quantitative data from the organizational-survey process, the organization was poised to enter the planning and implementation phases with goals in mind and areas to work on identified.

The first thing the department did as a result of this survey was to revisit the organizational vision and values. Department members made them consistent with the goals of community policing. Next, the department established a guidance committee to plan the change effort. Many of the committee members were people involved in the facilitated assessment. Their charge was to define more clearly the goals and outcomes sought, and engage a broader stakeholder base both internally and externally. This team later divided into three subcommittees to examine moving to geographic teams, establishing a unified problem-solving approach within the department, and developing partnerships that were more effective.

The chief also began focusing on the top management team to make sure that everyone was on board and that everyone was working to remove existing barriers to community policing. This involved changing supervisors' traditional roles with regard to delegation and empowerment in order to free up more energy for removing barriers to change. The chief, himself, also made an effort to remove resource barriers by stepping up efforts aimed at broadening political and financial support for change to include city council, business, and neighborhood partners.

Internal systems, such as performance appraisals, promotion, and policies, were also modified as a result of the facilitated assessment and survey data. The department redesigned the performance appraisal system to reinforce commitment to community-policing principles, and began placing heavy emphasis on support for and actions consistent with community policing in promotions. Multiple members of the department were also involved in reducing the rules and procedure manual to be consistent with the new organizational values.

Next Steps

The case example has shown the advantages of collecting data at the beginning of a change effort in order to jump-start the planning and implementation phases of change. However, by no means does the data-gathering process end there. Once a department has direction about how to plan and subsequently implement change interventions, the effectiveness of these interventions must be monitored and plans revised.

Monitoring the effectiveness of change involves the same data-collection techniques we have outlined in this chapter. Using the same data-collection methods throughout the change process can help to maintain the consistency in the types of data being collected, and can help to ensure the continuity of feedback to the organization. Continuous improvement dictates that improvement be measured and plans be revised based on progress and new goals. It is hoped that, as some changes are institutionalized, needed changes in other systems will become apparent and the data-collection and feedback processes will begin again.

Collecting data at the beginning of the change effort can provide the department with valuable baseline data to which future data can be compared. For instance, resurveying one year later would inform the department about its rate and degree of progress. We have worked with some departments who have resurveyed using the same survey instrument both times. Collecting subsequent data has always resulted in learning for these departments, particularly when followed by a reassessment of where the department is and where they want to be. More often than not, monitoring change allows department members to see and celebrate their progress in the areas where they have devoted effort, as well as to revise their goals to reach an even better place.

In sum, basing decisions on data diminishes the risk of initiating unnecessary change efforts or of targeting issues that are irrelevant to effective organizational performance. Data obtained through qualitative and quantitative methods can provide a wealth of information on topics that are critical to the success of the organization. For this data to be useful and have an impact, however, employees must have access to it and it must be presented in an unbiased manner to drive problem analysis and problem solving relevant to the data gathered. Over the years, this process has been found to be a very effective way of guiding and sustaining organizational development (French & Bell, 1999).

REFERENCES

Boles, J. G. (1999a). *Organizational survey summary feedback report: August 13, 1999.* Lansing, MI: Michigan State University, School of Criminal Justice, Regional Community Policing Institute.

Boles, J. G. (1999b). *Report on departmental planning session: June 23, 1999.* Lansing, MI: Michigan State University, School of Criminal Justice, Regional Community Policing Institute.

Bowers, D. G., & Franklin, J. L. (1972). Survey-guided development: Using human resources measurement in organizational change. *Journal of Contemporary Business, 1*(3), 43–55.

Burke, W., Coruzzi, C., & Church, A. (1996). The organizational survey as an intervention for change. In A. Kraut (Ed.), *Organizational surveys* (pp. 41–66). San Francisco: Jossey-Bass.

Cohen, S., & Turney, J. R. (1978). Intervening at the bottom: Organizational development with enlisted personnel in an army work-setting. *Personnel Psychology, 31,* 715–730.

Dunham, R. B., & Smith, F. J. (Eds.). (1979). *Organizational surveys: An internal assessment of organizational health.* Glenview, IL: Scott, Foresman.

Ford, J. K., Boles, J. G., Plamondon, K. E., & White, J. P. (1999). Transformational leadership and community policing: A road map for change. *Police Chief, 66*(12), 14, 16, 18û22.

French, W. L., & Bell, C. H. (1999). *Organizational development: Behavioral science interventions for organization improvement* (6th ed.). Upper Saddle River, NJ: Prentice Hall.

Hinrichs, J. R. (1996). Feedback, action planning, and follow-through. In A. Kraut (Ed.), *Organizational surveys* (pp. 255–279). San Francisco: Jossey-Bass.

Homan, P., & Devane, T. (1999). *The change handbook.* San Francisco: Berrett Koehler.

Jones, J. E., & Bearley, W. L. (1995). *Surveying employees: A practical guidebook.* Amherst, MA: HRD Press.

Kraut, A. (1996). An overview of organizational surveys. In A. Kraut (Ed.), *Organizational surveys* (pp. 1–14). San Francisco: Jossey-Bass.

Kraut, A., & Saari, L. (1999). Organizational surveys: Coming of age for a new era. In A. Kraut & A. Korman (Eds.), *Evolving practices in human resource management* (pp. 302–327). San Francisco: Jossey-Bass.

Neuman, W. L., & Wiegand, B. (2000). *Criminal justice research methods.* Boston: Allyn & Bacon.

Plamondon, K. E. (1999). *Organizational survey feedback report.* Lansing, MI: Michigan State University, School of Criminal Justice, Regional Community Policing Institute.

Plamondon, K. E., & Ford, J. K. (1999). *Organizational assessment instrument: Development, implementation, and findings.* Lansing, MI: Michigan State University, School of Criminal Justice, Regional Community Policing Institute.

Schein, E. (1999). *Process consultation revisited.* Reading, MA: Addison-Wesley.

Scholtes, P. R., Joiner, B. L., & Streibel, B. J. (1996). *The team handbook* (2nd ed.). Madison, WI: Joiner.

White, J. P., & Bloss, D. (1997). *Facilitated self-assessment of community policing.* Lansing, MI: Michigan State University, School of Criminal Justice, Regional Community Policing Institute.

CHAPTER 3

Citizen Input and Police Service
Moving Beyond the "Feel Good" Community Survey

Michael D. Reisig

At the dawn of the 20th century, it was common for citizens to provide input into the policing process. Officers would regularly talk to local residents about neighborhood problems (e.g., panhandling and drunkenness) as they walked the beat (Wilson & Kelling, 1982). Widespread accusations of corruption, political favoritism, selective enforcement, and administrative inefficiency soon brought about change in the policing process. Over time, police work evolved from informally dealing with order maintenance problems to fighting crime. The reform movement also brought with it new technologies (e.g., automobiles and communications equipment), as well

AUTHOR'S NOTE: This project was supported by grant #97-CK-WX-0010 from the Office of Community Oriented Policing Services, U.S. Department of Justice. The opinions, findings and conclusions or recommendations expressed in this document are those of the author, and do not necessarily represent the official position of the U.S. Department of Justice.

The author would like to express his gratitude to the many police professionals with whom he has worked in recent years, including Harold Barr, Jerry Boles, Tilman Crutchfield, Julie Liebler, Michael Madden, Chris Magnus, Steve Persons, and Ralph Soffredine.

as efficiency-oriented managerial practices (Leonard, 1951; Smith, 1940; Wilson, 1950). Despite efforts to improve police services by reducing crime and increasing efficiency, an unforeseen problem emerged: police-citizen communication began to break down, and police organizations became increasingly alienated from their communities (Reiss, 1992).

The movement to professionalize the police and the subsequent communication barriers resulted in a disconnect between the police and citizens in several communities across the United States. This state of affairs has had serious ramifications. Organization scholars have noted for some time that reliable feedback is necessary for the maintenance of processes that produce preferred outcomes (Katz & Kahn, 1966; Thompson, 1967). Despite their unique role in a democratic society, police organizations are no exception. Such breakdowns in communication have been blamed for the overemphasis placed on reactive policing strategies aimed at combating crime. Evidence suggests that the public is concerned not so much with crime, but rather with quality-of-life issues, such as neighborhood disorder. Contemporary police executives view crime differently from their predecessors. The prevailing view, which is commonly referred to as the "broken windows" thesis, posits that if minor public nuisances (e.g., public intoxication and graffiti) are left unchecked, the likelihood of predatory crimes increases, because would-be criminals assume that residents and governmental agencies are indifferent to neighborhood conditions (Wilson & Kelling, 1982). As a result, police officials have renewed their interest in working with citizens to identify and address local problems in the hopes of preventing more crimes of a serious nature.

The evolution of police departments from bureaucratic, efficiency-oriented, crime-fighting organizations to decentralized agencies focused on order maintenance and collaborative problem-solving activities has also brought about a renewed interest in citizen feedback. The contemporary approach commonly referred to as *community policing* entails much more than just acquiring citizen input (see Cordner, 1999; Mastrofski, 1993; Skogan & Hartnett, 1997; Trojanowicz & Bucqueroux, 1990); nevertheless, feedback regarding police services, neighborhood problems, and related issues remains a salient component.

Police executives actively involved in implementing community-policing initiatives have adopted numerous mechanisms to acquire citizen input. One common approach is the community survey, which entails the systematic collection of public attitudes, opinions, and perceptions regarding the police and quality of life, as well as self-reports of criminal victimization. Critics caution, however, that police officials sometimes rely too heavily on "soft measures" of police service to show that tax dollars are hard at work (Bayley, 1994). Police reformers take issue with such practices, and are quick to point out that research has consistently shown that a vast majority of citizens in communities across the United States are satisfied with the police (Bureau of Justice Statistics, 1999; Shaw, Shapiro, Lock, & Jacobs, 1998). Accordingly, reformers warn that results from community surveys should not be used as a mandate for the *status quo*, because these surveys provide little (if any) useful information pertaining to specific police practices (Mastrofski, 1981; Skogan, 1975; White & Menke, 1982).

This chapter highlights the usefulness of survey research as one way for police officials to collect meaningful citizen input. Doing so, however, requires that police personnel move beyond their reliance on traditional community surveys. Because surveys administered to general populations, which assess citizen satisfaction with the police in general terms, reveal widespread public support, critics commonly refer to this practice as "feel good" survey research. This chapter encourages current and future police executives to use community surveys in conjunction with other forms of information, such as encounter-level surveys, to improve, develop, and focus policing strategies. Given the widespread interest expressed by police executives and skepticism noted by critics, the chapter begins by focusing on a frequently used "soft" measure of police performance—citizen satisfaction with police services. After reviewing the relevant literature, an integrative strategy for collecting community feedback that provides straightforward, useful information to improve police services rendered during citizen encounters is outlined.

CITIZEN SATISFACTION AS FEEDBACK IN THE POLICE CONTEXT

A mountain of research exploring the dynamics of citizen satisfaction with police has been conducted over the past 30 years. Most of this work shows that a majority of people residing in cities and towns around the country express positive sentiments toward the police. Nevertheless, differences do exist. To help police professionals understand and address variation in public opinion, criminal justice researchers have continued to focus attention on citizen attitudes toward police.

Police Encounters and
Citizen Satisfaction

Early citizen satisfaction research was driven by the premise that public evaluations of police were a product of prior police encounters. Studies falling under the heading of the "experience with police" model focused on the type of police encounter and citizen expectations of police service in specific situations (Reisig & Parks, 2000). Results from these studies revealed that individuals who were subjected to aggressive police patrols frequently expressed negative opinions about the police. Additionally, crime victims also reported having felt "very angry" when officers failed to meet their service expectations, such as perform an investigation (Bordua & Tifft, 1971; see also Furstenberg & Wellford, 1973). Despite these findings, an important question lingered regarding how attitudes among citizens who have come into contact with the police differ from those who have not.

To make meaningful comparisons, such as between victims and nonvictims, researchers began to sample citizens who had and had not encountered the police. Using community survey data, researchers found that victims did not always express comments of a more negative nature about the police when compared with nonvictims. Victims who reported less satisfaction with the way police handled their situation, however, usually evaluated the police in less favorable terms than victims who were more satisfied (Smith & Hawkins, 1973; see also Brandl, Frank, Worden, & Bynum, 1994; Parks, 1976). These findings suggest, then, that the service police provide during encounters with crime victims influences satisfaction with the encounter.

In sum, early research governed by the experience-with-police model found that type of contact (e.g., voluntary vs. involuntary) was, to some extent, associated with citizen assessments of police performance. More important, however, was the finding that whether citizen expectations of police service were met or not influenced encounter-level satisfaction (i.e., citizen evaluation of a specific police contact). Although relatively straightforward, the usefulness of these findings in terms of police policy remained questionable. For example, should police departments stop initiating contact because it lowers citizen satisfaction? Also, fulfilling service expectations is contingent upon knowing what citizens expect in the first place.

Quality of Life
and Citizen Satisfaction

With the growing influence of community-policing reforms, the focus of police attitudinal research has changed in recent years. For example, many community-policing activities promote the building of collaborative relationships between the police and citizens. Community-policing advocates argue that these partnerships can be effective in identifying neighborhood problems and working toward finding solutions. Given this emphasis, researchers have become increasingly interested in the association between citizen quality of life and satisfaction with police.

The quality-of-life model posits that perceptions of neighborhood conditions (e.g., crime, social disorder, and physical decay) are associated with citizen satisfaction. For example, citizens who perceive neighborhood incivilities to be problematic will express sentiments that are significantly more negative about the police. Implicit here is the assumption that residents hold the police accountable, at least partially, for the quality of life in their neighborhood. The quality-of-life model posits also that citizens believe their neighbors share responsibility with the police for neighborhood conditions, and should help maintain neighborhood order and reduce crime (e.g., via formal police-citizen partnerships and informal neighborhood friendship networks; Reisig & Parks, 2000, pp. 610–611). To date, published research in this area is limited.

Studies using community survey data have found evidence in support of the quality-of-life model. For example, Cao, Frank, and Cullen (1996) reported that citizens who perceived higher levels of neighborhood disorder also expressed less confidence in the police. Additionally, these authors found that citizens who believed their neighbors were willing to assist in providing protection from crime also reported higher levels of confidence in police. Similarly, Reisig and Giacomazzi (1998) found that higher levels of fear of crime and perceptions of neighborhood crime were inversely associated with evaluations of the police. In combination, these two studies support the quality-of-life model's primary hypothesis: Citizens who rate the current state of their neighborhood in positive terms will also express higher levels of approval for their local police department.

The policy prescriptions that can be derived from quality-of-life research seem reasonable: Police would be well advised to implement community-policing initiatives that promote police-citizen partnerships focusing on ridding neighborhoods of crime and disorder. Of course, this conclusion rests on the assumption that citizen evaluations of local conditions are fairly consistent within neighborhood boundaries; unfortunately, there is evidence to suggest otherwise.

Taylor (1997) found that a significant proportion of variation observed in subjective quality-of-life indicators, such as fear of crime, was due to individual differences and measurement error (p. 68). In other words, widespread disagreement exists among area residents as to the condition of their neighborhood. A recent study using data from the Project on Policing Neighborhoods confirmed Taylor's (1997) findings. In particular, Reisig and Parks (2000) report that quality-of-life assessments among citizens living in the same neighborhoods differ considerably. Ironically, Reisig and Parks found that the most important determinant of overall satisfaction with the police was perceived neighborhood quality of life. The authors note that these findings pose a dilemma for police executives: Should agencies invest valuable resources to improve neighborhood conditions deemed problematic by area residents when citizens from the same neighborhood disagree on what problems actually exist?

Reisig and Parks's (2000) work also revealed that citizen satisfaction with specific types of police encounters (i.e., calls for service and traffic stops), which was the focus of earlier satisfaction police research, was an important component of satisfaction with the police in general. In particular, whether citizens were satisfied with calls for service and traffic stops influenced whether they were satisfied with the police in general. When compared to the results regarding quality of life, these findings may have more practical value. Can police officials more easily address the quality of police-citizen encounters by modifying official departmental procedures and training curriculums that shape officer behavior on the streets? To do so, as noted earlier, officials must develop a firm understanding of what citizens expect from police in different situations.

Reviving Encounter-Level Satisfaction Research

Recently published research suggests that a revival of encounter-level satisfaction research is under way. To better understand citizen expectations of police services, researchers have looked to the field of consumer psychology, where the link between expectation fulfillment and customer satisfaction has been explored in depth.

Research in consumer psychology suggests that customer satisfaction is determined through a four-stage process. First, consumers develop expectations regarding a service. Second, individuals assess services and, third, compare their assessments against expectations. Finally, customers judge whether the services rendered were better than, worse than, or equal to their original expectations. If services were better than expected, then levels of satisfaction with services will be higher when compared with consumers who felt that services did not measure up to their expectations (Oliver, 1980).

Is there a link between expectation fulfillment and citizen satisfaction with police service? Working closely with police managers, Reisig and Chandek (2001) identified several task-oriented behaviors that citizens might expect from officers during police encounters. It should be noted, too, that the department in question also expected their officers to perform each of the tasks that were identified. The authors' study focused on two types of police-citizen encounters: victims of breaking and entering and traffic stops. Task-oriented behaviors were not defined in terms of officer demeanor (e.g., courteousness), but rather referred to service-related tasks (both verbal behavior and physical activity) that the officer provided during the encounter. For example, an officer might offer a breaking-and-entering complainant advice on how to prevent future break-ins. Or, during a traffic stop, an officer may inform the driver how to go about taking care of the ticket. Reisig and Chandek hypothesized that as the disparity between citizen expectations and actual police service increase, levels of encounter-level satisfaction would decrease.

Results from their analysis demonstrated quite clearly that citizens who were the recipients of police service that measured up to or exceeded their expectations were significantly more satisfied regardless of whether the encounter was voluntary, as in calls for service, or involuntary, as with traffic stops (Reisig & Chandek, 2001, p. 94). When coupled with other research findings (see, for example, Chandek & Porter, 1998), it appears as though police behavior can significantly influence citizen satisfaction. It should be noted that the term "police behavior" is much broader than the task-oriented definition discussed above. Guided by past research, Reisig and Chandek (2001) also hypothesized that officer demeanor was associated with encounter-level satisfaction. Their findings indicated that demeanor-oriented police behavior was in fact a significant determinant of encounter-level satisfaction, as well as of global satisfaction (i.e., citizen satisfaction with the police department in general) in both samples (p. 93).

To sum up, recently conducted encounter-level citizen satisfaction research reaffirms what many observers have believed for some time: police behavior matters. What are the policy implications? First, it seems fairly straightforward that officers should behave in an out-wardly polite manner during citizen encounters. Second, police train-ing programs should not only focus on protecting officer safety, legal is-sues, and the like, but also train officers to identify, appreciate, and meet citizen service expectations.

Although social scientists often use multivariate models for testing hypotheses, practitioners frequently view such exercises as ivory tower techniques that provide little in terms of practical value. Admittedly, there is some truth to this view. However, extant satisfaction-based re-search does provide a firm empirical base for developing a mechanism whereby citizen input can be acquired to help guide organizational change.

AN INTEGRATIVE STRATEGY FOR
ACQUIRING CITIZEN INPUT

Despite the critics' claims, community surveys *can* provide useful in-formation to police professionals. In addition to periodically taking the community's pulse regarding general approval of the police, commu-nity surveys can also help direct initiatives to improve the quality of specific types of police-citizen encounters. Doing so, however, requires a more enlightened view of survey research in the policing context: a view that moves beyond the either-or dichotomy (i.e., community survey vs. encounter-level research), and incorporates both research strategies to form a two-stage, integrated mechanism for acquiring meaningful citizen input. Perhaps this point is best made by way of a hypothetical example.

The Middletown Police Department:
A Hypothetical Case

The Middletown Police Department (MPD) is a progressive agency that has actively implemented community-policing initiatives over a 10-year period. Their successes include the establishment of three storefront substations, the defining of patrol sectors in a manner con-sistent with existing neighborhood boundaries, the designation of community police officers assigned to specific neighborhoods, the im-plementation of neighborhood crime-prevention programs, and foot patrols in the downtown business district. The implementation of these initiatives was not always easy. Like police executives elsewhere,

MPD officials have had to overcome numerous obstacles, including political opposition, officer resistance, and budgetary constraints, to name just a few. Nevertheless, the overall mood among MPD personnel was that these changes brought about various positive outcomes, such as a reduction in public order complaints and a sense that citizen-police communication improved in recent years. Being a proactive department, however, MPD was far from complacent, and was interested in exploring additional ways that police service could be improved. To help them in their pursuit of quality police service, MPD executives and city officials determined that the time had come to conduct a community survey.

The results from the community survey revealed, not surprisingly, that a majority (62%) of Middletown citizens were generally satisfied with the MPD. Aware of the fact that community surveys most often reveal a fair level of support for police, MPD personnel looked beyond the approval rating for information that might help them improve police services. The survey also revealed that a majority of victims who reported a crime to the police were not satisfied with the way the police handled the situation. MPD's chief was troubled by this finding. Because she was aware that research shows that general satisfaction with police and encounter-level satisfaction are inextricably linked, she convinced her staff that efforts to improve encounter-level satisfaction among crime victims may result in increased levels of overall satisfaction.

Given limited available resources to address the issue, MPD officials determined that they should focus on the most prevalent type of crime in Middletown. The survey showed that the majority of victimizations involved vandalism. This information surprised few at MPD given that Middletown experienced very little in the way of violent crime, and official records and police perceptions confirmed that vandalism was most problematic. Next, MPD's supervisory staff studied the results concerning victims of vandalism, and found that these victims expressed low levels of encounter-level satisfaction. In other words, a significant proportion of victims of vandalism reported that they were not satisfied with how the police handled their situation. Given these results, MPD's staff concluded that these encounters appeared to be a good place to begin.

MPD next assembled a project team consisting of police officials from various ranks and a few "informed citizens" (i.e., citizens who reported to be less than satisfied with the way officers handled their vandalism complaint were contacted and encouraged to participate). Justification for creating a multirank team went well beyond "inclusion for the sake of inclusion," and helped to ensure that the project would benefit from individuals with different sources of knowledge and perspectives. For example, upper-level police managers at MPD possessed a strong appreciation for the organization's resources, the political environment, and where to find needed information (e.g., a list of potential citizen participants). Lower-level MPD supervisors had a strong sense of what officers should be doing on the beat, and patrol officers provided firsthand knowledge about police-citizen encounters. The inclusion of informed citizens was deemed useful given that these individuals could relate their experiences and interpretations of their encounters. MPD officials assumed that they might not fully understand what citizens expect from their officers. After forming the team, the job of identifying a set of task-oriented behaviors that the department and citizens both expect from officers during encounters with victims of vandalism began. Once complete, the team turned its attention toward formatting the survey. Guided by previous encounter-level research, the team decided that the survey should first present task-oriented behaviors and ask victims whether they "expected the officer" to act accordingly. Later in the survey, these items were presented again, but this time participants were asked whether the officers "actually performed these services." The format for survey items is provided in Figure 3.1.

Before locating a list of potential respondents, the research team addressed one of the primary concerns with this type of research—human recollection. Because the team planned to ask people to remember what police officers actually did during the encounter, they decided to focus their attention on residents who had been victimized in the previous three months. MPD's official records indicated that 156 citizens filed a vandalism complaint over this period. The project team determined that it had the means available to survey all of these victims. Before distributing the survey, the team sent out a notification card via the U.S. Postal Service to inform victims of the study. Unfortunately, 15 of the addresses were bad. In other words, these residents had moved or the information was invalid. Accordingly, the research team's list of potential respondents was reduced to 141 Middletown residents. Within two weeks following the mailing of the notification card, the first wave of surveys was mailed. Resident participation was quite high: Nearly 47% of those surveyed returned a useable survey. To achieve their predetermined goal of a 65% response rate, the research team decided that two additional waves should be administered. After completing three waves, the final response rate was 74%, or 104 citizens.

SECTION ONE:
In this section, we would like to ask you some questions about how you expected the officer to handle your vandalism complaint. Please check one response for each of the following items.

Did you expect the officer to arrive on the scene in a reasonable amount of time?	__Yes	__No
Did you expect the officer to attempt to locate witnesses?	__Yes	__No
Did you expect the officer to search for and collect evidence?	__Yes	__No
Did you expect the officer to give advice on how to prevent future vandalism?	__Yes	__No
Did you expect the officer to contact you after the initial report was taken to inform you of the status of your case?	__Yes	__No

SECTION THREE:
Now we would like to ask you some questions about how the officer actually handled your vandalism complaint. Please check one response for each of the following items.

Did the officer arrive on the scene in a reasonable amount of time?	__Yes	__No
Did the officer attempt to locate witnesses?	__Yes	__No
Did the officer search for and collect evidence?	__Yes	__No
Did the officer to give advice on how to prevent future vandalism?	__Yes	__No
Did the officer contact you after the initial report was taken to inform you of the status of your case?	__Yes	__No

FIGURE 3.1. Survey Item Format

The results from the survey (see Table 3.1) provided some good news for the MPD. Specifically, MPD officials judged that their officers were doing a more than adequate job arriving at the scene in a reasonable amount of time and attempting to locate witnesses. These judgments were made given existing organizational resources. For example, MPD supervisors reasoned that vandalism complaints are sometimes given lower priority out of necessity. Additionally, although officers are required to knock on the doors of neighboring houses when taking a report of vandalism complaint, officers are sometimes called away and cannot invest the time necessary to talk to potential witnesses. In short, the MPD was satisfied with these findings. MPD officials found the disparity between citizens' expectations of officers to collect evidence and the percentage that actually do so somewhat troubling. First, they were surprised that so few citizens actually expected such action

TABLE 3.1 Expectations and Actual Service Comparisons

Survey Items	Expected	Actual	Difference (+/–)
Arrive on the scene in a reasonable amount of time	85%	82%	–3%
Attempt to locate witnesses	63%	58%	–5%
Search for and collect evidence	50%	41%	–9%
Give advice on how to prevent future vandalism	79%	52%	–27%
Contact you after the initial report was taken to inform you of the status of your case	93%	41%	–52%

on behalf of the officer. That said, the leadership staff was most troubled because their officers are required to photograph damage to property and include at least one photograph with the report. They believed that this practice had clearly fallen below acceptable levels. Although this matter was discussed previously among the supervisory staff, MPD officials now believed the issue should be addressed with the officers. Simply put, noncompliance with this MPD policy would no longer be tolerated.

Perhaps most disturbing to the MPD management staff were the data pertaining to advising citizens about future victimization and follow-up contacts. First, a department-wide effort to establish and participate in neighborhood crime-prevention programs had been in place for several years prior to the survey. Officials believed strongly that officers should encourage victims of all sorts of crimes to join the crime-prevention program in their neighborhood. Doing so, they reasoned, was pertinent advice on how to prevent future crimes. After further analysis, however, MPD decision makers came to realize that many of the victims who reported that officers did not provide advice resided in neighborhoods where such programs were not in place. This piece of information led MPD officials to conclude that perhaps the time had come to consider developing crime-prevention programs in neighborhoods previously deemed less in need.

The results pertaining to follow-up contact were quite shocking. In previous meetings, the supervisory staff had considered making it departmental policy that officers make a good faith effort to follow up with all crime victims, even if only to say the case was still open. MPD officials were under the impression that most citizens did not expect officers to follow up on cases dealing with less serious crimes. The results from the survey changed their minds on the issue. Shortly after discussing the results, MPD's supervisory staff began the process of implementing procedures requiring officers to inform past victims of their case's status (either by telephone, mail, or in person). In the broad scheme of things, this change in policy was relatively minor. Nevertheless, MPD officials strongly believed that this minor adjustment would contribute significantly to levels of encounter-level satisfaction among victims of vandalism.

After the project was completed, the MPD planned to move on to other types of encounters, such as traffic stops, and repeat the process described here. In five years, they plan to conduct another community survey. If the minor alterations in departmental procedures take hold (and all else being equal), then they expect the 62% overall satisfaction figure to be higher.

CONCLUSION

This chapter has attempted to bridge the gap between criminal justice research and policing practices. In so doing, empirical findings were used to develop a coherent strategy for collecting citizen input to identify and help direct needed change in policing processes to produce preferred organizational outcomes—that is, to produce quality police service. The model focuses on encounter-level satisfaction that research indicates police executives have the most control over. In other words, although it remains relatively unknown the extent to which police can address quality-of-life issues (e.g., fear of crime) in a manner that will improve citizen satisfaction with the police in general, research suggests that meeting (or even exceeding) citizen expectations of police service will increase encounter-level satisfaction. Further, because research has shown that encounter-level satisfaction is linked to more general assessments of the police (Brandl et al., 1994; Reisig & Correia, 1997; Reisig & Parks, 2000), improving encounter-level satisfaction among citizens may also have a significant effect on general satisfaction. It is important to note that the strategy outlined in the hypothetical example is not static. Hence, police executives in search of a quick-change tool should shop elsewhere. The integrated model is best viewed as cyclical in nature. It requires a continued commitment among organizational members to ensure success. Whether meeting or exceeding expectations in specific situations will improve overall assessments of police agencies, however, is really a secondary concern. The salient issue should be whether changes result in service that is more responsive (see Mastrofski, 1999, p. 2). If the integrated model helps to produce this outcome, then individual applications can be judged a success.

It would seem shortsighted to conclude this chapter without noting a few of the technical details associated with conducting survey research that can greatly affect the quality of the data collected. Police agencies interested in using the integrated model should pay special attention to sampling, item construction, instrument design, and distribution (see Weisel, 1999). Survey researchers use numerous tricks of the trade to help ensure data quality. For example, Dillman (1978) recommends that first-class mail always be used. Reasons for doing so, according to Dillman, include the "image of importance it creates" (pp. 175–176). Delivering mail surveys using bulk rate not only lowers the perception of importance, but may also significantly delay the distribution of the survey to potential respondents. Fowler (1993) suggests that survey instruments begin by presenting "easy, straightforward questions that help 'get the respondent into' the survey" (p. 99). Survey items requiring more thought or dealing with more sensitive matters should be placed toward the middle or end of the instrument. Beyond these suggestions, empirical research shows that surveys with university sponsorship, prior notification, stamped returned postage, and artful presentation, on average, increase the percentage of the sample who return the survey (Fox, Crask, & Kim, 1988; also see Peak, 1990). Because these and other technical details can significantly influence the quality of the data, police officials interested in using survey research methods to collate citizen input need to pay careful attention to the technical details associated with conducting survey research.

Despite the value of survey research, limitations exist. For example, projects involving survey research may not be appropriate for departments experiencing budgetary cutbacks. Under such conditions, police executives may opt for a less costly mechanism for acquiring citizen feedback. Focus groups made up of informed citizens are one potential alternative (see Morgan, 1988; Stewart & Shamdasani, 1990). Using the case highlighted in the hypothetical example, police supervisors may have opted, instead of using an encounter-level survey, to conduct a series of focus groups whereby participants were asked questions similar to those presented in the survey, such as, "What did you expect the officer to do during the encounter?" or "Did the officer meet your service expectations?" Although focus groups are often less expensive, the technique usually fails to provide information that can be generalized to a larger population. Nevertheless, police officials may make the trade-off in the interest of improving police service when faced with budgetary limitations.

Police professionals often express reservations about carrying out surveys, because of the fear that the results will cast their efforts in a negative light. These concerns have increased in recent years as pressures to make results from surveys available to the public have also increased. Perhaps these self-protective fears can be eased somewhat by the following reminders. First, as mentioned previously, an overwhelming majority of community surveys conducted in communities across the United States show that most citizens are generally satisfied with their local police. Second, encounter-level surveys, which are designed to identify areas where police services can be improved, also frequently provide at least some good news. For example, MPD officials found that many citizens felt as though officers arrived on the scene in an appropriate amount of time and that officers did a good job attempting to locate witnesses. The supervisory staff was concerned with these two aspects of responding to vandalism complaints because of the less serious nature of these crimes and limited organizational resources. Information from the survey that indicated room for improvement did not focus solely on one group of MPD personnel. For example, the supervisory staff found that many of their officers were bucking the existing policy to collect evidence. Although it was found that citizens did not expect this from officers, supervisors believed that reemphasizing adherence to this policy would result in officers exceeding citizen expectations and improving encounter-level satisfaction. Also, MPD officials discovered that their assessment that some neighborhoods may not benefit from crime-prevention programs might have been misguided. The results from the survey prompted supervisors to reconsider their earlier conclusion. In sum, then, fears about the integrated survey strategy outlined here should be conditioned by the fact that a majority of citizens are quite satisfied with police service in general, and that the information generated from encounter-level research usually pertains to personnel throughout the chain of command. Facing up to areas of improvement does take initiative and an element of bravery, but the positive outcomes associated with doing so (i.e., improving police service) should provide the necessary impetus.

The notion that survey research can provide reliable citizen input to police organizations is far from new. In fact, three decades ago, Bordua and Tifft (1971) strongly encouraged police supervisors to regularly survey clients and use the information during the planning process (p. 181). However, cynicism among reformers concerning the utility of "feel good" community surveys has increased markedly in recent years. Earlier reviews of the published research in this area concluded that general assessments of police "do not tell administrators what actions to take in the face of low ratings from the population they serve" (Skogan, 1975, p. 58). Others have even suggested scrapping the collection of general citizens' assessments of police service altogether. For example, based on data pertaining to the distribution of citizen roles during police encounters and loosely knit theory of police demeanor, Mastrofski (1981) proclaimed,

> Survey research which focuses on the clients' perceptions and evaluations of specific encounters can provide more comprehensive, accurate, and interpretable data about the quality of police performance in these encounters than can survey research that asks citizens to render evaluations of all past encounters or impressions of entire programs or routine operations. (p. 399)

Two decades after Mastrofski's declaration, the empirical evidence appears, at least in part, to support his contention. In light of the above discussion, however, one is left with the impression that Mastrofski and others too hastily discarded the use of community surveys to evaluate police in general terms. As the integrated strategy presented above demonstrates, community surveys that include a variety of survey items, including citizen reports of police encounters, can help direct encounter-level research.

The driving theme of this chapter is that survey research can provide meaningful mechanisms for collecting citizen input to guide organizational change with regard to service delivery. Undoubtedly, a handful of ambitious reformers will balk at the integrative strategy outlined here because it is driven by a "evolutionary" change model—incremental change directed at processes to produce preferred outcomes. Ambitious change advocates in the world of policing, in comparative terms, appear less patient, and actively promote a more rapid change agenda (i.e., the "revolutionary" change model) whereby police leaders radically restructure their organizations' framework (i.e., move toward decentralization) and seek to initiate, to use Frederick Taylor's (1996) phrase, "a complete mental revolution on the part of the workmen [and women]" (p. 70). One must question such a rapid change agenda. History suggests that organizations change slowly, and that revolutionary initiatives can inhibit meaningful change by fostering resentment among organizational members who view radical initiatives as nothing more than window dressings or banner slogans. The approach espoused here is consistent with the various truths of police organizations: that organizational actions are intricately tied to budgetary allocations, innovation can be stifled by a determined few, much of police work is rooted in tradition, and police organizations throughout history have changed gradually. These truths strongly suggest that change in police organizations is best sought using an evolutionary model. The take-away message is that police officials interested in making meaningful incremental improvements while pursuing more ambitious organization-wide community-policing reforms may find the integrative strategy for acquiring citizen input outlined here a positive next step.

REFERENCES

Bayley, D. H. (1994). *Police for the future.* New York: Oxford University Press.

Bordua, D. J., & Tifft, L. L. (1971). Citizen interviews, organizational feedback, and police-community relations decisions. *Law and Society Review, 6*(2), 155–182.

Brandl, S. G., Frank, J., Worden, R. E., & Bynum, T. S. (1994). Global and specific attitudes toward the police: Disentangling the relationship. *Justice Quarterly, 11*(1) 119–134.

Bureau of Justice Statistics. (1999). *Criminal victimization and perceptions of community safety in 12 cities, 1998.* Washington DC: U.S. Department of Justice.

Cao, L., Frank, J., & Cullen, F. T. (1996). Race, community context and confidence in the police. *American Journal of Police, 15*(1), 3–22.

Chandek, M. S., & Porter, C. O. (1998). The efficacy of expectancy disconfirmation in explaining crime victim satisfaction with the police. *Police Quarterly, 1,* 24–40.

Cordner, G. W. (1999). Elements of community policing. In L. K. Gaines & G. W. Cordner (Eds.), *Policing perspectives: An anthology* (pp. 137–149). Los Angeles: Roxbury.

Dillman, D. A. (1978). *Mail and telephone surveys: The total design method.* New York: John Wiley.

Fowler, F. J. (1993). *Survey research methods* (2nd ed.). Newbury Park, CA: Sage.

Fox, R. J., Crask, M. R., & Kim, J. (1988). Mail survey response rate: A meta-analysis of selected techniques for inducing response. *Public Opinion Quarterly, 52,* 467–491.

Furstenberg, F. F., & Wellford, C. F. (1973). Calling the police: The evaluation of police service. *Law and Society Review, 7,* 393–406.

Katz, D., & Kahn, R. L. (1966). *The social psychology of organizations.* New York: Wiley.

Leonard, V. A. (1951). *Police organization and management.* Brooklyn, NY: Foundation Press.

Mastrofski, S. D. (1981). Surveying clients to assess police performance: Focusing on the police-citizen encounter. *Evaluation Review, 5*(3), 397–408.

Mastrofski, S. D. (1993). Varieties of community policing. *American Journal of Police, 12*(3), 65–77.

Mastrofski, S. D. (1999). *Policing for people.* Washington, DC: Police Foundation.

Morgan, D. L. (1988). *Focus groups as qualitative research.* Newbury Park, CA: Sage.

Oliver, R. L. (1980). A cognitive model of antecedents and consequences of satisfaction decisions. *Journal of Marketing Research, 17,* 460–469.

Parks, R. B. (1976). Police response effects on citizen attitudes and perceptions. In W. G. Skogan (Ed.), *Sample surveys of the victims of crime* (pp. 89–104). Cambridge, MA: Ballinger.

Peak, K. (1990). A research note on successful criminal justice survey research: A "personal touch" model for enhancing rates of return. *Criminal Justice Policy Review, 4*(3), 268–277.

Reisig, M. D., & Chandek, M. S. (2001). The effects of expectancy disconfirmation on outcome satisfaction in police-citizen encounters. *Policing: An International Journal of Police Strategies and Management, 24*(1), 88–99.

Reisig, M. D., & Correia, M. E. (1997). Public evaluations of police performance: An analysis across three levels of policing. *Policing: An International Journal of Police Strategies and Management, 20*(2), 311–325.

Reisig, M. D., & Giacomazzi, A. L. (1998). Citizen perceptions of community policing: Are attitudes toward police important? *Policing: An International Journal of Police Strategies and Management, 21*(3), 547–561.

Reisig, M. D., & Parks, R. B. (2000). Experience, quality of life, and neighborhood context: A hierarchical analysis of satisfaction with police. *Justice Quarterly, 17*(3), 607–630.

Reiss, A. (1992). Police organization in the twentieth century. In M. Tonry & N. Morris (Eds.), *Modern policing* (pp. 51–97). Chicago: University of Chicago Press.

Shaw, G. M., Shapiro, R. Y., Lock, S., & Jacobs, L. R. (1998). Trends: Crime, the police and civil liberties. *Public Opinion Quarterly, 62*(3), 405–426.

Skogan, W. G. (1975). Public policy and public evaluations of criminal justice system performance. In J. A. Gardiner & M. A. Mulkey (Eds.), *Crime and criminal justice* (pp. 43–61). Lexington, MA: D. C. Heath.

Skogan, W. G., & Hartnett, S. M. (1997). *Community policing, Chicago style.* New York: Oxford University Press.

Smith, B. (1940). *Police systems in the United States.* New York: Harper.

Smith, P. E., & Hawkins, R. O. (1973). Victimization, types of citizen-police contacts, and attitudes toward the police. *Law and Society Review, 8*, 135–152.

Stewart, D. S., & Shamdasani, P. N. (1990). *Focus groups: Theory and practice.* Newbury Park, CA: Sage.

Taylor, F. W. (1996). The principles of scientific management. In J. M. Shafritz & J. S. Ott (Eds.), *Classics of organization theory* (4th ed., pp. 66–79). Fort Worth, TX: Harcourt Brace.

Taylor, R. B. (1997). Crime, grime, and responses to crime: Relative impacts of neighborhood structure, crime, and physical deterioration on residents and business personnel in the twin cities. In S. P. Lab (Ed.), *Crime prevention at a crossroads* (pp. 63–75). Cincinnati, OH: Anderson.

Thompson, J. D. (1967). *Organizations in action.* New York: McGraw-Hill.

Trojanowicz, R. C., & Bucqueroux, B. (1990). *Community policing: A contemporary perspective.* Cincinnati, OH: Anderson.

Weisel, D. (1999). *Conducting community surveys: A practical guide for law enforcement agencies.* Washington, DC: U.S. Department of Justice.

White, M. F., & Menke, B. A. (1982). On assessing the mood of the public toward the police: Some conceptual issues. *Journal of Criminal Justice, 10*(3), 211–230.

Wilson, J. Q., & Kelling, G. L. (1982, March). Broken windows: The police and neighborhood safety. *Atlantic Monthly*, pp. 29–38.

Wilson, O. W. (1950). *Police administration.* New York: McGraw-Hill.

CHAPTER 4

Using Multiple Methods in Community Crime Prevention and Community-Policing Research
The Case of Project ROAR

Andrew L. Giacomazzi
Edmund F. McGarrell

Social scientists continually strive to find the most credible evidence in their quest to answer social science research questions. However, a variety of factors typically preclude the researcher from confidently stating that his or her findings represent "certain" evidence. A number of these factors relate to the nature of the social world, including the world's complexity. Social scientists often are put in the position of figuring out motivation for human behavior while taking into consideration its plausible and diverse influences, such as mass media, contacts with others, and past experiences (Schutt, 1996).

AUTHORS' NOTE: This project was supported by Grant Number 93-IJ-CX-0054 awarded by the National Institute of Justice, Office of Justice Programs, U.S. Department of Justice, September, 1993. The points expressed are those of the authors and do not represent the position of the National Institute of Justice.

Given the inherent complexity of the social world, researchers have attempted to use various methods—and techniques within those methods—to best measure variables central to their research questions. However, whether a researcher employs observations, surveys, or the use of available data, limitations for each of these methods readily are apparent. Despite these limitations, many researchers continue to use only one source of evidence as a means to answer their questions. According to Yin (1989), the isolated use of data sources likely is a function of a researcher's tendency to choose the data source with which he or she is most familiar. This results in researchers who not only announce which problem will be studied, but also select only a *single* source of data.

Using a single data source hampers the credibility of research in the growing fields of community policing and community crime prevention. As Lurigio and Rosenbaum (1986) note, all of the data sources described in this chapter have been used as the sole source of data for past community-policing and crime-prevention studies. Furthermore, according to Yin (1979), investigators in the past often relied primarily on crime data as a central outcome measure for evaluating community anticrime efforts. Given some of the inherent limitations of social science research methods, we argue that the triangulation method of combining multiple sources of information offers the best potential for reaching firmer conclusions regarding the effectiveness of community-policing programs.

In this chapter, we highlight some of the methodological issues of interest after our two-year evaluation of Project ROAR (Reclaiming Our Area Residences), a collaborative problem-solving program involving public housing residents in Spokane, Washington. First, we provide a brief overview of Project ROAR, followed by our research questions and a discussion of the research methods used to address these questions. We then provide a summary of the key research findings. The focus of the chapter is a discussion of the strengths and weaknesses of the research methods and the challenges faced in this type of evaluation research. We conclude by outlining the importance of triangulation in community-policing and community crime-prevention research.

PROJECT ROAR OVERVIEW

Project ROAR was established in Spokane, Washington, against the backdrop of strong support for locally based, collaborative partnerships that addressed disorder, crime, and fear of crime at the community level. This strong support arose out of the growing frustration among public housing residents that their neighborhood streets had been "taken over" by the disorderly and criminal. Key organizing events concerning the project occurred in late 1993, and Project ROAR officially was implemented with a media kick-off in January 1994.

Project ROAR is a public housing drug crime elimination program sponsored by the Spokane Police Department and the Spokane Housing Authority. The program reflects a public-private, interagency collaboration that seeks to empower public housing tenants in an effort to produce a safer neighborhood. The program targets a poor neighborhood in the central business district with a large elderly and transient population that is experiencing high rates of drug dealing and related crime and disorder problems.

Project ROAR builds upon the ideas of past and present community-based crime prevention and reduction efforts. The evaluation of the project provides insight into the effectiveness of such programs as they relate to the mobilization of public housing residents and the extent to which they can create positive changes in perceptions of safety, neighborhood disorder, and crime rates. The key elements of the program as originally conceived included the following: (a) opening a COPS (Community-Oriented Policing Services) Shop within the public housing area, (b) assigning neighborhood resource officers (community-policing officers) to the target area; (c) coordinating efforts with the city's Crime Prevention Center, located in the public housing unit; (d) hiring a resident resource coordinator; (e) creating an "adopt the tenants" program with local businesses; and (f) addressing physical target hardening and neighborhood improvements.

Research Questions and Design

The following research questions guided the evaluation of Project ROAR:

1. To what extent does Project ROAR, as implemented, reflect Project ROAR as originally conceived?

2. To what extent can Project ROAR be considered a comprehensive community crime-prevention program?

3. What effects might a collaborative anticrime program have on residents' perceptions of the quality of their neighborhood life, including perceptions of neighborhood inhabitants, satisfaction

with their neighborhood, fear of crime, and neighborhood physical and social disorder?

4. What effects might a collaborative anticrime program have on objective measures of physical and social disorder?

5. What effects might a collaborative, anticrime program have on levels of neighborhood crime?

6. What effects might a collaborative, anticrime program have on subjective perceptions of the level and quality of policing services?

The evaluation of Project ROAR reflected a process assessment and short-term impact assessment using a quasi-experimental design with a specifically matched comparison site constructed to be similar to the project site with regard to individual and neighborhood characteristics. The comparison site was used to make comparisons with regard to official crime statistics, objective measures of social and physical disorder, and survey research regarding perceptions of the quality of neighborhood life and the level of police services. For survey data and official crime statistics, trends for the city of Spokane also were compared with the project area.

Multiple sources of data were used to assess the implementation and short-term impacts of Project ROAR, including qualitative research in the form both of direct observations of all program meetings and activities, and of focus group sessions with Project ROAR participants, and survey research in the form of interviews with the Parsons' public housing residents, as well as with residents of the broader neighborhood and comparison neighborhood, and mail questionnaires for city residents. In addition, data regarding known offenses and arrests, as well as data from a social and physical inventory of neighborhoods, were used to evaluate the effectiveness of the project.

Key Findings

As noted earlier, we were interested in both the process of program implementation and the effect of the program on crime, disorder, and quality of life in the neighborhood. The process evaluation documented that Project ROAR led to the implementation of a number of activities. First, regular collaborative problem-solving meetings involving the police, housing authority, and residents occurred nearly four times per month. Second, social activities involving residents of the neighborhood and/or residents of the broader neighborhood occurred at a rate of nine per month during the project period. Our assessment also indicated that Project ROAR led to a large number of problem-solving efforts seeking to make physical changes in the neighborhood—either to improve the esthetic quality of the area or to make the area less attractive to criminal activity through target hardening. An additional indicator of the effective implementation of Project ROAR came from inspection of police arrest records. The police made the Project ROAR neighborhood a priority for proactive enforcement activity. Felony drug arrests nearly tripled when comparing the 24-month project period to the prior two years. Thus, our observations and interviews revealed that Project ROAR led to the implementation of a comprehensive community anticrime program (Popkin, Olson, Lurigio, Gwiasda, & Carter, 1995). This included law enforcement activity (both collaboration with the community and increased enforcement), community involvement, and situation crime prevention.

The key outcome measures employed in this study were citizen perceptions, official crime statistics, and objective measures of physical changes in the neighborhood. We also attempted, unsuccessfully, to collect objective measures of social disorder in the neighborhood. The most powerful effects came from the survey data, with the crime statistics and measures of physical changes in the neighborhood suggesting more modest program impact.

In terms of citizen surveys, there were large increases in resident satisfaction with the neighborhood, and a significant number of residents reported positive physical changes in the neighborhood and decreases in such visible social disorder as drug dealing and prostitution. There were also large decreases in fear of crime within the building and in the neighborhood. Additionally, resident perceptions of the police improved significantly by the end of the two-year evaluation period. The degree of the change in perceptions was consistent over a number of indicators and contrasted a citywide sample of Spokane residents that revealed very little change in citizen perceptions during the two-year project period.

The changes in official crime data were modest. There was a reduction in reported burglaries and robberies during the project period. It attained statistical significance when contrasted with the citywide trend, but not when contrasted with the comparison area.

The physical inventory survey involved trained observers measuring physical disorder variables, such as abandoned buildings, graffiti, broken windows, and litter, as well as indicators of target hardening, such as BlockWatch signs, fencing, lights, and security cameras. The findings revealed some signs of improvement. For example, there was evidence of reduction in abandoned buildings, but there was an increase in graffiti. There were also increases in signs of target hardening. The findings and the issues related to our various evaluation methods are discussed in more detail in the subsequent sections.

DISCUSSION OF RESEARCH METHODS
AND IMPLEMENTATION

Four sources of data used to assess the implementation and impact of Project ROAR suggest that the program is comprehensive in scope, consisting of law enforcement approaches, community involvement, and situational crime-prevention activities. In addition, the project resulted in significant changes in the positive direction with regard to public housing residents' perceptions of the overall quality of their neighborhood life, and substantial positive changes in their perceptions of police services. In addition, official crime statistics indicate that Project ROAR likely has led to a crime suppression effect in the project area between the years 1994 and 1995. Although these data represent evidence of the successful implementation and desired outcomes of Project ROAR, several notable limitations of our methods and techniques clearly stand out.

Process Evaluation

The process evaluation component of this study ideally was suited to address the research question of the extent to which Project ROAR fit the criteria of a comprehensive community crime-prevention program. Popkin et al. (1995) describe a comprehensive program as one that includes law enforcement activities, community involvement, and situational crime-prevention activities. The findings reported above suggest that Project ROAR, indeed, is comprehensive in nature.

Yet another reason for our collection of program implementation data was an attempt to improve upon past community crime-prevention evaluations. Lurigio and Rosenbaum (1986) note that the great majority of previous community crime-prevention program evaluations have failed to distinguish between the program *in theory* and the program *in practice,* thereby leading to serious problems with construct and external validity. As such, this study presented a thorough qualitative and quantitative account of the implementation of Project ROAR through observational research (see Giacomazzi, McGarrell, & Thurman, 1997).

During the two-year period beginning in January 1994 (the official kick-off month for Project ROAR) and ending in December 1995, direct observations were conducted of all meetings subsumed under Project ROAR, including the resident association meetings and its subcommittees, the improvement committee meetings, the business owners' association meetings, COPS meetings, and other special meetings conducted under the auspices of Project ROAR. Direct observation was also undertaken during many of the neighborhood social activities that were initiated by Project ROAR's social committee. In addition, systematic observations were conducted of all other activities undertaken through Project ROAR, including press conferences, police substation activities, tenant crime-prevention training, collaborative grant meetings, and the hall-monitoring BlockWatch program.

All observations were recorded using the narrative method. Those researchers who attended a particular activity completed a "contact form" for the event. Contact forms were created in an effort to track the type of activity, the date of the activity, the number of individuals in attendance, and the nature of any discussion. After completing a contact form, researchers placed it in an appropriate file for all activities occurring in that particular month.

These systematic observations were used to develop a comprehensive, descriptive account (on a month-by-month basis) of the nature of the program as implemented. In addition, data were collected on the number and types of meetings, workshops, open houses, and training sessions (by month) for the evaluation period, and the number and types of social activities undertaken under the rubric of Project ROAR.

However, we acknowledge the limitations associated with the use of observational research methods in general, and our specific approaches, in obtaining observational data in a comprehensive program such as Project ROAR. According to Rossi and Freeman (1989), observational methods are a preferable source of data for monitoring programs as long as the observer is not obtrusive; obtrusiveness, in essence, leads to reactive effects among participants who are observed, thereby threatening measurement validity.

Initially, the *complete observer* method was used; however, this method evolved into the *observer-as-participant* approach as Project ROAR key participants became increasingly familiar (and comfortable) with the evaluation team. By the end of the evaluation period, evaluators became *participant observers* in some aspects of Project ROAR, namely as staff volunteers at the COPS Shop located within the public housing complex.

Although the reactive effects of observation undoubtedly were reduced as the evaluators developed rapport with the project participants and entered into a role as project volunteers, the argument can be made that the evaluators themselves—in their role as project participants—may have threatened the integrity of the project by influencing its activities. Quite simply, the question here is whether other outcomes may have been observed had some of the evaluators not been involved in the project. This question is not easy for us to answer. However, given the limited role the evaluators had in the project implementation (a few hours per week as volunteers at the COPS Shop), and that these evaluators worked and/or resided in the broader neighborhood anyway, we contend that the impact that the evaluators had—as evaluators—in the implementation and success of Project ROAR was limited. Nonetheless, the above issue again brings to light the complexities of obtaining valid process evaluation data for community crime-prevention programs.

Another, perhaps even more important, rationale for conducting the process component of the evaluation using observational research concerned our interest in the so-called black box problem. According to Rossi and Freeman (1989), process components to evaluations are necessary to avoid slipping into the black box problem, where only inputs and outcomes are examined without paying attention to how or to whether certain inputs may be used to effect a predicted outcome. Our process evaluation component sought to provide direct, empirical evidence that the project was indeed implemented as outlined in *theory*. However, our findings suggest that Project ROAR participants did much more in their crime-prevention effort than originally conceived (Giacomazzi, McGarrell, & Thurman, 1996), leading to three problems which we highlight below.

First, given the increase in the number and frequency of Project ROAR meetings, by the end of the first year of the evaluation, it became virtually impossible to collect observational data regarding all program functions as we initially set out to do. Time and resource constraints were factors that contributed to this. In addition, as project activities expanded, especially after the opening of the COPS Shop in the public housing facility, the evaluators were not systematically contacted about meetings and activities under the rubric of

Project ROAR as they had been during the first year, when the project was smaller in scope.

A second and related problem concerned an effort by project participants to broaden the focus of Project ROAR. Initial Project ROAR activities were conceived as consisting of a rather small group of people representing public housing residents, the police department, the housing authority, and local business owners, that would focus on the area within and immediately surrounding the public housing facility. However, by the end of the second year of the evaluation, the project expanded to the broader neighborhood. The new focus of the project was a neighborhood revitalization effort that would attract individuals from the broader neighborhood—and city, for that matter—by creating a new market and arts district. With new community groups and activities spinning off from the more well-established Project ROAR groups and activities, it became difficult for the evaluators to know with certainty whether the neighborhood revitalization effort was, in fact, still Project ROAR.

Our first two points lead us to the third. Given the increase in and frequency of activities surrounding Project ROAR, which we felt we adequately captured in our process evaluation research, we are left with the original problem that we intended to overcome with the process evaluation in the first place, namely, the black box problem. Although our plan was to collect survey data at specific intervals corresponding to the implementation of new project activities, these activities increased at a rate that precluded us from "disentangling" them from other activities. Therefore, it was not possible adequately to answer the question, "What could have been left out of the project for the project to have still been a success?"

Survey Research

Four waves of face-to-face interviews were conducted with representative samples of the public housing residents, and they suggest that Project ROAR resulted in changes in the positive direction with regard to perceptions of the overall quality of neighborhood life, and substantial positive changes in their perceptions of police services. Indeed, the magnitude of shifts in perceptions of the residents was often quite striking. Further, the consistency in the reports across several dimensions of citizen's perceptions suggest that the program truly did have a positive impact on the quality of life of the residents of this public housing facility. These included the belief that positive physical and social changes had occurred in the neighborhood, that streetwalking prostitution and open drug sales had declined, and that the residents felt considerably safer in the building and the neighborhood. Similarly, there was significant improvement in the resident's perception of the police. These changes translated into a dramatic increase in the percentage of residents expressing satisfaction with the neighborhood (from 38% to 89%) and a corresponding decrease in residents reporting dissatisfaction with the neighborhood (from 62% to 11%). Clearly, at the level of perceptions, all indications are that Project ROAR had a profound positive impact.

Despite these findings, our data collection was hampered by a number of problems that introduced validity threats. First, though our overall response rates for the public housing residents' interviews were acceptable, they were lower than one might expect from such a small group of people (Wave 1, $N = 29$, 58%; Wave 2, $N = 32$, 64%; Wave 3, $N = 31$, 62%; Wave 4, $N = 28$, 56%). These rates beg an answer to the question of the external validity of our findings (i.e., to what extent did those who refused to participate differ in their views from those who participated?). In addition, as the interviews progressed to the third and fourth waves, questionnaire items became familiar to the residents, some of whom complained that they felt they had just answered the questions a short while ago. As indicated by our response rate for wave four, several former respondents could not be convinced to participate in "yet another" face-to-face interview.

We also conducted a citywide mail survey on many of the same items included in the residents' interviews. The intent was to conduct two such sets of interviews and to oversample from both the Project ROAR area and the comparison area. Despite oversampling four times the rate of other Spokane neighborhoods in the hopes of gaining sufficient numbers of respondents from these two neighborhoods, we did not end up with sufficient numbers of respondents to draw conclusions about these two areas (even though we used the Dillman "total design method" with three waves of follow-up and a final phone call). The city survey, however, did allow us to look for trends among city residents as a whole. Given differences in method of administration (face-to-face interviews vs. mail surveys), direct comparisons between the Project ROAR residents' interviews and the city survey could not be made. To the extent that trends among the residents do not track with citywide trends, however, we gain confidence that the change is likely the product of Project ROAR.

Finally, a sample of project-area residents (non–public housing residents) and comparison-area residents was drawn in January 1996. A subset of items from the public housing residents' questionnaire was used to determine any differences between project-area residents and comparison-area residents with regard to perceptions of the quality of neighborhood life and perceptions of police services. Unfortunately, in several of the locked residential buildings, limited access was granted to researchers. This resulted in a convenience sample, and thus our use of these interviews was limited to certain qualitative observations offered that tended to support our more systematic observations and survey research efforts (see Giacomazzi et al., 1997).

Offenses Known and Arrest Data

Twenty-four months of pre-program implementation crime data and 24 months of post-program implementation data were collected from the Spokane Police Department's Crime Analysis Unit for the period beginning January 1, 1992, and ending December 31, 1995. The Crime Analysis Unit routinely collects reported crimes only for burglaries, robberies, and sex offenses. Given the small number of reported sex offenses in both the project and comparison areas, statistics for burglaries and robberies were analyzed. The crime of *burglary* is defined as any unauthorized entry into a residential or commercial dwelling. The crime of *robbery* is defined as any use of force or the threat of force for purposes of committing a theft. In addition to the above crimes tracked by the Crime Analysis Unit, felony drug arrest data collected by the Special Investigations' Unit also were analyzed here for the 24 months prior to the implementation of Project ROAR and the 24 months following its implementation. Here, drug arrests were identified by type of drug used, and included both trafficking and possession.

Data for the crimes outlined in the preceding paragraphs were collected both for the project and comparison areas, in addition to the city of Spokane. Although it was expected that crime totals would differ between the project and comparison areas, analysis of these data concentrated on crime trends over time and proportional differences in the three areas.

It is recognized that one of the possible effects of such a program as Project ROAR is that drug-dealing activity and associated neighborhood crime simply will be displaced from the project area to other areas of the larger downtown core or to other Spokane neighborhoods. As such, the analysis of crime data made an initial step in capturing potential displacement effects by examining crime trends for the entire city of Spokane and the larger downtown area. It is also important to examine for the possibility of diffusion of benefits (Green, 1996). Given the extension of the Project ROAR study through a grant by the National Institute of Justice and the improved geographically coded crime data in Spokane, the issue of displacement versus diffusion will be addressed in the second phase of the evaluation.

Because we were dependent upon the Spokane Police Department for our official statistics, and because the department had not yet begun to track calls for service using their computer-aided dispatch system, these data were not available at the time we completed the evaluation of Project ROAR. Therefore, we were limited to tracking reports of burglaries, robberies, and felony drug arrests over the two-year evaluation period. Of course, any use of official crime data in community crime-prevention research, whether in the form of calls for service or official arrests, creates a problem of interpretation. Changes in the levels of reported crimes and arrests often are deceiving. The overarching goal of community anticrime programs in general, and Project ROAR specifically, typically is to affect a change in the amount of crime and disorder in a specific area; however, determining which direction of the change actually is an indicator of program success remains problematic.

Physical and Social Inventory of Neighborhoods

A block-level physical and social disorder inventory was conducted in April 1994 for baseline data for the project, and in October 1994, April 1995, and October 1995 for post-program implementation data. The inventory was conducted for 44 blocks—the combined total number of blocks in the project and comparison areas—and was modeled from the work of Perkins and his colleagues (Perkins, Meeks, & Taylor, 1992; Perkins, Wandersman, Rich, & Taylor, 1993).

For purposes of data collection, independent raters walked through all of the blocks of both the project and comparison sites and recorded observations of the physical and social environment. Interrater reliability checks determined that levels of interrater agreement were high. Each block-level inventory began with the raters recording the street name and cross streets, date, time, and the estimated temperature. Immediately thereafter, the social environment inventory was conducted. For exactly one minute, raters recorded the social activity on the block, recording the number of individuals present outside, their gender, approximate age, and their behavior. Behavior categories included *pedestrian, working, hanging out, illegal activity,* and *other.*

After the one minute elapsed, the physical environment inventory commenced. Here, raters recorded the number of guardianship items, lighting items, and disorder items found on each block. Because blocks varied in length, the physical environment inventory (per block) lasted anywhere between 5 and 40 minutes. It also should be noted here that the social environment inventory actually continued simultaneously with the physical inventory, but focused only on "social incivility." Throughout the physical inventory, raters recorded the frequency or number of the following on the block: loitering youths, young adults hanging out, panhandlers, open prostitution, open drug sales, and public drunkenness.

The social and physical inventory data show little change in the physical and social environment during that same period. To some extent, however, particularly in terms of social disorder, we believe this reflects our measurement strategy. Although recorded levels of social disorder both in the project and comparison areas were minimal and did not significantly change from 1994 to 1995, two important points stand out. First, although the researchers attempted to be as unobtrusive as possible in their data collection procedures, the very nature of the inventory required them to mark a form indicating the presence and levels of social disorder. Typically carrying clipboards, the researchers often were mistaken for police officers or code enforcement officials. Furthermore, because of their "official-looking" appearance and their presence on a given block, it is the conventional wisdom of the research team that they, indeed, may have contributed to low levels of social disorder while conducting research on a particular block.

Second, although one would expect at least some indicators of social disorder in the project area, for most of these blocks this simply was not the case. Aside from the reason delineated above, this may have been due to the fact that observations were recorded on weekdays, typically between the hours of 10 a.m. and 2 p.m., when less social disorder would be expected to occur. The fact that the interview data so clearly pointed to reductions in social disorder leads us to question the reliability of our observational data on social disorder.

Although it is clear that having visible observers walking the streets at midday is *not* a vehicle for attaining reliable and valid measures of social disorder, the goal of developing such measures remains a challenge for community crime-prevention researchers. During the course of the project, members of our research team had opportunities through ride- and walk-alongs with police officers, interviews in resident apartments, and similar situations to observe substantial amounts of social disorder, particularly after dark. This included open drug sales, solicitation of prostitution, street-side drinking, fighting, and large groups of teens "taking over" sidewalks. Yet measuring such activity raises challenging sampling and measurement issues. Our initial attempts revealed that reliability issues are significant problems to be overcome. Observer's definitions of activities, such as loitering or threatening behavior, may be influenced by the observer's background as well as by simple realities, such as proximity to the behavior. Ethical considerations are also likely to arise when observers systematically record illegal activities. Koper's (1995) observational study in Minneapolis suggests that sampling and reliability issues are not insurmountable. Yet this type of strategy, involving a researcher sitting in a parked car at crime hot spots during high crime periods, raises issues of personal safety for the researchers.

Despite these challenges, the development of these measures is important. In our case, although our impressions of the significant reduction in social disorder are consistent with resident's interview findings, our inability to have reliable measures of social disorder during the pre-intervention period preclude more refined answers to the question of whether the perceptions are matched by observed change on the streets.

Though the physical inventory data suggest some positive program effects, especially with regard to fewer abandoned buildings, target hardening, and signs of guardianship in the project area, several caveats should be mentioned here. The evaluation team had the impression that small changes, changes that were not likely to have had much impact on the quantitative data captured in the physical inventory, could have a significant effect on resident impressions of their environment and on police intervention. For example, although the number of unbroken lights in the project area did not significantly change between 1994 and 1995, residents continually spoke of their appreciation of increased lighting in the parking lot behind the resident building that had previously been dark and where much loitering had occurred in the evening hours. Similarly, police officers spoke of their appreciation of the cooperation of the business owners in the area to allow the fencing-off of the alleyways as a way of hindering the movement of drug dealers and patrons. The strategic placement of these barriers may be more meaningful than the increase from 0.95 barriers per block to 1.7 barriers per block as found in the data from physical inventory. In addition, survey data and informal observations by the research team suggest that numerous improvements to the physical environment were undertaken and completed through Project ROAR efforts, including improvements to the façades of buildings and improvements to side-walks, among others. These improvements simply were not captured in the quantitative data gleaned from the physical environment inventory.

Finally, the increases in graffiti in the project area from 1994 to 1995 initially were a surprise to the evaluation team, considering that the elimination of graffiti was considered a high priority in 1995. In fact, the Spokane Police Department worked with the juvenile court to have some youths paint over graffiti in the area as part of their community service obligation. In addition, a city ordinance was passed requiring property owners to clean up graffiti, or volunteers from the COPS Shop would paint it for them. Three pieces of information may at least partially explain the increases found in the physical inventory. First, the decision rules for the raters conducting the physical inventory required them to count large amounts of graffiti (typically occurring in the railroad viaducts in the project area) as a single instance of graffiti if the space between graffiti markings was less than the width of the rater's hand. Survey research and informal observations by the evaluators indicate that a significant amount of graffiti was removed under the viaducts, but may not have been captured in the quantitative data.

Second, Spokane Police Department officials were not surprised at the increases in graffiti in the project area because graffiti has been substantially increasing citywide. The increases in graffiti in the comparison area appear to support this explanation. Finally, because graffiti removal is considered a constant battle, the data generated from the physical inventory may be an artifact of the timing of the data collection.

Quasi-Experimental Design

Community crime-prevention evaluations also face challenges in implementing research designs that can maximize clear answers to the research questions. In an ideal situation, the program would be implemented in randomly chosen locations and compared to randomly selected control areas (Sherman et al., 1997). The reality, of course, is that programs are typically implemented in areas selected for political reasons, including the real and perceived nature of the crime problem, citizen action, funding opportunities, and related factors. Having chosen a target area, researchers are forced to select a comparison area. The reality of communities, however, is that no two areas are alike, and the researcher is forced to consider a variety of compromises. In the case of Project ROAR, there was no other public housing facility in the city: The remainder of public housing was in scattered site units. The comparison site chosen was the area the research team believed the "best" available location given demographic and physical characteristics of the two areas.

A related concern has to do with the possibility that the comparison may undergo unanticipated changes during the evaluation. During the project period, neighborhoods throughout Spokane were mobilizing and requesting increased police presence in the form of police substations, increased foot and bicycle patrol, and related community-policing initiatives. The Spokane Police Department would have responded to such requests from our comparison neighborhood as if it were any other neighborhood in the city. This did not occur during our evaluation, but the possibility of having a "treatment" provided to the comparison area is likely to be common in community crime-prevention research.

CONCLUSION

The intent of this chapter has been to highlight the findings of a two-year process and outcome evaluation of Project ROAR and to discuss the use and limitations of the research methods in this endeavor. The results of this research are encouraging, especially as they pertain to the ability of a number of diverse groups, including public housing residents and the police, to work collaboratively on effecting positive change both in the social and physical environment in an area that, by its very nature, is at high-risk for failure for such efforts (Skogan, 1990).

Future research endeavors require an assessment of the extent of crime displacement and a discussion of crime control benefits. Additionally, as Hope (1995) has noted, the multicausal nature of programs like Project ROAR calls for study of the specific factors within a comprehensive program such as this that tend to result in change.

For purposes of this chapter, we focused on the particular data-collection methods and design used to assess the implementation and outcome of Project ROAR, and have noted both the limitations of these methods and problems surrounding our operationalization of these techniques. Below, we summarize the lessons we have learned in this endeavor:

- The importance of reliable project participants who are willing to keep evaluators informed of expanded project activities cannot be overstated.

- Innovative and creative means to elicit higher survey response rates in impoverished urban areas should be tried. This may include a coordinated effort with area merchants to provide incentives (such as coupons) in exchange for the completion of surveys.

- Coordination with residential managers in the comparison area would have resulted in greater access to residents in the area for survey data collection.

- Whenever possible, calls-for-service data should be used in place of the more limited information collected through the Uniform Crime Reports.

- Reliable and valid measures for physical and social disorder need to be developed. Raters should have common definitions of physical and social disorder, and the means to collect these data should be as unobtrusive as possible.

- The combination of qualitative and quantitative data in community crime prevention and community-policing evaluations will improve the confidence evaluators have of their results. In our case, small changes in the quantitative data had quite an impact on residents and their environment as measured through interviews and direct observation.

Although there are both benefits and drawbacks to the use of observations, survey research, and official data in social science research, evaluators—including ourselves—should continue to triangulate, striving for the collection of data that will allow us to more confidently conclude what—if anything—has led to the desired effect. Though the complexities of the social world typically preclude evaluators from achieving a high level of certainty in their results, in our case the confluence of several independent streams of imperfect evidence allows us more confidently to conclude that Project ROAR was a success. We hope we have shown that this is easier said than done.

REFERENCES

Giacomazzi, A., McGarrell, E. F., & Thurman, Q. C. (1996, March). *Community polic-ing and public housing: A process evaluation of a collaborative strategy to reduce crime, fear, and disorder in Spokane, Washington.* Academy of Criminal Justice Sci-ences Conference, Las Vegas, NV.

Giacomazzi, A., McGarrell, E. F., & Thurman, Q. C. (1997). *Reducing disorder, fear, and crime in public housing: An evaluation of a drug crime elimination program in Spo-kane, Washington* [Final report to the National Institute of Justice]. Washington, DC: U.S. Department of Justice, Office of Justice Programs, National Institute of Justice.

Green, L. (1996). *Policing places with drug problems.* Thousand Oaks, CA: Sage.

Hope, T. (1995). Community crime prevention. In M. Tonry & D. P. Farrington (Eds.), *Building a safer society* (pp. 21–89). Chicago: University of Chicago Press.

Koper, C. (1995). Just enough police presence: Reducing crime and disorderly by optimiz-ing patrol time in crime hot spots. *Justice Quarterly, 12*(4), 649–672.

Lurigio, A. J., & Rosenbaum, D. P. (1986). Evaluation research in community crime pre-vention: A critical look at the field. In D. P. Rosenbaum (Ed.), *Community crime prevention: Does it work?* (pp. 19–44). Beverly Hills, CA: Sage.

Perkins, D. D., Meeks, J. W., & Taylor, R. B. (1992). The physical environment of street blocks and resident perceptions of crime and disorder: Implications for theory and measurement. *Journal of Environmental Psychology, 12*(1), 21–34.

Perkins, D. D., Wandersman, A., Rich, R. C., & Taylor, R. B. (1993). The physical envi-ronment of street crime: Defensible space, territoriality and incivilities. *Journal of Environmental Psychology, 13*(1), 29–49.

Popkin, S. J., Olson, L. M, Lurigio, A. J., Gwiasda, V. E, & Carter, R. G. (1995). Sweeping out drugs and crime: Residents' views of the Chicago Housing Authority's Public Housing Drug Elimination Program. *Crime and Delinquency, 41*(1), 73–99.

Rossi, P. H., & Freeman, H. E. (1989). *Evaluation: A systematic approach.* Newbury Park, CA: Sage.

Schutt, R. K. (1996). *Investigating the social world: The process and practice of research.* Thousand Oaks, CA: Pine Forge Press.

Sherman, L. W., Gottfredson, D., MacKenzie, D., Eck, J., Reuter, P., & Bushway, S. (1997). *Preventing crime: What works, what doesn't, what's promising.* Washing-ton, DC: U.S. Department of Justice, Office of Justice Programs.

Skogan, W. G. (1990). *Disorder and decline: Crime and the spiral of decay in American neighborhoods.* Berkeley, CA: University of California Press.

Yin, R. K. (1979). What is citizen crime prevention? *Review of Criminal Justice Evalua-tion.* Washington, DC: Law Enforcement Assistance Administration.

Yin, R. K. (1989). *Case study research: Design and methods.* Newbury Park, CA: Sage.

Part II

Changing the
Police Culture

CHAPTER 5

Styles of Patrol in a Community-Policing Context

Stephen D. Mastrofski
James J. Willis
Jeffrey B. Snipes

In the late 19th century, American police re-
formers promised that officers would be selected, trained, and super-
vised to fit an ideal mold (Berman, 1987; Fogelson, 1977; Walker,
1977). The ideal officer was committed to law enforcement, free of corruption, and well versed in the latest crime fighting methods. Nowa-
days, community-policing reformers encourage officers to exercise initiative and creativity in deciding how to achieve community-policing
"values," but they still expect them to adhere to certain behaviors:
to engage fully the people on their beat; to treat them in a civil, caring fashion; to be proactive in identifying problems and taking preventive action; and to reinforce informal institutions that will maintain
order.

AUTHORS' NOTE: Supported under award #91-IJ-CX-0030 from the National Institute of Justice, Office of Justice Programs, U.S. Department of Justice. Points of view in
this document are those of the authors and do not necessarily represent the official position of the U.S. Department of Justice. The authors are grateful for the cooperation of the
Richmond Bureau of Police for making this study possible

Given the diversity of community-policing approaches, we should expect some variance in the ideal type of community-policing officer—depending on the model promoted in a department. In the literature on community policing, some advocate a no-nonsense, aggressive—and, if necessary, forceful—approach to even minor offenses and disturbances (Sykes, 1986; Wilson & Kelling, 1982). This is characterized as the "broken windows" approach (Bratton, 1998; Kelling & Coles, 1996). Others suggest that a more gentle, friendly, concerned, or low-key method is what should characterize community policing, one that conveys a sense of both equity and lawfulness, one that seeks to combine punishment with integration of the subject of police attention into the community of upstanding citizens (Braithwaite, 1989; Braithwaite & Pettit, 1990; Eck & Rosenbaum, 1994; Independent Commission, 1991; Trojanowicz, 1991). We term this model "community building." One could easily overstate the differences between these two models, but they alert us to the importance of attending to the particular model employed by a department to learn what ideals it wishes to promote. Once we know this, we can conduct an assessment of behavior that compares practice to the department ideal. We can also compare behavior patterns in a community-policing framework to those noted in times that predate community policing. This is particularly important because—except for anecdotal accounts—there has been no observation-based assessment of police work styles under community policing.

This chapter characterizes the work styles of patrol officers in the Richmond, Virginia, Bureau of Police at a time when it was in the midst of implementing community policing. We focus on important choices officers made on their own in the field: on the nature and frequency of proactive encounters with the public and how members of the public were handled once contact was made, however initiated. We note the extent to which different styles conform to the community-policing approach advocated by department leaders, and we note the extent to which our inductively derived typology of police styles conforms to the pattern found in previous research.

RESEARCH ON PATROL STYLES

Scholars often stereotype police officers according to observations about their occupational subculture, but researchers have also established that officers vary in how they perform their work. Several scholars offer typologies of police attitude, operational style, and behavior (Broderick, 1977; Brown, 1981; Muir, 1977; White, 1972). Worden (1995) notes that despite differences in departments and research methods, the typologies are congruent in what they tell us about police officers' belief systems. Three value orientations capture much that is important in guiding the behavior of police: views of human nature, preferences for processes versus outcome, and acceptance and moral integration of the coercive aspects of police work.

Although there may be some correlation between these dimensions of police outlook, research shows that they are sufficiently independent to produce interesting combinations in the real world. Worden (1995) identified five types of officers found across these studies. *Professionals* have a tragic perspective on human nature, are process oriented, and are comfortable with using their coercive power. They acknowledge a broad police role, and are as comfortable providing mundane services as dealing with dangerous offenders. *Tough Cops* are also at ease with their coercive power, but they are cynical and outcome oriented. They focus on serious crime. *Clean-Beat Crime Fighters* are cynical and comfortable using coercion, but they are process-oriented, and therefore less selective in their choice of enforcement targets. They value the promotion of both social order and due process. Quite different from the Clean-Beat Crime Fighter, *Problem-Solvers* have a tragic view of the human condition, are uncomfortable with coercion, and are outcome oriented. They want to improve the quality of life for individuals and neighborhoods, but they prefer to avoid arrest and to seek alternative informal solutions. Rather than relying on formal rules and procedures, they like to have the freedom to fit their actions to the particulars of a situation, whenever possible responding to the community's preferences. *Avoiders* are cynical, uncomfortable with coercion, and do not score high on either process orientation or outcome orientation. As their name implies, they avoid work, especially that which is challenging, and they have no apparent goal except to avoid trouble for themselves.

These types are distillations that officers may actually resemble in varying degrees. There have been just a few attempts to replicate the original research on which they were based, and those have not been confirmatory (Hochstedler, 1981; Snipes & Mastrofski, 1990). Community-policing reforms have implications for the kinds of "ideals" about police outlook and practice that are set before officers and public as the right approach to street-level practice. The potential of the ideal type is given in the high-visibility profiling of individual officers, a practice common in both the local and national press (Norman, 1993). This promotes a singular vision of community policing in powerful, personal terms, although it surely overrepresents the degree of officers' commitment to the department's model. It is to Richmond's model we now turn.

Richmond and Its Community-Policing Program

During the study's fieldwork in 1992, Richmond had 621 officers to serve about 203,000 residents, 55% of whom were black, 43% white, and 2% other. The department was in the middle of a five-year plan to implement community policing. This was undertaken by a new chief, hired in 1989 with a mandate to replace the department's legalistic policing with community policing. The department expected all patrol officers to engage in community policing. Its values were formalized in a mission statement developed by a task force of police and community members. The chief placed special emphasis on the partnership aspects of community policing. He wanted to gain the trust of citizens in the most alienated, high-crime neighborhoods.

A number of programs were designed to build bridges to Richmond's neighborhoods: Neighborhood Watch, Drug-Free Zones, foot and bike beats in troubled areas, and school safety programs. Officers were instructed to get involved with neighborhood groups, business associations, schools, and churches. Community-policing training, though limited, stressed positive relations with citizens and working with neighborhood groups. The department had initiated a policy of "creative failure"; officers who tried to solve a community problem innovatively would not be punished if they did not succeed, as long as it was a good faith effort. The department did not deliver a strong message about a "community-policing way" to treat "problem" citizens. Department leaders valued aggressive pursuit of drug traffickers and violent offenders, but the chief and precinct commanders also encouraged experimentation with nonarrest alternatives.

Some structural changes had also been implemented to facilitate community linkages: decentralizing decision making to the precinct commanders, allowing permanent beat assignments, and creating a small patrol unit in each precinct freed from responding to calls for service in order to engage intensively in special community policing activities. One of these efforts was a "weed and seed" project in two high-crime neighborhoods, funded by the U.S. Department of Justice.

The department participated in a government-wide coordination of municipal service delivery structured to respond to neighborhood demands through monthly meetings with residents and businesses. The chief frequently declared that hiring and promotion decisions would be based upon candidates' motivation and skill in engaging in community policing. Precinct commanders encouraged officers to park their vehicles and take the time to walk the beat. Richmond's approach incorporated the most common structural elements reported by departments whose leaders characterized them as engaged in community policing (Wycoff, 1994).

The department had not yet set forth its performance appraisal checklist of ideal officer practices, but the dominant message emphasized community building. Several individual officers had been featured by the local press as exemplars of the department's new approach, and these stories stressed community building. Field interviews with officers suggested that the community-outreach message had made a clear impression (though not necessarily positive) on the vast majority of officers, who defined community policing in Richmond as heightening the frequency and improving the quality of personal contact between the police and the public. Involvement, the helping hand, and initiative were themes repeatedly stressed by the leadership. How closely officers fit their own practices to those ideals is the focus of our analysis.

Data and Methods

Ride-along observations were conducted with Richmond patrol officers during the spring and summer of 1992. Field researchers observed in each patrol beat on all three shifts and with members of patrol units assigned special functions. A total of 125 ride-along sessions were conducted, most lasting 10 hours. Most officers patrolled by themselves, although some were observed with partners. Observers accompanied officers throughout the shift, taking brief field notes on officers' activities and encounters with the public. Officers were debriefed after many encounters about their view of what had just transpired (Mastrofski & Parks, 1990). Officers were guaranteed confidentiality.[1] Observers interviewed officers about their views of community policing at convenient times during the ride-along. Observers were trained to take brief field notes at times and in a manner that would not distract the officer or citizens present. Within 15 hours of completion of the ride-along, observers prepared a detailed narrative account of events that occurred during the ride-along and coded key items associated with these events according to a protocol available on personal computers at the research office.

Of the 120 observed officers, 17 were observed at times when their job assignments, the weather, or the length of the observation period provided insufficient opportunities to determine their style of engaging the public. Of the remaining 103 officers, 91 are used in this chapter's analysis; 12 who were observed on more than one shift are excluded for comparability's sake.[2]

Qualitative analyses are based on a review of the narrative description of events on each ride. These accounts were used to characterize how officers handled citizens. Styles of policing were derived inductively. We began with a series of questions sensitive to various aspects of the department's approach to community policing. Four general areas were covered: (a) handling of suspects and wrongdoers; (b) handling victims, complainants, and service recipients; (c) mobilizing the community; and (d) problem solving. Because there was little observed activity relevant to the last two categories, analysis concentrated on how officers dealt with people where enforcement or order maintenance was an issue and with people in need of assistance.

To classify the officer's patrol style, a researcher read each narrative at least three times. Categories of police style emerged from the qualitative analysis, which began by looking for the kinds of decisions that officers could make about how to interact with the public. Two types of decisions were considered: (a) the frequency and nature of interventions officers initiated on their own (proactively), and (b) how officers dealt with citizens once involved in encounters. For the latter type of decision, we focused on the extent to which officers attempted to establish rapport with the public and serve them.

Quantitative data were used to determine the nature and extent of officer proactivity in initiating public encounters. We divided encounters into three categories: (a) those oriented only to dealing with a suspected criminal or troublemaker (enforcement only);[3] (b) those oriented only to dealing with citizens in need of assistance (i.e., crime victims or requesters of other services); and (c) those involving both suspects and those in need of assistance. Because we are interested in choices that *officers* made, we counted only those encounters where the officer, not some other party, was the mobilizing force (Reiss & Bordua, 1967). We created measures of officer proactivity by dividing the number of officer-initiated encounters by the amount of unassigned time available to the officer (i.e., all time not spent on activities assigned by the dispatcher or supervisor). These counts were applied to the styles of policing determined in the qualitative analysis.

Given the limited time span of observation of each officer in our sample, we are unable to provide an estimate of the stability of the behavior patterns each officer exhibited. Indeed, our prior research leads us to expect a high degree of variability in the work styles that officers exhibit (Snipes & Mastrofski, 1990). Obviously, it would be preferable to have observed each officer for several observation sessions to establish the extent to which a given style predicted his or her pattern of behavior. We must thus regard our observations as providing a snapshot of each officer captured at a particular point in time, and therefore subject to a degree of variability. Our confidence in the stability of these characterizations is increased somewhat by our "debriefing" conversations with officers, conducted after many of their interactions with the public. Here the officers were given an opportunity to describe their thoughts about what had transpired and to construct a justification for their actions. It seems likely that such accounts would be heavily influenced by their long-term orientation to their work. Even so, we are mindful of the tenuous linkage between what people say and what they do, and we caution the reader not to overinterpret the "styles" we observed.

STYLES OF POLICING

Our analysis revealed four distinctive officer styles, three of which are similar to those found in previous research (e.g., Worden, 1995). To minimize confusion, we have adopted Worden's (1995) characterization of those three styles: *Professional, Tough Cop,* and *Avoider.* A fourth style showed a different combination of behavioral proclivities, so we assign it a different name: *Reactor.* The 91 officers were distributed as follows: Professional (19%), Reactor (43%), Tough Cop (27%), and Avoider (11%). Table 5.1 shows the results of the quantitative analysis of officer proactivity, discussion of which is integrated with the results of the qualitative analysis in the following sections. We note that differences among the means are not statistically significant at the conventional level ($p < 0.05$), and no *posteriori* contrasts between any two groups are statistically significant.[4]

TABLE 5.1 Officer Proactivity by Patrol Style: Proactive Encounters per Hour of Discretionary Time

	N	Enforcement Only Mean (SD)	Service Only Mean (SD)	Enforcement and Service Mean (SD)
Professionals	17	0.33 (0.22)	0.17 (0.15)	0.03 (0.08)
Reactors	39	0.25 (0.25)	0.10 (0.13)	0.03 (0.08)
Tough Cops	25	0.38 (0.34)	0.07 (0.12)	0.02 (0.06)
Avoiders	10	0.17 (0.15)	0.08 (0.09)	0 (0)

NOTE: A proactive encounter is one initiated by the officer, not the dispatcher, supervisor, or citizen.

The Professional

Professionals initiated encounters for both enforcement and nonenforcement and tried to create partnerships with the public. They showed the highest overall rate of proactivity. They initiated enforcement-only encounters at about twice the rate of service-only encounters, but their inclination to do the latter was substantially greater than any other group. These officers enacted the community-policing tactics advocated by the department. They were willing to engage the public just to establish a closer relationship. They were often friendly, even with troublemakers, but they demanded respect. Although they rarely engaged in elaborate problem-solving projects, they tended to take a long-term perspective about addressing problems in the situation at hand.

Sense of the Beat. Professionals had a very strong sense of territorial possession (Mastrofski, 1983; Muir, 1977; Rubinstein, 1973). They developed knowledge of their beat as a point of pride:

> Officer A then asked where Citizen B [a small-time drug runner] was staying. Citizen B responded that he was staying with a friend, mentioning the general area. Officer A then asked for his specific address, but Citizen B said he couldn't recall. Then, Officer A said that he knew he was staying at X, naming a specific address. Citizen B responded with widened eyes and surprise in his voice, "Damn! You know more about me than I do!" At that, Officer A said, "Right!" and chuckled, bringing

even a smile to Citizen B's face. Officer A continued, "I makin' *you* my project. I don't wanna see you knocked off 'fore summer's out. Don't be messin' with those guys [drug dealers]," he said, in a tone that conveyed a bit of request, persuasion, and command.[5]

Professionals resented other officers encroaching upon their territory. They were confident about how things worked on their beat, and they liked to impose their own style of policing. One Professional said that he would not want any other officers to patrol *his* beat, and he had once had to run an officer off his beat because he was not policing *his* way. This sense of belonging to the beat and the community increased the Professional's feeling that he had a personal stake in the welfare of the community. He felt responsible to the community, and felt that they should reciprocate. They *both* shared the beat. The Professional did not view himself as an external protector, but as a concerned, specially empowered partner who was acting in the best interests of the community. Confronting someone suspicious who was standing on a street corner in his beat, one officer expressed it this way:

> What you doin' standin' on this corner? You got no business on this corner. I don't want you selling no drugs here. This is *my* corner. Get your ass off my corner! You ain't got no right to stand on *this* corner, 'cause this is *my* corner, and *your* sorry ass don't belong here!

Caring for People on the Beat. Professionals did not engage in superficial, "public relations" encounters with the people on their beat. They viewed casual conversations instrumentally—an opportunity to get to know who was on the beat, what they were doing, and what they needed. Professionals frequently took pains to assist people. One officer told a woman that she wanted to give her mother a ride home from the hospital. When the observer later asked the officer about department rules forbidding police from giving rides to the public, she replied that people like this woman deserved anything she could do to help her, and if that meant breaking department rules, "I don't care. If there is [such a policy], I'll take the day off . . . or I'll use the cruiser. This is my job, helping these people." Another Professional checked twice a day on an elderly man who lived alone. The officer had been doing this every workday for five or six years. Another encouraged women to use social service agencies and attempted to find jobs for those on welfare.

Many Professionals took a special interest in children, who seemed to them more reachable. Professionals also took opportunities to perform small services. One officer regularly offered to follow up his initial visit to a crime victim with a visit or telephone call. Another offered to call someone to bring a woman more insulin syringes; her supply had been stolen. Her television had also been stolen, so he offered to return and engrave her new television. Furthermore, Professionals made their services widely available, even to those in trouble with the law:

> Officer E stops in a dry cleaners and speaks with the owner. Officer E asks him about an upcoming court appearance. Officer E is very concerned. Citizen 1, a black male in his 60s, says that it is scheduled, and his lawyer is planning to fight. Officer E asks if he will be okay away from work. Citizen 1 says nothing will happen, because he has enough help. Officer E wishes Citizen 1 good luck and tells him to call if there is anything he can do. Officer E leaves. In the debriefing, Officer E said that someone served a 12-year-old probation violation on the man, and was pursuing it. The officer said that he had met that man as soon as he started working [this beat], and he has known him all of this time. Now, he gets a 12-year-old warrant served on him. Officer E thought it was ridiculous, since it was obvious that Citizen 1 had moved on and wasn't causing any problems.

Talking and Teaching. As with Muir's (1997) Professional, the Richmond Professional enjoyed talk, worked at developing language skills, and used them to teach citizens about government, law, and fairness, and how to take care of themselves. Professionals explained actions; they saw that it was often more important for a citizen to *learn* a lesson than to receive punishment, even if deserved. For example, a young motorist, suspected of involvement with drugs, was stopped, but the officer could find no legal justification for searching the car. Instead,

> he then said that he would cut the kid a break, and walked back to the car. He asked Citizen 1 to step out of the car, and had him walk back by the trunk. Officer 1 then said in a very patient, almost fatherly tone, "Look, I'm going to give you a break today. I could cite you for three violations. You don't have a city sticker. You don't have a pink slip for the vehicle inspection, and your tail pipe is about ready to fall off. I figure that you don't know that these things are violations. I know it's not

your car, but you have to understand that whenever you use someone else's car, you take responsibility for that car, for everything that's wrong with it. When you get into that car, you're saying, 'I'm responsible for this car, whatever it's like.'" He then explained what each of those things meant, and how to correct them. He then said, "Now listen to me carefully, because I want you to go directly home to your daddy and explain all this to him, all that I'm telling you."

Dealing with people who break the law to effect their own justice can be quite challenging (Black, 1983). The officer must deal with the paradox of "face" (Muir, 1977, Chapter 7):

Officer G then turned to Citizen 2 and said, as if he were talking to a peer, "I know this ain't easy, and what I think you should do won't be either. But for the time being, until we get this straightened out, I think you should take some precautions. I know you got to prove yourself, your manhood, and this guy provokes you, but if you could just stay away from the pool for a while, that would help." Citizen 2 said that he could do that, that he wasn't looking for a fight, but he wouldn't back down from one either. Officer G then said he understood Citizen 2 didn't want to back down from a fight, but if he could avoid one altogether, that would make things easier for his mama and for them. Citizen 2 agreed.

The Professionals wanted to put suspects at ease, letting them know the procedure they were going to put them through, thus avoiding unnecessary hostility and resistance:

At this point, Officer X got out his handcuffs and Officer Y explained that they would have to cuff him, that it was for his own protection (implying, but never saying, that if he were uncuffed the officers might interpret some of his actions as an effort to escape or resist and would have to harm him). Officer Y explained this in a very calm, reassuring, matter-of-fact way. He said that he would test the substance, and if it came up negative, he would be released; but if it came up positive, he would go to jail. Was he sure it wasn't drugs? Citizen 1 was sure. Citizen 1 also wanted to know why the officers could search without a warrant. Officer Y very calmly summarized the law on

search and seizure for Citizen 1, stating they had seen a substance that looked like drugs in plain view, they had a right to
search further and to cuff him—again emphasizing for his own
protection.

Order Maintenance. Professionals established order according to their
own moral sensibilities, but they were steeped in the beat, its people's
wants and needs. Professionals established specific rules about the line
between tolerable and intolerable disorder. To the outsider, they might
appear arbitrary and whimsical, but to those indoctrinated on her beat
they made sense (Bittner, 1967):

> Officer Z stopped at one of the corner stores on her beat. She
> asked how things were going, and Storeowner 1 said the drug
> dealers were not bothering them as much anymore. In the de-
> briefing afterwards, Officer Z said that she had been going to
> the store for at least a year. Storeowner 1 and Storeowner 2
> were very nice, and helped out the neighborhood as much as
> possible. Officer Z said that they give the local kids candy, and
> get the local drunks to help them unload the supply truck when
> it comes. Officer Z pointed to a group of men sitting under a
> tree not too far from the store. Office Z waved and the drunks
> waved back. Storeowner 1 and Storeowner 2 gave the drunks
> money when they worked for them. "These aren't your typical
> drunks, because they work for a living. They make good money
> too. They come under the tree in shifts, so there is always a
> group under the tree. They don't bother anyone, and they drive
> off the drug dealers. Storeowner 1 likes having them around,
> and so do I. I don't mess with them."

After establishing rules of order, Professionals were careful to enforce them. Whatever leniency they offered had clear limits:

> Driving down the street, the officer saw several elderly black
> males sitting on a front stoop. The officer pointed to Citizen 1,
> a man about 60, saying in a commanding voice, "This is the
> *second* time I've told you. Third time, I get your signature. I
> want you outta here! You understand?" Citizen 1, obviously
> under the influence of alcohol, nodded, vigorously assenting,
> and moving away immediately, putting the bottle down. Citi-
> zen 1 said that, yes, he understood and that it wouldn't happen

again. Citizen 1 thanked the officer and shuffled off from the group as we headed in the opposite direction. In the debriefing the officer said of Citizen 1, "He had respect. He's okay. I know him, so I give him some slack. Sometimes these drunks will drop a dime, but tomorrow I'll arrest his ass if he's here. All these guys know me and how I operate. I don't hassle them, but they know my rules. They know how I operate."

Professionals saw themselves as guardians of the neighborhood. They strove to deliver on threats as well as promises. They prided themselves in impressing potential troublemakers with their capacity to know who was doing what. They drew heavily on their memory of names and faces, their knowledge of neighborhood activities, and the connectivity of events on the beat. When they did arrest someone, they wanted to be sure that the citizen deserved it, and that it could be accomplished in a way that did not diminish their reputation for fairness.

Professionals tried to get the community to police itself. Most often, this meant serving as the eyes and ears of the police. This was sometimes done through the department's programs (e.g., Neighborhood Watch), but more frequently it was organized on an *ad hoc* basis:

> Officer Q saw Citizen 1 and Citizen 2, both white males, ages 55–60 and 25–30 respectively, sitting on the porch of a house that was well kept. Officer Q stopped the car and hollered hello to the men. The men walked over to the car, and Officer Q asked them if they knew about the drug problems. They said that they did know about them, but that the problems were mainly on another block. Officer Q told them that they could help keep the drugs away by calling him if they saw any dealing or use in their area. Officer Q gave Citizen 1 and Citizen 2 cards and instructed them on how they could reach Officer Q's pager. He also explained that if they did contact him about a suspicious person, he could not arrest the person just on that information, but told them that he would watch for that person, and try to get enough information to establish probable cause for arrest.

Professionals also promoted self-policing in many domestic disputes. This might mean encouraging a parent to take a different approach with a child or advising a citizen to avert future conflict by avoiding another person. One Professional spent much of her shift trying to sort out cross-complaints between former lovers. The woman was considering filing a request for a warrant on her former boyfriend, because he had allegedly abused her daughter. The man claimed that the daughter's injury was completely unintended and that he was not culpable, but that his former girlfriend was just seeking revenge, because he was now with another woman. The officer committed much effort to explaining legal rights and obligations to each, while also forcefully arguing the importance of staying away from each other. She, like other Professionals, tried to show citizens how to use the law to secure justice (Muir, 1977, pp. 118–125).

Problem Solving. Professionals were more likely than other officers were to engage in problem solving—that is, proposing longer-term solutions to problems rather than merely resolving the immediate situation. One officer was trying to organize the businesses on his beat into a merchant's association as a way of aiding communication between the police and the business owners. Other officers used existing agencies to deal with the problems they encountered. One officer noticed that some door locks on abandoned apartments were broken, which encouraged the use of these abodes as drug-dealing dens. If the locks were not broken, they were the type that makes it difficult to open the door from the inside. Rooms protected by these doors were favored by drug dealers: When the door closed, the person was trapped inside the room. This particular officer was working with the project manager to get the system changed. Most of the observed problem-solving efforts were small scale and *ad hoc,* not projects of the scope reported in the literature on problem-oriented policing (Eck & Spelman, 1987; Goldstein, 1990).

The Reactor

Reactors, the largest group of officers in the sample, were characterized by a disinclination to initiate encounters to offer assistance to citizens, but they were willing to oblige when "deserving" citizens explicitly asked for help and were able and willing to use it. Their reactive style did not extend to enforcement, however. In this regard, Reactors actively initiated encounters with the public to investigate suspicious circumstances and deal with troublemakers and law violators. The overall rate of Reactors' proactivity was lower than that of Professionals and Tough Cops. They were midway between Professionals and Avoiders in their enforcement-only proactivity, and similar to Tough Cops and Avoiders in their service-only proactivity.

Reactive Assistance. Reactors seldom went out of their way to initiate help to citizens on their beat, but when citizens requested it, they were inclined to accommodate, often with a considerable degree of effort. They seemed to have merged the department's current model to the more traditional reactive vision of police work, characterized by one officer as "you call, we haul." However, when summoned by citizens, Reactors were usually friendly:

> The officer asked the Citizen if she had made the call. The Citizen responded very calmly, yes, because she wanted to make sure that a man she knew wasn't still in the house. The Citizen explained that she had already talked to other police officers that day, and they advised her to take a warrant out on him. The Citizen had gone to do just that, and realized he had the keys to the house. The Citizen wanted the officer to go into the house with her to make sure the man wasn't there. The Officer said he would be more than happy to go with her. The Officer [and another Officer] escorted the Citizen inside the house. The Citizen checked the downstairs and upstairs and was sure the man was no longer there. "I want to thank both of you very much. I really appreciate this," said the woman. "No problem, that is what we are here for. Call us if you need anything else," responded the officer.

The Reactor took time to be reassuring or helpful and offer praise if appropriate:

> My Officer began talking with Citizen 1. She sat down in a chair next to him and addressed him by his first name. She asked him if he had lost his job. He said no. The Officer asked if he had a fight with his girlfriend. He said yes; that they had been separated for three months. The Officer asked if he had been drinking. The Citizen said no; he was an alcoholic, but he hadn't had any alcohol for three days because he didn't have any money. The Officer said that it was good that at least Citizen 1 had not resorted to stealing. "You have enough respect for yourself and others not to steal," she said. "That's something you can be proud of."

The Reactors showed that they cared about the citizens they encountered, and this was poignantly revealed in the amount of time they were willing to devote to the citizen:

Citizen 3 [a traffic violator in an accident] began to cry and the
Officer consoled her, telling her it wasn't as bad as she thought;
she should thank God that no one was hurt; this was an accident, and accidents do happen; she should explain the slippery
road conditions to the judge in court; and, if Citizen 3 had a
good driving record, the judge would likely offer that her driving record would be kept clean if she went to driving school.
Citizen 3 stopped crying and signed the citation. The Officer
advised Citizen 3 to let the insurance companies handle everything and not to agree to pay Citizen 1 any money out of her
own pocket if he should call and ask her for money. The Officer
then asked Citizen 3 if she had any way to get home. Citizen 3
said that she did not, so the Officer said that he would drive her
home. He then drove Citizen 3 home, telling her again that she
should be thankful that everyone was okay, and that she
shouldn't be worried about the citation. Citizen 3 nodded, and
thanked the Officer for her ride home.

Selectivity of Assistance. Reactors complained about the lack of help
from the public, and displayed a propensity to engage in helping activities only when citizens initiated the idea. Reactors considered this entirely within the spirit of community policing—letting the people decide
what police should do, and that to deserve a special partnership arrangement, citizens had to make the effort. The citizen had to demonstrate a
desire for the officer's help before receiving it; others went further:

> Having just returned from a five-hour orientation on commu-
> nity policing, Officer X said with some satisfaction, "It [com-
> munity policing] means that we can tell them [citizens] that if
> they don't cooperate, they can't complain about crime and po-
> lice services."

Reactors were inclined to be selective in other ways, too. Citizens
who were down-and-out, irrational, and incoherent—who did not appreciate what police were trying to do—were less deserving of special police effort:

> [Citizen 2 was slightly incoherent, had no shoes, and was lying
> on the ground in the middle of the city]. Citizen 2 came up
> clean [on the warrant check], and the officer walked back over
> to Citizen 2. "Do you want me to call Crisis Center?" the Offi-

cer asked Citizen 2, matter-of-factly. "The problem, Mr. W, is you can't stay out here. The neighbors will keep complaining, and I'll have to keep coming out here. Is there some place you can go?" the Officer asked Citizen 2. Citizen 2 asked the Officer, where did the Officer want Citizen 2 to go? The Officer said he didn't care, as long as he moved on. Citizen 2 said he had some place he could go. After this, Citizen 2 would try to talk to the Officer and the Officer, not appearing interested, would always cut him off to say something to me or the security officer who was still there.

One officer opined that people who pay taxes deserve better treatment than those who do not, and another officer was more comfortable interacting with "church-going types." The Reactors were more likely to be frustrated with the people on their beat or unsympathetic to their plight:

Officer L approached Citizen 1 (a white female in her 20s) and asked her sternly why she had left headquarters without swearing out a warrant. Citizen 1 meekly said that she was scared of her boyfriend, and would rather just leave town than have him arrested. Officer L angrily responded, "Oh, so you just decided to waste our [Officer L and Officer N] time by having us bring you all the way downtown for nothing. Well, you deserve to be whipped by your boyfriend. And if he does whip you and give you crack and you wind up with a crack baby, don't go around saying the system doesn't work; 'cause it's trying to work for you!"

Initiating Enforcement. Reactors were quite comfortable with initiating *enforcement-oriented* encounters with the public. They were quick to approach citizens who might be engaged in illegal activity, just to let them know that they were on patrol. One officer liked to pull people over for suspected drunk driving; another liked to make traffic stops as an excuse to run a check on the driver's identification. Although not exceptionally aggressive in terms of enforcement, they clearly identified this area as the place where initiative mattered in police work.

Reactors bore some similarities to Muir's (1977) Reciprocators—officers who needed clients who recognized and appreciated the kinds of service they could provide (pp. 92–97) and were stymied when they did not (pp. 137–140). Like Reciprocators, Reactors were willing to devote considerable time and effort when they found a citizen who appreciated what they could offer. Unlike Muir's Reciprocators, however, Reactors were less imbued with a tragic perspective, less inclined to assume a there-but-for-the-grace-of-God orientation to social outcasts. Further, unlike Muir's Reciprocators, they were at ease with their capacity to intrude on citizens, to coerce—as long as the situation fit an enforcement framework.

The Tough Cop

Tough Cops enacted a narrow role; they focused on crime fighting. The quantitative analysis shows that they were the most active in initiating enforcement-only encounters and about the same as Reactors and Avoiders in initiating service-only encounters. Tough Cops were cynical: impatient with complex disorders in which people could not be quickly sorted into "good" or "bad." They liked to impose their own reading of a situation without much investigation, and took easy umbrage if someone questioned their interpretation.

Role as Crime-Fighter. Tough Cops viewed themselves as deliverers of justice—but in a restricted domain—when there was a clear violation of the law. They were angered by the department's expectation that they serve as Jacks-of-all-trades. One Tough Cop said that he would rather be a "law enforcer than a babysitter." Another said, "I love my job. I'm here to bring about justice." This officer engaged in the following encounter, displaying her zest for full enforcement:

> The Officer noticed a car that was illegally parked in front of a business in a shopping center. "The thing that pisses me off, is there are plenty of parking spaces in the parking lot." A woman headed towards the car, and the Officer put on the P.A. [public announcement system], "Don't move that car!" very forcefully. The Officer got out and put a ticket on the car without saying a word or even looking at the woman . . The Officer spotted an illegally parked car at X Plaza. "Gotcha you!" the Officer said with a certain amount of glee. The Officer put a ticket on the car.

Another officer was very angry when he had to direct traffic around a broken-down car; he would rather be catching drunk drivers. A similar frustration was voiced by another who preferred to pursue drug dealers, driving at a high speed to scare them into dropping something.

The Quick-Fix. The Professional and the Reactor took some time to put citizens at ease when they encountered them on their beats. The Tough Cop preferred to resolve situations as quickly as possible, especially those fraught with factual and moral complexity:

> Officer T commented that he had never spent this much time on a domestic [call] before. The Officer said that it's a bad thing for a cop to show bias, since it jeopardizes his or her profession-alism. Officer T said that when it comes to domestic disputes, he doesn't hesitate to arrest both parties if necessary, and "let the judge work it out later." The Officer said that the best tactic for handling domestics is to do whatever is necessary to stop the dispute as quickly as possible, and to not play marriage counselor and try to solve the couple's problems.

Tough Cops were frustrated by those calls that they considered time-consuming and worthless; they often found it difficult to disguise their impatience with the situation:

> Officer D does not appreciate having to leave his beat to do what he considers to be wasteful calls that are time-consuming but don't accomplish anything. These include calls like someone saying a kid is playing on a pay phone, or someone is playing music too loudly during the day, or petty arguments. At the beginning of this shift, when Officer D got several of these kinds of calls right in a row, he became angry and arrived at the scene with an attitude that this was *not* going to take much time, if he had any say in the matter.

Officer as Authoritarian. The Tough Cops preferred to take charge im-mediately and were quick to impose their authority on anyone involved. They demanded complete respect, taking offense at the slightest demurral. They relied mostly on coercive power rather than skill in con-versation, as in these two examples:

> "Those people who are polite and treat you with respect, I give them a break. People who don't respect me, I hook [arrest] them quick." The Officer said that he doesn't let stuff get out of

hand, and he never has any problems. "When I do have a problem, I take care of it quick. If he hits me, I'll try to cave-in his skull."

Citizen 1 becomes louder as the child does not answer. The Officer physically blocks Citizen 1's path as she tries to go upstairs to the other children. Citizen 1 demands to go upstairs to see the other children. The Officer tells her she can't. Citizen 1 tries to push past the Officer, scratching her in the process. The Officer loses her temper completely, *"You scratched me, you bitch!"* Citizen 1 shouts back, "I didn't do anything to you." The Officer goes to put her in handcuffs. Citizen 1 swings at her. The Officer pounces on top of her, screaming, "Come on, dammit! I want to fight you!" Officer 2 jumps in and the Officers handcuff the suspect.

Cynicism About the Public. Tough Cops felt alienated from most of the people on their beat. Caring service or "partnerships" were unthinkable:

Shortly after Citizen 1 left, the officers said goodbye to Citizen 2 and left as well. Citizen 1 was nowhere to be seen when we came out of the house. At a nearby residence, we heard two people in a verbal argument. One of the children from Citizen 2's apartment, who had followed us outside, told the Officer that the neighbors were fighting. The Officer said, "Tell them to call 911 and wait in line." We then left.

One Tough Cop separated people into "ticks and turds," and another estimated that 95% of the people in the United States were criminals, rehabilitation was a joke, and the police were "banging their heads against a stone wall" with the war on drugs. The Tough Cop is this study's analog to Muir's (1977) Enforcer, quite willing to impose his or her "justice" on a public perceived as mostly undeserving of their protection.

The Avoider

Avoiders were reluctant to engage in any type of encounter. They rarely initiated contact with the public and were loath to seek opportunities to help. They showed the lowest overall proactivity, substantially below Reactors and about half that of Professionals. When dispatched to an assignment, Avoiders attempted to get by with as little effort as possible, showing little concern for the needs and requests of citizens.

If the Avoider sensed that a citizen might not immediately submit to police authority, he or she attempted to get out of the situation as easily as possible, even if that meant not addressing an important problem:

> The Officer said she thought the Citizen was a drunk, but he was acting too weird. The Officer said that all she wanted was a cup of coffee, and she didn't really feel like dealing with the Citizen. The Officer said she might have cuffed him, and charged him with being drunk in public, but all the other units were tied up, and she thought there might have been a struggle and she didn't want to tackle the Citizen alone. The Officer said she called for a supervisor to cover her ass. The Officer said if she had cuffed the Citizen, he would have been back on the streets in four hours, so, this way, he would at least be out of her hair for a few days.

This officer also stated, "Why should I look for trouble? The trouble is going to find me anyway," and that all she wanted to do was to "put in her time and go home." Similarly, another Avoider with over 20 years experience believed that he had now earned the right to let the younger officers run the radio calls and "hustle." He remained logged off from calls until all the paperwork was completed, and he avoided traffic stops too.

Avoiders preferred to dodge the community—and if that were not possible, then to make the contact as brief as possible:

> Citizen 1 said she wanted to know how she could find out who the owner of the home was. "City planning, Crisis Center, City Assessor. I don't know who could give you that information," Officer 1 said to the Citizen. The officers walked next door and there were about five people sitting outside. Officer 2 asked if he could see the person whose name appeared on the lease. "This isn't my beat, and I don't know you people. You and your neighbor need to work out something. Otherwise this will probably be settled in court," Officer 1 said, sounding frustrated. In the debriefing, Officer 1 said that she was tired of answering X precinct's calls. "It wasn't my beat, it wasn't my precinct. I didn't give a damn what they did."

When opportunities presented themselves to improve the relation-ship between the police and community, the Avoider chose to ignore them:

> The Officer asked what the [previous] officer had told her, and Citizen 1 said he told her to get out a warrant. The Officer then said, "Well, why did you call us again when you know I'm going to tell you the same thing? You were told by the other officer last time. I'm not going to tell you something different." And then we got back in the car and left.

Avoiders scorned the people on their beat. They expressed no sympa-thy for the plight of the poor, and several disliked or were bewildered by blacks:

> The two citizens begin a slight argument about the money to do the laundry. The Officer interrupts, and says that this is ri-diculous and that they really must not want to do anything about the situation if something this small starts a fight. Citi-zen 1 is obviously insulted by the remark. The Officer asks her what she thinks the situation is doing to the child. Citizen 1 re-sponds, as if insulted, that she does everything for the child. The Officer is clearly disgusted with the lot. The Officer waits in silence.

Their cynicism justified dodging work. Some carried miniature TVs in their patrol cars, left their shifts early, made 30-minute personal calls, "milked" dispatched assignments, avoided writing reports, and dis-played a reluctance to answer calls. Avoiders took neither a short- nor long-term interest in handling citizens' problems. In many of their en-counters, they appeared aloof, apathetic, and indolent. They had the Tough Cop's cynicism, but they lacked any sense of mission. They fit neatly into Muir's (1977) category of the same name.

STYLES OF POLICING IN A COMMUNITY-POLICING CONTEXT

We have presented four distinct approaches to patrol work occurring within the same department. Professionals fit the official department ideal. Reactors seemed to have adapted some aspects of the community-policing "philosophy" to their preferred work style. Tough Cops and Avoiders routinely engaged in practices that were antithetical to the department's new ideal.

Our study cannot determine the extent to which the department's efforts to shape street-level police styles actually altered practice, because we do not have observations of officers before the organization undertook its community-policing program. However, we can examine the relationship between officers' attitudes toward community policing (expressed in response to specific questions from the observers)[6] and the style of policing they exhibited on the beat (see Table 5.2). Positive officers show a much stronger inclination to be Professionals (about 3.8 times that of negative officers), and negative officers show a stronger inclination to be Avoiders (about 3.6 times positive officers). Reactors and Tough Cops fall in the middle, showing much smaller differences. It is not surprising that attitude toward community policing is associated with behavioral style of policing. What is remarkable is that the association is not stronger. Although a positive attitude toward community policing increases the likelihood of yielding police work more compatible with the department's community-policing ideals, it is far from a guarantee. Possibly for some officers, a shift in values was not accompanied by a shift in skills, a potentially important element in predicting some aspects of police behavior (Mastrofski, Ritti, & Snipes, 1994). The Tough Cops and Avoiders who were positively oriented to community policing ($N = 14$) may have lacked the communications skills of the Professionals.

Shift Work and Police Style

An alternative source of influence on an officer's operational style is the distribution of opportunities available to the officer while on the job (Mastrofski et al., 1994). Opportunities for involvement with the public can vary according to the time of day. What citizens are in the beat, what they are doing, and the kinds of problems they are likely to experience are heavily influenced by social and economic patterns of behavior closely tied to time of day (Rubinstein, 1973, pp. 63–64). Many police feel that community policing is most appropriately done on the day shift, and that disorder control and enforcement opportunities (for more serious crimes) are concentrated on the other two shifts. Many officers on the evening shift argued that there simply was not much time available to engage in "social niceties" on this shift, which

TABLE 5.2 Style of Patrol by Attitude Toward Community Policing (in percentages)

	Attitude Toward Community Policing	
	Negative	Positive
Professionals	8.3	30.2
Reactors	47.9	37.2
Tough Cops	27.1	27.9
Avoiders	16.7	4.7
(N)	(48)	(43)

$p < 0.05$

they regarded as the most active of the three. Perhaps, then, the distribution of officers across the operational style categories is heavily influenced by the distribution of officers according to work shift.

Table 5.3 shows the bivariate distribution of officer styles according to work shift. The distribution of officers by style changes significantly according to work shift. A substantially larger portion of the day-shift officers displayed behavior most consistent with the department's model of community policing (Professionals), but they were far less apparent on the other two shifts.[7] It is difficult to know what underlies this distribution. It may be that the opportunities to engage in the aspects of community policing captured in our analysis *are* dependent upon the shift. It may also be the case that officers attracted to community policing are also more attracted to (or able to obtain) day-shift work, whereas those who are less attracted to a community-policing style are more inclined to seek work on the other shifts

We can explore this issue by examining the relationship between officers' feelings about community policing and their behavior. If officers are predisposed to do community policing (as revealed in their attitudes), and the opportunity to do community policing (as revealed in shift work) does not make a difference, then the relationship between attitudes and behavior (as reflected in their operational style) should remain constant across work shifts. However, if opportunity matters, then the strength of the relationship should depend upon work shift. Table 5.4 suggests that the latter is the case, although the number of cases is insufficient for a statistical test for independence. Positively oriented officers are far more likely to show Professional patterns on the day shift (compared to negative officers) than they are on the evening/midnight shift.

TABLE 5.3 Style of Patrol by Work Shift (in percentages)

	Work Shift		
	Day	*Evening*	*Midnight*
Professionals	33.3	7.1	4.8
Reactors	40.5	39.3	52.4
Tough Cops	16.7	35.7	38.1
Avoiders	9.5	17.9	4.8
(*N*)	(42)	(28)	(21)

$p < 0.05$.

Community Policing and Police Styles: A New Paradigm?

Our analysis did not produce a radical divergence from previous police operational style typologies. Three of the four were quite consistent with those identified by Worden (1995). A case study of one department in the midst of implementing community policing hardly constitutes a conclusive test for assessing the nature and extent of change, but it affords us the opportunity to look for patterns suggestive of trends.

Those officers who most closely fit the Richmond community-policing ideal were readily classified in the Professional category, one which Muir (1977) argued was preferable to all others. We note, however, that Richmond's Professionals did not engage much in the kinds of activities that reformers have proclaimed as "new and different" about community policing: mobilizing large numbers of citizens to improve public safety (usually by dealing with neighborhood and business groups), and engaging in problem-oriented policing projects, as characterized in the literature. Our observers frequently heard officers declare that community policing was not new, but only what had long constituted good police work, a refrain often heard from supervisors and administrators as well. From this perspective, Richmond's experience with community policing could hardly be expected to have produced a paradigm shift. It seems more likely that, if anything shifted, it was the distribution of officers across different operational styles.

The Reactor category offers a subtle qualification to this judgment, however. Reactors really fit into none of the prior categories. They were fairly proactive on enforcement matters, but not on incidents that only offered the prospect of providing assistance. Once involved with

TABLE 5.4　Style of Patrol by Work Shift and Attitude Toward Community
Policing (in percentages)

	Day Shift		Evening/Midnight Shift	
	Negative Attitude	Positive Attitude	Negative Attitude	Positive Attitude
Professionals	10.5	52.2	6.9	5.0
Reactors	57.9	26.1	41.4	50.0
Tough Cops	10.5	21.7	37.9	35.0
Avoiders	21.1	0.0	13.8	10.0
(N)	(19)	(23)	(29)	(20)

$p < 0.05$.

the public, they offered their assistance selectively, only if citizens asked. They were not as openly hostile to socially marginal people as were Tough Cops and Muir's Enforcers, but they were not inclined to help them out, even if asked. This group held a plurality of officers; it would be useful to know how many were behavioral styles in transition from some other style. Were these officers who were once Tough Cops whose behavior was being modified by community-policing pressures? Or, were these officers once Professionals now becoming disillusioned with community policing? We can only speculate, but the possibility raises the intriguing proposition that community-policing efforts in Richmond did little to restructure police styles at the extremes (Professional and Avoider), but perhaps had their greatest effect in the middle.

CONCLUSION

We have examined police styles in a department implementing a model of community policing that stressed a proactive, community-building approach. We found considerable diversity among officers. Only one in five (Professionals) exhibited behavior consistent with the leadership's ideal of how officers should deal with the public. Almost two in five officers showed styles distinctly at odds with the department's ideal, infrequently initiating helping encounters and making little effort to establish closer rapport with the community (Tough Cops and Avoiders).

The largest group, slightly more than two in five officers, showed a mixed pattern not observed in previous research on police work styles: a willingness to improve rapport with the public, but only on a reactive and selective basis. These officers furthermore sustained a fairly high level of proactive enforcement. However, if these officers represent an evolution from the Tough Cop or Avoider styles, this would represent "progress" toward the department ideal.

That the vast majority of officers, when observed by outsiders, should show patrol styles outside the department's ideal will not surprise most seasoned officers or students of policing. Nonetheless, this stands in striking contrast to the perspective offered in the press, by anecdotal accounts, and even through some systematic surveys—that police officers are taking to community policing as *the* wave of the future (Weisel & Eck, 1994). When we look at actual street-level practice, the picture is much fuzzier, at least in Richmond.

These observations were made early in the department's efforts to move to a community-oriented model. The study confirms a common-sense assumption that is often lost in the promotion of this reform: A rapid, wholesale change in patrol officers' behavior is not likely. One can find many limitations in the department's implementation at the time of the study, but reports from other departments suggest that its experience is not atypical of others (Greene, Bergman, & McLaughlin, 1994; Sadd & Grinc, 1994; Trojanowicz, 1994; Weisel & Eck, 1994). Moreover, in Richmond, as perhaps around the nation, many officers can accept community policing because it is presented and perceived as a distillation of the best the craft has *long* produced. Whether the department's sponsorship of community policing stimulated more officers to pursue styles closer to the community-policing ideal than previously is beyond our capacity to determine. Longitudinal observation studies of individual officers could help establish such effects. For example, they could help determine whether the Reactor style observed here is merely a reflection of officers in transition between traditional styles found in studies of the 1970s, or whether it represents the emergence of a previously unidentified style of policing.

The relationship between officers' views about community policing and their behavior is noteworthy, not so much for the strength of the relationship, but because it is not stronger. This relationship is strongest on the day shift, where officers reported having the greatest opportunity to do community policing. Consistent with the propositions of expectancy motivation theory (Mastrofski et al., 1994), this suggests that performance requires that the worker have the will *and* perceive the opportunity to enact the prescribed work role. This means that departments such as Richmond may need to make special efforts to show officers what community policing requires on the evening and midnight shifts.

We must be cautious about the generalizability of these findings. Other models of community policing could easily produce different results. Even the same department, when the reform has matured, could yield different patterns. It is not at all clear what those patterns might be. Police, tend to be wary of management-generated improvement campaigns. They are skeptical of "new brooms," especially if they fail to deliver on their promises. Many Richmond officers who supported community policing also feared that the department and city government would fail to sustain long-term support, especially support that "put meat on the bones" of the new model: reigning in calls for service, providing more practical training, encouraging supervisors who support community policing, supplying adequate equipment, and staffing of line and support functions (Mastrofski, Willis, & Snipes, 1993). Given the characteristically short tenure of police chiefs and the evanescent quality of community-policing reforms in some of the pioneer departments, the officers' concerns seem rational.

The Richmond officers' anxieties about the trajectory of their organization's change should direct our attention to the larger structures having major implications for the patterns of street-level policing. Analyses such as ours need to be fitted into a broader, but currently underdeveloped, agenda of cross-department research. Wilson's (1968) classic comparative study of police department structure still stands as the most significant statement of the relationship between police organization structure and street-level performance. Scholars have since become sensitive to the diversity of individual patrol styles extant at the street level within a single department, but we know little about what different organizational structures in different environments mean for the patterns that emerge. Community-policing advocates hope that the reform will generate a renaissance in experimentation with organizational forms. If police organizations do become more diverse structurally, they will present researchers with an opportunity to learn whether and how structural change affects the everyday work of police officers.

A final comment about the utility of this sort of research is in order. Most of the literature assessing the implementation of community policing relies upon surveys of police officers to gauge their reactions to community policing. Although survey data can be useful, this type of research is unable to tell us much about the actual behavior of officers on the street, which surely must be *the* gold standard of implementation. Our research shows that when the standard is the behavior an officer displays, rather than the officer's philosophy, the picture is far more complex than can be revealed through simple expressions of officer attitude toward community policing. Research from this data set has been published in several outlets, and has been used to determine the extent to which officers committed to community policing are influenced by extralegal factors, such as the race or sex of suspects, compared to the influence of legal considerations (e.g., the strength of evidence; Mastrofski, Worden, & Snipes, 1995). These data have also been used to test whether officers committed to community policing are more successful in getting citizens to obey them than officers with weaker commitments to community policing are (Mastrofski, Snipes, & Supina, 1996). In both cases, the results were positive for the prospects of community policing in Richmond, at least according to the expectations of the department's top leadership at the time. The ultimate benefit of such research is to offer a *realistic* appraisal of what has been accomplished by community policing at the street level, where the police and public experience it.

NOTES

1. To protect the identity of officers whose actions are described here, we have randomly altered some of the personal characteristics used to portray them.
2. These officers present an interesting, but only suggestive, picture of the stability of police behavior. Five of the 12 officers received identical style classifications on all observed rides, but the remaining officers received different classifications. Adding the five consistent officers to the distribution makes no substantive difference, altering the percentage in each category no more than 1%. Of the remaining seven officers, those displaying what we came to call the Reactor style (see our discussion in the Styles of Policing section) showed the greatest tendency to instability.
3. Because of the ambiguity of roles when there are disputants present (each claiming that the other is in the wrong), encounters with disputants were grouped in the "suspect" category, since both disputants are considered potential "troublemakers."
4. The F ratio for the between-group differences for *all* proactive encounters summed (not shown in Table 5.1) approaches statistical significance ($p < 0.06$). The contrast test used was Tukey's HSD (honestly significant difference), $p < 0.05$.
5. This and the following excerpts are taken from observers' notes.
6. Officers were asked to describe Richmond's community-policing program and then to give their opinion about it. These open-ended questions were followed by additional probes about the best and worst things about it and about what problems patrol officers face in making it work. In most cases, officers went well beyond cursory responses to these open-ended questions. Based on these responses, the observers classified officers

into one of five categories: very negative, negative, mixed, positive, and very positive. For this paper's analysis, "negative attitudes" included officers who were classed as having very negative, negative, or mixed views of community policing. Positive officers were those who held positive or very positive views.

7. A chi-square test for independence was performed with the evening and midnight shifts collapsed into one category (to create a sufficient number of cases in each cell), yielding a chi-square statistic significant at $p < 0.01$.

REFERENCES

Berman, J. S. (1987). *Police administration and progressive reform: Theodore Roosevelt as Police Commissioner of New York.* New York: Praeger.

Bittner, E. (1967). The police on skid-row: A study of peace keeping. *American Sociological Review, 32,* 699–715.

Black, D. (1983). Crime as social control. *American Sociological Review, 48*(1), 34–45.

Braithwaite, J. (1989). *Crime, shame and reintegration.* New York: Cambridge University Press.

Braithwaite, J., & Pettit, P. (1990). *Not just deserts: A republican theory of criminal justice.* Oxford, UK: Clarendon Press.

Bratton, W. (1998). *Turnaround: How America's top cop reversed the crime epidemic.* New York: Random House.

Broderick, J. (1977). *Police in a time of change.* Morristown, NJ: General Learning Press.

Brown, M. (1981). *Working the street: Police discretion and the dilemmas of reform.* New York: Russell Sage.

Eck, J. E., & Rosenbaum, D. P. (1994). The new police order: Effectiveness, equity and efficiency in community Policing. In D. P. Rosenbaum (Ed.), *The challenge of community policing: Testing the promises* (pp. 3–23). Thousand Oaks, CA: Sage.

Eck, J. E., & Spelman, W. (1987). Who ya gonna call? The police as problem-busters. *Journal of Research in Crime and Delinquency, 33*(1), 31–52.

Fogelson, R. (1977). *Big city police.* Cambridge, MA: Harvard University Press.

Goldstein, H. (1990). *Problem-oriented policing.* New York: McGraw-Hill.

Greene, J. R., Bergman, W. T., & McLaughlin, E. J. (1994). Implementing community policing: Cultural and structural change in police organizations. In D. P. Rosenbaum (Ed.), *The challenge of community policing: Testing the promises* (pp. 92–109). Thousand Oaks, CA: Sage.

Hochstedler, E. (1981). Testing types: A review and test of police types. *Journal of Criminal Justice, 9*(6), 451–466.

Independent Commission on the Los Angeles Police Department. (1991). *Report of the Independent Commission.* Los Angeles: Author.

Kelling, G. L., & Coles, C. M. (1996). *Fixing broken windows: Restoring order and reducing crime in our communities.* New York: Free Press.

Mastrofski, S. D. (1983). Police knowledge of the patrol beat: A performance measure. In R. R. Bennett (Ed.), *The police working environment: Policy issues for the eighties* (pp. 45–64). Beverly Hills, CA: Sage.

Mastrofski, S., & Parks, R. B. (1990). Improving observational studies of police. *Criminology, 28*(3), 475–496.

Mastrofski, S. D., Ritti, R., & Snipes, J. B. (1994). Expectancy theory and police productivity in DUI enforcement. *Law and Society Review, 28*(1), 113–148.

Mastrofski, S. D., Snipes, J. B., & Supina, A. E. (1996). Compliance on demand: The public's response to specific police requests. *Journal of Research in Crime and Delinquency, 33*(3), 269–305.

Mastrofski, S. D., Willis, J. J., & Snipes, J. B. (1993). *Community policing: The street officer's view.* University Park, PA: Pennsylvania State University.

Mastrofski, S. D., Worden, R. E., & Snipes, J. B. (1995). Law enforcement in a time of community policing. *Criminology, 33*(4), 539–563.

Muir, W. K. (1977). *Police: Streetcorner politicians.* Chicago: University of Chicago Press.

Norman, M. (1993, December 12). One cop, eight square blocks. *New York Times Magazine*, pp. 63–69, 76, 86, 89–90, 96.

Reiss, A. J., & Bordua, D. J. (1967). Environment and organization: A perspective on the police. In D. J. Bordua (Ed.), *The police: Six sociological essays* (pp. 25–55). New York: John Wiley.

Rubinstein, J. (1973). *City police.* New York: Farrar, Straus & Giroux.

Sadd, S., & Grinc, R. (1994). Innovative neighborhood oriented policing: An evaluation of community policing programs in eight cities. In D. P. Rosenbaum (Ed.), *The challenge of community policing: Testing the promises* (pp. 27–52). Thousand Oaks, CA: Sage.

Snipes, J. B., & Mastrofski, S. D. (1990). An empirical test of Muir's typology of police officers. *American Journal of Criminal Justice, 14,* 268–296.

Sykes, G. W. (1986). Street justice: A moral defense of order maintenance. *Justice Quarterly, 3*(4), 497–512.

Trojanowicz, R. C. (1991). Community policing curbs police brutality. *Footprints, 3,* 1–3.

Trojanowicz, R. C. (1994). *Community policing: A survey of police departments in the United States.* Washington, DC: Federal Bureau of Investigation.

Walker, S. (1977). *A critical history of police reform.* Lexington, MA: D. C. Heath.

Weisel, D. L., & Eck, J. E. (1994). Toward a practical approach to organizational change: Community policing initiatives in six cities. In D. P. Rosenbaum (Ed.), *The challenge of community policing: Testing the promises* (pp. 53–72). Thousand Oaks, CA: Sage.

White, S. O. (1972). A perspective on police professionalization. *Law and Society Review, 7,* 61–85.

Wilson, J. Q. (1968). *Varieties of police behavior: The management of law and order in eight communities.* Cambridge, MA: Harvard University Press.

Wilson, J. Q., & Kelling, G. L. (1982, March). Broken windows: The police and neighborhood safety. *Atlantic Monthly*, pp. 29–38.

Worden, R. E. (1995). Police officers' belief systems: A framework for analysis. *American Journal of Police, 14*(1), 49–81.

Wycoff, M. A. (1994). *Community policing strategies.* Washington, DC: Police Foundation.

CHAPTER 6

Dual Responsibilities
A Model for Immersing Midlevel Managers in Community Policing

Mark E. Alley
Elizabeth M. Bonello
Joseph A. Schafer

> It is possible to identify a desired culture and to specify strategies
> and activities designed to produce change, but without the change
> process becoming personalized, without individuals being willing
> to engage in new behaviors, without an alteration in the
> managerial competencies demonstrated in the organization, the
> organization's fundamental culture will not change.
>
> *K. S. Cameron and R. E. Quinn (1999)*

Much of the emphasis of the community-policing movement has been on the changing roles of patrol officers and sergeants. Community policing evokes images of patrol officers meeting with neighborhood groups, walking foot beats, and working with children. Consistent with this view, the focus of researchers and practitioners has been on moving officers away from their traditional law enforcement roles and toward working collaboratively to resolve quality-of-life issues in the neighborhoods they serve. Given their extensive interactions with patrol officers, the vital role that sergeants play in community policing and the need to redefine their role have been widely recognized.

Largely absent in the discussion about community policing are discussions of how community policing affects (or should affect) the role and function of midlevel managers. Such an oversight is unfortunate, because midlevel managers play a crucial role in changing the culture of the organization and thus determining the success of any police innovation. This chapter explores the role of midlevel managers in community-policing agencies, considers one method of immersing midlevel managers in community policing, and suggests how obstacles to the successful implementation of this model can be overcome.

THE ROLE OF MIDLEVEL MANAGERS

Police organizations have traditionally been characterized by highly centralized decision making, formalized communication structures, strict functional specialization, hierarchical command models, and a dense vertical distance between line officers and administrators (Fogelson, 1977; Walker, 1977). This type of structure is inconsistent with the move to community policing, which requires highly adaptive and flexible systems for responding to citizen needs. The midlevel manager is a key linking pin in driving the organizational culture change required for the successful move to community policing. For midlevel managers to be drivers rather than barriers to change, the roles of these managers must change. This section examines the traditional role of midlevel managers and the need to change roles to drive cultural change in police organizations.

Traditional Roles

Within the traditional paramilitary structure, midlevel managers have played a critical role in overseeing operations, acting as lynchpins between "street cops" and "management cops" (Reuss-Ianni, 1983), and establishing how policies and practices would actually be enacted on the street level (Lipsky, 1980). For the officers working on patrol, the midlevel managers represented the day-to-day face of a police department's administration.

Midlevel managers and their subordinates have traditionally had a command-and-obey relationship, with the managers being concerned with controlling and regulating the behavior, discretion, and conduct of patrol officers. Ensuring that officers complied with departmental policies and procedures has been the means by which midlevel managers maintained order and control over their shifts. The result has been that midlevel managers have extended "the reach of management into the day-to-day operations of police departments by standardizing and controlling both organizational procedures and officer performance" (Kelling & Bratton, 1993, p. 9).

Particularly in large agencies, midlevel managers have been a vital link between top management, who issued orders, and patrol officers and their sergeants. Although an officer ultimately answered to top management, the midlevel managers have had far more influence over how the officer operated on a daily basis. Midlevel managers operate in a "complex environment," linking subordinates, administrators, and the community (Trojanowicz, 1980). In some cases, they serve as insulation between the line officers and the department's administration. As the "man in the middle," a midlevel manager could not create policy, but did have the capacity to determine which policies would be emphasized. These managers have traditionally controlled their shifts by determining how officers would apply policies on the street, telling officers what was expected of them, and letting officers know whether their performance was meeting these expectations (Rubinstein, 1973; Van Maanen, 1983; see also Miller, 1977; Trojanowicz, 1980).

New Roles for Cultural Change

A key factor contributing to the failure of planned organizational change efforts is the lack of attention paid to the organization's culture (Cameron & Quinn, 1999). Clearly, the move to community policing must involve a change to the underlying police culture, which generally favors formal hierarchy, strict control, and adherence to clear rules and regulations. Often, administrators do not know how to create change at this level. Changing the behavioral patterns of midlevel managers is a key catalyst to department-wide cultural change.

Unfortunately, many agencies that have moved toward community policing have allowed midlevel managers to continue their traditional control function while expecting patrol officers and sergeants to adopt new roles and to discover innovative ways of delivering police services. One explanation for this may be that many police administrators have learned from past experience to view middle management as a source of resistance to change (Kelling & Bratton, 1993). In the 1970s, police departments across the country attempted to implement "team policing" in an effort to enhance their efficiency and efficacy.

These efforts largely failed to achieve their desired outcomes, and the approach was subsequently abandoned. A key factor contributing to the failure of team policing was middle management's view of team policing as a threat to the power and authority of midlevel managers (for supporting research, see Gaines, 1994; Walker, 1993; Wycoff & Kelling, 1978). Consequently, midlevel managers engaged in both active and passive resistance, which significantly impeded the successful implementation of team-policing programs.

More recently, the Washington State Police had similar experiences in its efforts to implement a collaborative problem-solving program. Midlevel managers, who had initially "expressed the highest expectation for community policing, became highly *cynical* as the program unfolded, . . . grew suspicious of the motives of agency mangers, or became impatient with the pace of change being achieved" (Zhao, Lovrich, & Gray, 1995, p. 166). Although it may be tempting for police administrators to bypass the struggle of changing the role of midlevel mangers, experience has shown that midlevel managers play a critical role in organizational change.

ENGAGING MIDLEVEL MANAGERS IN COMMUNITY POLICING

The move to community policing requires managers to focus less on controlling and directing and more on encouraging participation from officers and citizens, encouraging creativity, and diffusing innovations throughout the department. As noted by Cameron and Quinn (1999), this move to a bolder, more forward-looking organizational approach does not mean that managers should now allow everybody to do as they wish, de-emphasize hard work, or neglect a focus on tangible results. Instead, the move to community policing must be seen within an overall culture change. This requires a commitment to "clarify for all concerned what the new cultural emphases will be, to identify what is to remain unaltered in the organization in the midst of change, and to generate specific action steps that can be initiated to create momentum toward culture change" (Cameron & Quinn, 1999, p. 77).

As the most meaningful and most commonly seen representatives of the administration, midlevel managers are symbolically important to the change to community policing, particularly at the cultural level. Once the new cultural emphases have been clarified, cultural change ultimately depends on individual behavioral changes that demonstrate and reinforce the new values that the administration hopes to have adopted by the entire department. Holding midlevel managers accountable for a geographic area is one way of engaging them in the community-policing change initiative. The engagement in the process must encourage them to demonstrate behaviors that are consistent with the values of community policing.

Geographic Accountability

Geographic accountability is one of the cornerstones of community policing. Community policing requires that officers foster a sense of trust with the public, establish ongoing community alliances, develop an understanding of a neighborhood's problems, and enact meaningful solutions to community problems. If officers are to be effective in these efforts, they need to have responsibility over a finite geographic area for an extended period. The purpose of assigning officers to the same area for a prolonged period is to increase their sense of ownership, thereby creating an incentive to engage in problem-solving activities aimed at reducing disorder and crime in their areas.

For at least four reasons, midlevel managers must be included in the assignment to and accountability for specific geographic areas. First, accountability is a fundamental aspect of community policing. If an organization is truly to embrace the community-policing philosophy, then employees at every level must be held accountable for crime that occurs in their area. Omitting midlevel managers from geographic accountability would, in essence, be leaving them out of the community-policing movement. Alternatively, holding them accountable for the neighborhood problems and criminal activity in a geographic region forces them to become engaged in community policing.

Second, it is illogical to hold officers and sergeants to a higher level of accountability than midlevel managers. Hierarchical police organizations assume greater responsibility with each level of command, but if midlevel managers are not accountable for a geographic region while officers and sergeants are, an imbalance of power is created with lower-ranking officers having greater responsibility than higher-ranking midlevel managers. This imbalance is inconsistent with the paramilitary structure found in most police agencies, and can be avoided by holding midlevel managers responsible for a geographic region.

Third, in many problem-solving situations, patrol officers and sergeants need the support of midlevel managers. Midlevel managers have the ability to secure resources, gain cooperation, and alter officers' schedules—things that sergeants are often unable to accomplish. For example, a community-policing officer worked for months trying to resolve a problem involving middle school students who routinely wandered off campus into an adjoining neighborhood. The residents believed replacing a missing gate would solve the problem, but the officer and his sergeant were unsuccessful in their attempts to convince the school district to purchase a new gate. When the area lieutenant learned of the situation, he brokered a deal with the school district that resolved the issue. The police department purchased a new gate and the school district took on the responsibility of locking and unlocking the gate each day. Neither the officer nor the sergeant was in a position to accomplish what the midlevel manager was able to achieve. Assigning midlevel managers to geographic areas gives them a personal stake in the outcome of problem-solving efforts. This is important, because often the successful outcome of a problem-solving initiative relies on the active involvement of the midlevel manger

The Move to Dual Responsibilities

The role of midlevel managers in community-policing organizations differs from their traditional role in significant ways. Community policing seeks to empower officers to make decisions and to take action based on their firsthand knowledge of their neighborhoods and their understanding of the department's values and mission. It also requires that midlevel managers provide subordinates with the skills and resources to serve as independent and innovative employees, rather than as programmed automatons (Braiden, 1992). If community policing is to be effective, patrol officers need to be granted more freedom and liberty to identify problems and enact solutions. Such behavior cannot be achieved in a highly controlled, by-the-book environment. A strict manager-subordinate relationship is inappropriate in a community-policing organization, because if officers are to be effective, they need to be given latitude to exercise their own best judgment (Trojanowicz & Bucqueroux, 1994). The heavy emphasis on controlling officers' behavior that is fundamental to traditional policing is in direct conflict with the innovative and creative role that patrol officers are asked to assume in community policing. Kelling and Bratton (1993) recognized this inconsistency, and noted that "this conflict is not of their own making; midlevel managers are victims more than culprits in a process that catches them between conflicting role demands (control your officers so that all former expectations can be met *versus* encourage your officers to be creative and self-initiating)" (p. 10). Midlevel managers can reconcile this conflict by adopting a new role as facilitator and coach—they must shift their focus from regulating personnel to supporting their problem solving efforts (Peak & Glensor, 1999).

Although police departments engaging in community policing still maintain a hierarchical structure, the relationship between layers of that structure is significantly altered. Unlike the traditionally strict command-and-obey relationship between midlevel managers and officers, community policing calls for a relationship that is less rigid and more supportive. Community policing does not eliminate a midlevel manager's right to issue orders and expect obedience, nor should it do so; emergency situations necessitate that someone be in charge, and community policing does not alter this fact. What does change under community policing is the more routine nature of the relationship between supervisors and officers. In nonemergency situations, community policing allows officers to exercise more freedom and discretion in performing their duties. It recognizes that the officer who is on the street day after day may be the person with the most knowledge about a community problem and how that problem might best be resolved. To resolve community problems, officers need flexibility and support, not restrictions and orders, from their midlevel managers.

A major function of midlevel managers in community policing is to coordinate problem-solving efforts in their geographical area. Though sergeants are expected to recognize problems in their team areas and to direct their officers' response to those problems, it is the responsibility of midlevel managers to ensure that sergeants are fulfilling this role. Midlevel managers should assist sergeants with problem identification and work with them to ensure that sergeants know how to access and utilize all available information, such as calls for service, crime trends, and crime mapping. Regular meetings with midlevel managers and sergeants can serve as a forum where midlevel managers guide sergeants and coach them in their role as problem solvers.

Another important role that midlevel managers play in community policing is that of problem-solving facilitator. As noted above, midlevel managers are in a position to accomplish things that patrol officers and sergeants cannot achieve. Midlevel managers can facilitate problem solving through scheduling extra officers, authorizing overtime, assigning officers to work exclusively on a specific problem, and gaining cooperation from outside agencies and other divisions within the department. Midlevel managers can also acquire needed resources, such as unmarked cars and funds for special purchases. Additionally, midlevel managers can give guidance to sergeants and officers about possible strategies for addressing problems. Because midlevel managers oversee a larger geographic area than sergeants do, midlevel managers are in a position to have knowledge about what strategies have worked in the past and what pitfalls to avoid.

In addition to their geographic responsibilities, midlevel managers are also expected to oversee their shifts. This temporal responsibility is similar to that of midlevel managers in traditional police organizations, but this does not mean that midlevel managers are to maintain the *status quo* of controlling officers' behavior. Rather, community policing dictates that midlevel managers create an environment where it is safe for officers to make decisions and to take risks. Midlevel managers must be less authoritarian and more supportive while still maintaining standards of excellence and ensuring quality performance from the officers on their shifts.

We are advocating that midlevel managers in a community-policing organization be held accountable for a geographic area in addition to their shift. This model has the potential to be problematic and may initially seem overwhelming to some midlevel managers. The remainder of this chapter explores the difficulties associated with dual responsibilities, and suggests ways of dealing with them.

THE CHALLENGES OF DUAL RESPONSIBILITY

Two major conflicts arise when midlevel managers are given the dual responsibilities of a shift and a geographic area. This section focuses on these challenges and provides some recommendations on actions that can be taken to minimize the conflicts that naturally occur with the move to community policing.

Handling Shift and Geographic Responsibilities

The first challenge is the temptation for midlevel managers to focus on their traditional shift responsibilities and to neglect their geographic duties. One lieutenant explained this by saying, "I'm aware of my sector responsibilities, but the reality is that my shift duties are staring me in the face, so that's where my attention goes." This is not surprising given that midlevel managers are knowledgeable of, and comfortable with, their role as a shift supervisor. Assigning geographic accountability to midlevel managers adds a new dimension to their job that includes unfamiliar and perhaps uncomfortable tasks.

Second, midlevel managers struggle with geographic accountability because it extends over a 24-hour period. This means that midlevel managers are responsible for the activity that occurs in their geographic sector around the clock, *even when they are off duty*. Likewise, a midlevel manager is responsible not only for the sergeants and officers assigned the shift the midlevel manager works, but also for those who are assigned to the midlevel manager's geographic region throughout the day. This is a dramatic departure from traditional shift-based responsibility. It is likely that during their initial adjustment, midlevel mangers will experience frustration and the feeling that they have lost control. For example, a veteran lieutenant who was given responsibility for a geographic region questioned, "How can I be accountable for stuff that happens when I'm home in bed?" Another expressed frustration, asking, "How am I supposed to know what my team sergeants and officers are doing when I'm on day shift and two-thirds of them are on afternoons and nights?"

As midlevel mangers become accustomed to their new dual responsibilities for a shift and a geographic region, it is probable that they will confront problems with time management, communication, and coordination difficulties. Fortunately, with proper training and modifications of their traditional responsibilities, it is possible for midlevel mangers to overcome these obstacles with minimal difficulty. Balancing the demands of dual responsibilities requires that midlevel managers be relieved of some of their traditional duties, create a means of cross-shift communication, and coordinate their efforts amongst themselves.

Strategies for Meeting the Challenges

Often, when organizations alter an employee's job description, they add responsibilities without eliminating any of the employee's preexisting duties. The net result is an expansion of the job description that may exceed what can reasonably be accomplished during a normal workweek. Experience has shown that if geographic accountability is added to midlevel managers' duties without eliminating some traditional functions, midlevel managers are likely to become frustrated because of the expanded demands placed on them. One lieutenant expressed this, saying, "To me, community policing means that in the same 40-hour week I'm expected to do all the stuff I've always done plus a whole lot more." A critical step in the process of redefining the midlevel managers' role is a thorough analysis of the duties they perform.

The objective is to identify tasks that can be eliminated or reassigned to other personnel, thereby freeing up time that midlevel managers can devote to their geographic responsibilities. Assigning geographic responsibility to midlevel managers should *change* their job duties, not simply expand them. An examination of how the lieutenant quoted above spent his workday revealed that he routinely did clerical tasks that could have been done by office personnel. He also performed some duties that "had always been done," but that were unnecessary. For example, the lieutenant had been making made daily entries into a logbook that was designed to track the number of hours worked by individual employees between regularly mandated training. This record had been kept for many years, but the department had adopted a new payroll system several years earlier that made this logbook obsolete and unnecessary. Delegating jobs that do not require the attention of a midlevel manager and eliminating unnecessary duties makes time available to be spent focusing on geographically based issues.

Coordinating the efforts of officers who work an assigned area over a 24-hour period presents significant communication difficulties. It is critical that the midlevel manager encourages and facilitates regular communication across shifts by establishing open lines for the sharing of information. Advances in technology, such as voice and electronic mail, can ease the difficulty of cross-shift communication. One midlevel manager used his department's voice mail system to create group lists that allowed a person to record messages that were then sent to the midlevel manager, the sergeants, and every officer who worked in the geographic area. This simple yet effective way of communicating enabled officers assigned to the same area to work together as a team despite the fact that they worked opposite shifts.

An example of the telephone messaging technology involved a complaint that a lieutenant received regarding a problem house whose renters frequently had loud parties. The house was in poor repair, the grass was overgrown, and there was trash strewn throughout the yard. The complainants also thought that middle school students used the house as a hiding place while skipping school. The lieutenant shared this information by recording a single voice mail message and sending it to the sergeant and officers assigned to that area. The day-shift officer began checking the house for truants, and ultimately referred the children to protective services. The afternoon-shift officer advised the landlord of the problem and contacted the building department to arrange for an inspection of the house. The night-shift officer cited the residents for disturbing the peace. The officers coordinated their actions and kept their sergeant and lieutenant informed of their progress by sending voice mail messages to all of the team officers. Electronic mail can be used in the same way to communicate effectively and efficiently across shift lines.

Lack of technology does not necessarily prohibit effective communication between officers working different shifts. A logbook can be kept in a central location, in which officers, sergeants, and midlevel managers record problems, actions taken, and requests for assistance. Another tool that has been used by agencies is to create a file that all of the officers working in a geographic area can access. Each major problem in the area is assigned its own file; officers can use the file to review the history of the problem, actions that have been taken by other officers, and guidance from the sergeant or midlevel manager. Of course, communicating in person is also essential for building relationships among officers who work different shifts but who are expected to function as a team. Ideally, midlevel managers should arrange for monthly meetings for all the officers assigned to the same geographic area.

The form of communication among officers working the same geographic area is less important than ensuring that information is actively and regularly shared. Our experience has been that officers may initially be hesitant to "bother" their coworkers with updates about problems in their geographic area, but with the encouragement, example, and insistence of the midlevel manager, effective communication across shifts can be achieved.

Another factor essential to the successful balancing of dual responsibility is coordination and cooperation among midlevel managers on all shifts. The on-duty midlevel manager is naturally concerned with temporal issues, including calls for service and time-based problems, such as truancy, which only occurs during the day shift. However, for geographic accountability over a 24-hour period to be effective, midlevel managers on every shift must be committed to allowing and encouraging officers to attend to their geographically based duties. The off-duty midlevel managers must rely on the on-duty midlevel manager to protect and promote their geographic interests.

Ensuring that midlevel managers on all shifts are cognizant and respectful of their fellow midlevel managers' geographic interests requires consistent communication among the midlevel managers. The failure of midlevel managers to communicate regularly affords officers an opportunity to skirt their responsibilities by taking advantage of the midlevel managers' ignorance. For example, a night-shift lieutenant was irritated because the day-shift officer assigned to the lieutenant's geographic area routinely reported that she did not have time to work on geographically based problems because she was overwhelmed with her temporal duties. When the night-shift lieutenant eventually discussed this with the day-shift lieutenant, they were surprised; the day-shift lieutenant revealed that the same officer had been neglecting her temporal duties while claiming that she was occupied with her geographic duties. This type of manipulation can be avoided by frequent communication and coordination among midlevel managers.

CONCLUSION

It is clear that the transition from a traditional style of policing to community policing presents administrators with a number of challenges. Experience has shown that midlevel managers are essential to the success of organizational change, yet the temptation remains to pay little or no attention to midlevel managers and to allow them to continue doing their traditional duties while the organization focuses on changing the roles of patrol officers and their sergeants.

The overriding theme of this chapter is that a successful move to community policing required a fundamental cultural change. Too often, new initiatives are seen as isolated programs or techniques rather than "as fundamental shifts in the organization's direction, values, and culture" (Cameron & Quinn, 1999, p. 9). More specifically, we have argued that rather than being an isolated change, the task of redefining the role of midlevel managers can be a significant part of a larger cultural shift. Thus, midlevel managers must be immersed in the transition to community policing, not left out of it, and we have offered a suggestion for how this can be achieved through the assignment of dual responsibilities for a shift and a geographic area. This model is not without difficulties; however, our experience has shown that dedicated midlevel managers can successfully manage both a shift and a geographic region when they are given guidance and direction from their administrators.

There are many factors that affect the success of assigning midlevel managers dual responsibilities. For example, the leadership of the chief of police is critical. Midlevel managers need a clear mandate that explains why they are being required to restructure their job duties and take on additional responsibility. Research has shown that when leaders provide midlevel managers with a clear understanding and a strong vision of where the department is headed, midlevel managers are willing to shoulder additional responsibility and to be leaders in the implementation process (Kelling & Bratton, 1993). The chief must clearly and concretely define the role that midlevel managers are expected to perform and provide guidance on how this may be accomplished. In doing so, the chief has an opportunity to demonstrate the coaching and encouraging roles that midlevel managers are expected to assume with the sergeants in their geographic sector.

Likewise, as the role of midlevel managers is modified, their performance evaluation and reward systems must also change. If midlevel managers continue to be evaluated based on their traditional functions, it is likely that they will continue to focus on their shifts and controlling officers' behavior at the expense of their geographic responsibilities. Ideally, new performance appraisals should be designed with the input of midlevel managers *before* the change in roles is implemented. This process will allow midlevel managers to share in redefining their role and to gain better understanding of what is expected of them.

As the community-policing movement matures, we hope that more researchers will focus their attention on the changing role of midlevel managers. Although it has long been recognized that midlevel managers are important in the organizational change process, police administrators have been given little guidance on specific ways to alter the role of midlevel managers. The importance of clearly defining this new role should not be underestimated, because it may require police organizations to rethink how they select, socialize, and train their midlevel managers.

REFERENCES

Braiden, C. R. (1992). Enriching traditional roles. In L. K. Hoover (Ed.), *Police management: Issues and perspectives* (pp. 87–116). Washington, DC: Police Executive Research Forum.

Cameron, K. S., & Quinn, R. E. (1999). *Diagnosing and changing organizational culture.* Reading, MA: Addison-Wesley.

Fogelson, R. (1977). *Big-city police.* Cambridge, MA: Harvard University Press.

Gaines, L. (1994). Community-oriented policing: Management issues, concerns, and problems. *Journal of Contemporary Criminal Justice, 10,* 17–35.

Kelling, G. L., & Bratton, W. J. (1993). Implementing community policing: The administrative problem. *Perspectives on policing, 17,* Washington, DC: U.S. Department of Justice, Office of Justice Programs, National Institute of Justice.

Lipsky, M. (1980). *Street-level bureaucracy: Dilemmas of the individual in public services.* New York: Russell Sage.

Miller, W. R. (1977). *Cops and bobbies: Police authority in New York and London, 1830–1870.* Chicago: University of Chicago Press.

Peak, K. J., & Glensor, R. W. (1999). *Community policing and problem solving: Strategies and practices* (2nd ed.). Upper Saddle River, NJ: Prentice Hall.

Reuss-Ianni, E. (1983). *The two cultures of policing.* New Brunswick, NJ: Transaction.

Rubinstein, J. (1973). *City police.* New York: Farrar, Straus & Giroux.

Trojanowicz, R. C. (1980). *The environment of the first-line police supervisor.* Englewood Cliffs, NJ: Prentice Hall.

Trojanowicz, R. C., & Bucqueroux, B. (1994). *Community policing: How to get started.* Cincinnati, OH: Anderson.

Van Maanen, J. (1983). The boss: Front-line supervision in an American police agency. In M. Punch (Ed.), *Control in the police organization* (pp. 275–317). Cambridge, MA: MIT Press.

Walker, S. (1977). *A critical history of police reform.* Lexington, MA: D. C. Heath.

Walker, S. (1993). Does anyone remember team policing? Lessons of the team policing experience for community policing. *American Journal of Police, 12*(1), 33–55.

Wycoff, M. A., & Kelling, G. L. (1978). *The Dallas experience: Organizational reform.* Washington, DC: Police Foundation.

Zhao, J., Lovrich, N. P., & Gray, K. (1995). Moving toward community policing: The role of postmaterialist values in a changing police profession. *American Journal of Police, 14*(3/4), 151–171.

CHAPTER 7

Organizational Change and Development

Fundamental Principles, Core Dilemmas, and Leadership Challenges in the Move Toward a Community-Policing Strategy

J. Kevin Ford

*T*he movement to community policing signals an attempt to redefine the role and responsibilities of police agencies. The roles and responsibilities change from a focus on routine patrol to more emphasis on direct interaction with citizens, an emphasis on prevention rather than reaction to crime activity, and a geographical focus in which officers are more accountable to an area rather than simply performing police functions. The goal of this shift is to promote a more "customer-based" organizational transformation that incorporates extensive partnerships with the community, as well as greater integration of police efforts within the agency. To be effective, the transformation requires an informational, problem-solving approach to the continuous improvement of police services (Ford, Boles, Plamondon, & White, 1999).

Transforming a police agency requires an intensive effort at organizational change and development. The organizational change must be both nurtured and managed. The research and practice of organizational change and development has clear implications for the effective transformation of police agencies to community policing. This chapter provides an organizing framework for thinking about and pursuing a transformation to community policing. More specifically, this chapter (a) examines the fundamental principles of organizational change and development, (b) describes implications of these principles for initiating and implementing a transformation to community policing, and (c) highlights key leadership challenges that must be addressed in the move to community policing.

FUNDAMENTAL PRINCIPLES OF ORGANIZATIONAL CHANGE AND DEVELOPMENT

Organizational change and development is a field of inquiry that emerged in the late 1940s and early 1950s. One of the first fairly comprehensive change and evaluation studies was done by Coch and French (1948) as they examined factors that influenced resistance to change. They reported that resistance to change could be minimized by communicating the need for change and allowing the people affected by the change to participate in planning it. The late 1940s also saw the development of the laboratory training movement that focused on improving interpersonal relations, self-understanding, and awareness of team dynamics by managers.

Since these early works, the field has evolved into an integrated framework of theories and practices capable of solving or helping to solve important problems confronting the human side of organizations (Porras & Robertson, 1992). Thus, organizational change and development (OD) is about people and organizations, and about people in organizations and how they function. OD is also about planned change— about getting people (individuals, teams, and cross-departments) and systems (human resources, management, patrol, and administration) to function more effectively. Planned change involves common sense, hard work, time, goals, and the use of valid knowledge and information about the organization and how to change it.

In particular, OD has been defined as a top-management supported, long-range effort to improve an organization's problem solving and renewal processes, particularly through a more effective collaborative diagnosis and management of organizational culture—with special emphasis on formal work team, temporary team, and inter-group culture—with the assistance of a consultant-facilitator and the use of the theory and technology of applied behavioral science, includ-ing action research (French & Bell, 1995). This lengthy definition high-lights the systematic nature of the OD effort, which requires a firm hand on managing the process of change while at the same time allow-ing individuals within the organization to initiate action and move the change process forward. Managing a change process requires a particu-lar way of thinking about and relating to people and institutions, and of understanding and promoting human growth. Even more so, manag-ing a change process requires a mode of acting and being that helps in-dividuals within the agency to see the need for change, creating a vision for change, eliminating obstacles to change, encouraging risk taking and nontraditional ideas, recognizing and rewarding improvements, invigorating the change process, and developing the means to ensure leadership development (Mirvis, 1989).

Although there is a whole host of tools in the toolkit of OD, it is the set of values and assumptions that separate OD change agents from typical organizational consultants. These assumptions include the fol-lowing: that (a) individuals have the capacity for growth, (b) individuals desire to grow, (c) individual and organizational goals can be compati-ble, (d) the open expression of feelings and emotions are good, and (e) collaboration is preferable to competition. Some key values that OD change agents often espouse include concepts such as freedom, respon-sibility, self-control, justice, human potential and empowerment, dig-nity, respect, integrity, work, authenticity, openness, and an accep-tance of diversity (see French & Bell, 1995).

There are a number of foundations that underlie the theory, the practice, and the art of OD. They provide the knowledge base from which effective change efforts are planned and implemented. Three key foundations are systems thinking, high involvement, and continuous learning (Ford, 1999).

Viewing Organizations
as Integrated Systems

Systems theory pervades all of the theory and practice of OD. It in-volves consideration of the interdependency, interconnectedness, and interrelatedness of the parts within the organization that constitute the whole. An organizational system can be characterized by a continu-ous cycle of input, transformation, output, and feedback, whereby one element of experience influences the next. For example, a simple call for service at a traffic accident involves input both from the citizen, who makes the call, and from the dispatcher, who relays information to the responding officer. The throughput is the officer responding to the call and performing the functions of a patrol officer at the scene of an accident. The outcome includes how well the officer has performed his or her duties and the reactions of the citizens to the officer's actions. The feedback loop includes such issues as supervisory acknowledgment that the officer responded appropriately, that the reports were filed, that the problem was resolved in a timely manner, and that citizens affected by the accident liked the way the officer handled the case. Even in this simple case, a variety of people, from citizens, dispatchers, supervisors, and the officer, are involved in making this "system" effective.

Thus, systems thinking is the process of seeing the whole, including the underlying structures in complex situations (Senge, 1990). There are four key consequences of viewing organizations from a systems perspective. First, issues, events, forces, and incidents are not viewed as isolated phenomena, but are seen in relation to other issues, events, and forces. Second, there is an analysis of events in terms of multiple rather than single causation. Third, one cannot change one part of a system without influencing other parts in some ways. Fourth, if one wants to change a system, one changes the system as a whole, not just its component parts.

In addressing an organizational issue from a systems perspective, one must maintain a focus on stakeholders—those who have interests relevant to this particular issue. Such a perspective attempts to understand the points of view of each interested party. In particular, one must understand and acknowledge that there is a possibility of both conflicting and common interests among stakeholders. By identifying the various stakeholders with strong underlying interests or concerns, it is possible to compare and contrast those interests. This focus can begin the process of finding creative solutions that meet some of the goals or interests of each party while getting the parties to recognize that the competing interests have some validity (Ford & Fisher, 1994). The analysis of stakeholder interests includes both the resolution of conflicts within and across stakeholder groups and the pursuit of common concerns. Thus, the systems framework forces one to consider to what extent and in what ways the interests of the various stakeholders are involved in decision making and in what ways attempts are made to foster common rather than competing interests regarding a change effort.

A systems perspective also takes into account the issue of organizational levels. The levels perspective posits that organizational events
should be viewed within their larger contexts. This means that activities at one organizational level cannot be considered in isolation
from influences at other levels within the organization (Ostroff & Ford,
1989). For example, a strategic policy concerning the purchase of
new technology cannot stop with activities related to purchasing equipment; it must also address a variety of related personnel issues concerning the safe and effective use of that equipment, the training of
personnel, and the change in how information is acquired and communicated in the organization. Consequently, a systems approach recognizes that there is unique information available at all levels of the organization and that sharing that information is essential to planning
and implementing effective programs.

High Involvement

The underlying assumptions of OD specialists about people focus
on their potential for growth and development. Not surprisingly, then,
a second principle of change is the need to involve and empower those
who will be most affected by the change. The issues of participation
and involvement have had a long history in the field of OD and change.
Participation and involvement is extended broadly, rather than being
restricted to management.

Research and practice has indicated that increased involvement
and participation is desired by most people, has the ability to energize
performance, produces better solutions to problems, and greatly en-
hances acceptance of decisions. In a transformation process, a number
of positive outcomes can arise from involving employees in resolving
organizational issues and problems. These include increased trust and
confidence between supervisors and employees, increased communication and information flow, more effective decision making, increased
self-control, enhanced problem solving, and higher performance and
quality goals (see Lawler, 1992).

However, these results can occur only if employees are involved in
all stages of an OD effort, from initial diagnosis of the organizational
system and problem, through the development of action plans for improvement and the evaluation of the effectiveness of the action plans,
to the determination of what new actions or interventions are needed
to improve organizational effectiveness continually. Empowerment
and participation are much harder to incorporate into an organization

than one might think. We can all buy into the notion that people should be given the autonomy and authority to do their jobs effectively. What we often fail to realize, though, are system issues, such as conflicting stakeholder interests and differences across levels, that make implementation quite difficult. Nevertheless, an effective application of the principles of participation, involvement, and empowerment can have a transformational effect on the organization's culture and norms over time (Schein, 1985).

Some rules of thumb to consider in empowering others include the following: (a) involve all those who are part of the problem or part of the solution; (b) treat those closest to the problem as the relevant experts; and (c) provide the support and power needed to have decisions made by those who are closest to the problem (Wellins, Byham, & Wilson, 1991). Enacting these rules of thumb requires an analysis of the assumptions and beliefs that currently exist in the organization relevant to involvement. One assumption that needs to be checked is if leaders truly believe that frontline employees can and should make the majority of decisions that affect how they do their work. Another assumption to test is whether leaders feel that the union is likely to renegotiate traditional work rules to permit greater flexibility and autonomy. A third assumption to test is whether leaders are willing not only to adjust responsibility downward, but radically to change their own leadership roles and responsibilities—from direction and control to facilitation and delegation. A fourth assumption is that leaders are aware that high involvement strategies are a lengthy, time-consuming, and labor-intensive process and that they are willing to make that investment for a better future. Unless organizations are willing to face these types of assumptions and work on them, high involvement is not possible.

A Continuous Learning Perspective

A third fundamental principle of organizational change and development is the need to set up processes so that learning can occur within that organization as change is developed and implemented. The success of new initiatives in work settings such as community policing relies on the expertise of individual police officers and the coordinated efforts of team members (Geller, 1997). Various private and public sector organizations have begun to acknowledge the importance of learning and knowledge creation as a key method for improving productivity and for delivering effective services (Senge, 1994). Consequently, organizations have become more interested in how to build learning capabilities in the workforce—often labeled "intellectual capital" (Stewart, 1997)—on an ongoing basis. This organizational learning cycle has been labeled *continuous learning*.

The goal of continuous learning is to encourage everyone in the organization—employees, line managers, supervisors, and technical personnel—to become actively engaged in expanding their skills and improving organizational effectiveness (Senge, 1990). Learning becomes an everyday part of the job rather than being confined to formal training sessions in the classroom. Employees can learn skills of others in their work unit (cross-training), teach other employees in areas of expertise, and learn from one another on a day-to-day basis. Thus, though learning and development are clearly rooted in individuals, organizations can attempt to create the context for a positive learning environment.

Creating a learning organization requires a heavy investment in training that is closely tied to the strategic direction of the organization. With this training investment must come the support from supervisors and coworkers that encourages individuals to attend training, provides opportunities for trainees immediately to apply the trained knowledge and skills to the job, and invites trainees to share ideas gained in training with others. Another key characteristic of a learning organization is the ability of its employees to find or make opportunities to learn from whatever situation is presented. Thus, individuals in a learning organization must be given opportunities to work on projects outside the normal routine where they can gain new knowledge and skills. A learning organization also recognizes that mistakes can provide for valuable learning experiences for individuals and teams. In addition, learning on the job and trying out new ideas is encouraged. In a learning organization, such constraints as unclear task assignments, unrealistic time pressures, and poorly trained support staff can interfere with individual efforts to innovate and learn on the job (see Tannenbaum, 1997).

The backbone of these efforts to develop a continuous learning orientation is the development of problem-solving skills. Problem-solving skills include the ability to identify the gap between the aims of a improvement effort and the reality of the current state of the system, the analysis of root causes of the gap, the identification of improvement options, the choice of which improvement option has the greatest potential to add value to the organization, and the evaluation of the effectiveness of the improvement effort.

IMPLICATIONS FOR THE TRANSFORMATION
TO COMMUNITY POLICING

Systems thinking, high involvement, and continuous learning are difficult concepts to put into practice in an organization. The reality of organizational life is that most people, because of time pressures, organizational norms, or individual preferences, focus more on single than multiple causes and local issues rather than larger-scale organizational systems issues. Most organizations focus on efficiency and the development of specific roles and responsibilities rather than on enhancing integration across functions or encouraging innovation, risk taking, and decision making at the lowest levels possible. Most organizations want individuals to be up to date on technical skills, but spend little time and energy on building a learning culture that focuses on continuous improvement and development of people and systems within the organization.

For those leaders who attempt to make the transformation to community policing "happen," the change process is also quite ambiguous. The reality of any transformation effort is that there is no clear, best way to make change happen in an organization (Vail, 1989). The concepts of systems thinking, high involvement, and continuous learning provide the principles, but not the blueprint, of how to prepare, plan, and implement these concepts in an organization or how to combine these principles into a strong force for change.

A useful way to describe and systematically examine the realities one faces in a transformation effort is to consider the series of dilemmas that must be faced. The next section defines dilemmas, then discusses three key dilemmas where decisions must be made that can have a major impact on what type of community-policing initiative is initiated and how likely it is to be successful.

Dealing With the Dilemmas of Change

Encountering dilemmas is inherent in any change effort. Dilemmas are important, because they represent key choices underlying any change effort involving difficult decisions. How these dilemmas are faced is sure to cast a long shadow over future activities and affect the success of the change effort. There are three characteristics of a dilemma.

First, a dilemma involves choices where no one alternative is clearly superior. If there is a clear choice, then there is no dilemma. Sometimes, a choice seems clear to some, but not to others. The situation will only be experienced as a dilemma by people who are torn between or among what they see as the alternative possible choices. Thus, dilemmas can be experienced at the individual, group, or organizational levels—depending on the degree to which there is shared awareness and understanding of the situation. The recognition of alternatives inevitably points toward data collection, which could be formal or informal. It is only via data collection that it is possible to define clearly the problem, clarify the choices, and gauge consensus.

Second, a dilemma is characterized by trade-offs associated with each of the choices. Trade-offs involve situations where making one choice limits or constrains alternative choices—these are cases where it is not possible to, as they say, have your cake and eat it, too. Again, if one alternative does not have any associated trade-offs or drawbacks, then the situation is not a dilemma. This does not mean that trade-offs or drawbacks might not be discovered later—bringing the realization that there was actually a dilemma being faced. In the absence of this awareness, however, the choice is not experienced as a dilemma. Also, there may not be consensus in a group or organization that trade-offs need to be made, or there may be wide differences of opinion regarding how to value the alternative choices—leading to situations where some people experience a dilemma and others do not. Thus, the issues around trade-offs relate to the interpretation of data to generate knowledge. Recognition of trade-offs depends not just on the development of individual knowledge, but also on the development of shared knowledge about the issues.

Third, dilemmas involve significant, irreversible consequences. If subsequent events and decisions would proceed unaffected regardless of the decisions made, then there is no dilemma. That is, there are some decisions that involve alternatives in which no one choice is superior and where the choices involve trade-offs, but there is no dilemma because the consequences are minor or easily reversible. Consequences are significant either because they have a very deep effect on some or many people, or because they have a broad effect on many people. Consequences are irreversible where a subsequent change in the decision is either not possible or very complicated. Often, some people will experience a situation as involving significant, irreversible decisions while others will not. In time, however, if it was a dilemma, the significance and the irreversibility will become evident. This highlights the critical importance of moving beyond shared knowledge to action. It is in taking action (or not taking action) that a decision becomes irreversible.

In the case of movement toward community policing, the combination of the three elements of a dilemma becomes evident as a series of choice points or pivotal events. These events are pivotal in that the future course of the community-policing initiative is, in effect, on the table. The way the three elements of the dilemmas are addressed is critical, because the particular choices will have implications for subsequent efforts. Even failing to act at one of these pivotal events represents a choice, with its attendant consequences. Thus, dilemmas are important because they involve choices among alternatives that involve trade-offs, and these choices are both important and irreversible. Though it is important to anticipate the pivotal events, effective organizational change depends on taking the time to reflect and identify lessons from past events and choices.

Organizational Change Dilemmas

Dilemmas do not happen all at once. They arise over time in an iterative series of choice points or pivotal events. Sometimes, the events can be widely spaced in time. It is also possible for them to follow closely after each other or even occur simultaneously. These pivotal events can be categorized and labeled according to the fundamental principles of systems thinking, high involvement, and continuous learning. This categorization provides a way of systematizing what we know about the root cause of dilemmas when moving towards community policing. These are the areas of the greatest struggles in attempting to meet the aim of becoming a community-policing agency. They represent areas in which efforts can become derailed. Three important dilemmas for change towards community policing are described below.

Systems-Thinking Dilemma: Incremental Versus Frame-Breaking Change. The enormity of a change to community policing often leads agencies to take small steps, hopefully to create the opportunity to make larger change possible. These small first steps, such as dedicating a few officers to community policing or setting up a community officer unit, are seen as a way of making incremental progress and learning from these initial steps.

A systems perspective, though, highlights possible problems with this incremental approach. This incremental approach contends that something new can be put into place without having much impact on other systems in the agency. From a systems perspective, the opposite will happen: The new entity will receive much attention as it becomes a salient aspect that officers must consider in terms of what this means for the organization and where it is going. The incremental step approach also ignores the issue of multiple causation for a problem or issue, and can lead to cynicism that community policing, in terms of having a few officer riding bicycles and talking to community groups, is going to "solve all our problems."

A frame-breaking or transformational approach contends that there needs to be an overarching vision for a change effort. In a sense, with this approach, everything about how an organization is structured; how it is managed, how work gets accomplished, and how the organization interacts with the external world is "on the table" and negotiable. From this wide-open agenda on improving police effectiveness, a realistic vision can be crafted that helps to clarify the direction in which the policy agency needs to move. This vision can then be articulated as a message of transformational change that can be effectively communicated to customers, stakeholder groups, and employees. Without a sensible, realistic, and bold vision, a transformational effort can easily dissolve into a list of confusing and incompatible projects that leads the police agency to dead ends (see Kotter, 1995, for a discussion of these issues).

Research supports the conclusions that these types of frame-breaking efforts can lead to more sustained change efforts than incremental efforts. Miller and Friesen (1982) found change that is both concerted and dramatic was more associated with effective change efforts than piecemeal and incremental changes. Similarly, Gersick (1991) cites research from a variety of disciplines that supports the notion that fundamental change "cannot be accomplished piecemeal, slowly, gradually, and comfortably" (p. 34). She contends that transformational change is "punctuated"—that there are periods of relative calm and stability as the change process is initiated, followed by revolutionary change that challenges the fundamental or core values and belief systems of an organization. Goldstein (1990) summarizes this punctuated change perspective by stating that change must be viewed as a nonlinear rather than linear process.

The notion of frame-breaking or transformational change emphasizes the need to develop a bold vision, take steps to implement that vision, and push continually for the change effort to be successful. This does not mean that transformational change can happen in a hurry.

Most transformational efforts take years to accomplish. For example, I have been part of a transformational effort to move a private sector operation from a traditional assembly to a team-based, self-directed, quality-first type of operation. It took over five years for the organization to make a complete transformation to a new way of organizing. The steps towards progress were slow, but continuous. Only over time did the new ways of organizing lead to a major change in how people behaved, to where systems thinking, empowerment, and continuous learning became standard operating procedure. The transformation to a new way of organizing only began to have bottom-line impacts on organizational outcomes, such as increased sales and profitability, after seven years. Ten years into the transformational effort, the CEO of the company recently mentioned that the change effort is still unfolding and, in a sense, is a never-ending search for continuous improvement. This example highlights that the organization had a frame-breaking strategy, and yet had the patience to implement, reinvent, and institutionalize the overall strategy over a period of years.

High-Involvement Dilemma: Centralized Versus Decentralized Control. The concept of high involvement is usually first initiated by the police chief through the formation of a team of police personnel that cuts across levels and functions to examine the implementation of community policing. This guidance team might be given the charge to examine what types of geographical areas should be created, how they are to be created, how officers should respond in each area, what training officers will need, and other important issues to "get the transformation going." This level of involvement, though necessary, is not sufficient to drive the change process through implementation and institutionalization. What is often missing is an early analysis of how the existing hierarchical structure of command and control needs to change to be consistent with the move to community policing. This requires an in-depth examination of what "high involvement" means on a day-to-day basis, because the purpose of the traditional command-and-control hierarchy is to minimize the need for involvement, and instead rewards doing "what I am told to do" (Katzenbach, & Smith, 1993).

The change dilemma involves the structural issues around centralization and decentralization of control in the transformation to community-policing efforts. Centralized decisions regarding how the community-policing initiative is going to be set up and mandates regarding how officers are to behave or perform their duties differently have the advantage of speed, consistency, and coordination with parallel initiatives. Yet this centralized process feeds into the existing hierarchical control and leads to a lack of flexibility in adapting to local circumstances. The lack of change in the existing hierarchy while one is trying to push a change effort can increase frustration with the change process, and lead officers to speculate that they are supposed to change while individuals higher up in the hierarchy do not have to. In addition, mandates often lead to getting what one paid for: activity that somewhat resembles community policing, but that does not necessarily meet the overall objective behind the mandate of building effective teams of officers focusing on meeting customer needs.

Decentralization of control and day-to-day decision making can lead to a community-policing approach that is more closely aligned with local needs. However, the decentralization process is likely to introduce variation and inconsistency across settings in how community policing is implemented by each supervisor within a geographic area. It can also lead managers to feel as if they have lost control of their organization, because accountability shifts from organizational numbers (e.g., number of arrests) to the more nebulous service concept of meeting customer needs. Discussions about decentralization are important, because they put to the test the assumptions of leaders regarding high involvement.

In reality, transformation efforts require both centralized and decentralized control. The dilemma, then, is to know when and what type of control needs to be centralized and what can be decentralized (Cutcher-Gershenfeld & Associates, 1998). Thus, there is a perpetual process of trying to achieve an effective balance between the two. A key issue, then, is what aspects of the community-policing initiative could be decentralized to lieutenants or sergeants, and what aspects have to remain centralized.

The development of a transformational strategy for change must come from the leadership of the agency (with input from others). The overarching vision and specific goals of the move to community policing must be centralized, so that the agency is all pointed in the same direction. For example, a transformational strategy may state that the agency will be split into geographical districts with teams of officers responsible for each area. The strategy may also have as one goal that, within the first two years, over 80% of the officers will have made a formal presentation to a community group.

Once the strategy and goals are specified, the critical issues of how to enact the strategy and what is the best way to meet the goals of the transformation process require a decentralized approach. In this way, each geographical area can be viewed as a small organization that needs to determine how the strategy and goals are to be met. For example, one geographic area may focus attention on community surveys as a way of gathering data to enhance knowledge of that area before taking action. Another area may focus on the analysis of crime data and on targeting problem sectors. A third area may focus more on setting up community meetings and then using the meetings to identify and classify problems to be addressed. This degree of flexibility or decentralization calls for new roles and responsibilities for leaders. Leaders are needed who can set up administrative systems that aid and encourage creative community-policing efforts rather than leaders who focus on standardizing community-policing practices across the agency.

Continuous Learning Dilemma: Short- Versus Long-Term Perspective. A continuous learning perspective requires a major change in norms in police agencies (Geller, 1997). Police agencies were not developed with a community-policing perspective in mind. The focus in traditional police agencies is on taking action and reacting rather than on systematically gathering data to drive new knowledge, which will in turn drive new ways of acting and reacting. In addition, the structures and processes were developed to support a traditional command-and-control orientation. Limitations of this traditional model are typically the main reason cited for the transformation effort to community policing. Nevertheless, there were good reasons why the command-and-control system was developed: It was in response to the mandate for police agencies to maintain social order and control crime. This mandate does not disappear when an agency decides to transform itself into a community-policing agency.

The underlying dilemma, then, is how to maintain efficient daily operations that satisfy a variety of stakeholders while at the same time allocating time, resources, and energy towards addressing critical system issues to change the organization towards a continuous learning and improvement orientation (Sitkin, Sutcliffe, & Schroeder, 1994). This dilemma involves the inevitable tension between the need to maintain existing operations and the need to restructure and improve work practices (Cutcher-Gershenfeld & Associates, 1998). This dilemma gets at the heart of whether the organization truly believes or has faith that working on transforming the agency will have large payoffs or benefits down the line. Though it may be difficult to measure the exact short-term benefits, it is clear that recurring problems do lead to frustrations and questions regarding the usefulness of a community-policing approach to the agency. Without efforts to maintain or enhance enthusiasm for dealing with key system problems, the long-term success of the transformation effort is compromised.

This dilemma calls for serious attention to and discussion about how to establish new roles and responsibilities, how to facilitate a move to a different way of relating to people within and outside the organization, and how to reallocate resources (e.g., time, money, and effort) to allow continuous learning efforts to grow into a new set of norms for the agency. For example, officers not only will have new roles and responsibilities relevant to problem solving and proactive policing methods, but also will need to be more integrated with other police functions, such as crime analysts and police investigators. The new roles and responsibilities cannot just be an add-on or be implemented as additional tasks to be done in the officer's spare time. To drive learning, police personnel must be given the time and resources to meet and identify problems with the community, to work with other police personnel as a team of responders to identified community needs, and to be freed from the chains of the 911 dispatcher to work proactively on solving problems and monitoring progress. Police personnel must also be able to share innovative solutions with others so as to build a continuous learning orientation.

This behavioral change on the part of police personnel is often expected, but they are not given the support needed to drive and sustain those new behaviors. To facilitate behavioral change, changes to the formal reward systems are clearly one part of this equation. The reward system has to change to encourage new roles and responsibilities and closer integration of efforts across functions and departments within a police agency. Nevertheless, time and resource allocation issues are often overlooked as critical to the long-term success of the community-policing change effort.

LEADERSHIP CHALLENGES FOR
TRANSFORMING POLICE AGENCIES

The above dilemmas are threshold issues that, if ignored, will continue to resurface as roadblocks to subsequent efforts. If they are effectively addressed, they help drive subsequent activity. Note, however, that there is never a "right" answer to the dilemmas, nor are the dilemmas ever completely "put to bed." At best, the dilemmas are addressed with creativity, with constancy of purpose, and in ways that anticipate future dilemmas. The difficulty of change efforts is high, but the potential payoffs are large.

Many large- and small-scale change efforts fail to meet their aims for a variety of reasons. This section focuses on the challenges faced by leaders as they facilitate and guide a change effort to transform a police agency to a community-policing perspective. By meeting these challenges, leaders and their agencies will be in a better position to identify and to address the dilemmas of organizational change (Zhao, Thurman, & Lovrich, 1995).

In particular, OD specialists highlight the important role that leadership plays in the preparation, planning, implementation, monitoring, and institutionalization of any change effort (Rothwell, McLean, & Sullivan, 1995). This calls for leaders to take on new roles and responsibilities as change agents, facilitators, and motivators. How well leaders enact their new roles and responsibilities will have a major impact on the success of the transformation effort (Kotter, 1990).

Preparing the Organization: Creating a Sense of Urgency for the Change

One challenge is the need for the leaders of the police agency to establish a clear sense of urgency for the change (French & Bell, 1995; Kotter, 1995). This sense of urgency must be felt by others in the organization, because the transformation process requires a number of highly motivated individuals willing to cooperate to drive the transformation, manage the change process, and motivate others to work for, rather than against, the change.

This willingness to cooperate must go beyond simple compliance with authority to become of a commitment to a vision or plan for a better police agency. This level of commitment is more likely to occur when the organization is in a crisis that is easily seen by individuals within the organization. For example, a manufacturing company showing revenue drops that could lead to its going out of business has a ready-made sense of urgency for "doing something different" that can be used as a lever for change.

The leadership challenge for policing is how to create this sense of urgency given the lack of a survival crisis. Police agencies are not going to become less legitimate, nor are they going to be eliminated if they do not "do something different." There will always be a public mandate for the types of services that police departments provide. In fact, the move to community policing requires more effort with a similar level of resources, which inevitably lead police personnel to question, "Why are we doing this?"

Police leaders must begin by having a firm belief that changing the way the agency is run is both critical and worth the effort. The leaders must then emphasize to staff and officers alike that the *status quo* is not good enough, that business as usual cannot be tolerated, and that the move to community policing as a philosophy of doing business differently might be a strategy worth pursuing. On the other hand, leaders must also be open to alternative perspectives of what the real problems facing the agency are and disagreements as to whether community policing is the right direction to take to solve those problems. True transformation requires a debate within an organization to shape and mold the change effort to meet the challenges faced by the police agency.

One technique for bringing underlying issues to the surface to create a sense of urgency is to complete strength, weaknesses, opportunity, and threat (SWOT) analysis across various functions and levels in the organization. The SWOT analysis asks participants (a) what the police agency is currently doing well, (b) where the agency is weakest and could improve, (c) what opportunities exist to change the agency for the better, and (d) what threats exist to changing or challenging the *status quo*. Once the SWOT analysis is completed, the philosophy behind community policing can be described and then examined in relation to the existing strengths, weaknesses, opportunities, and threats in the agency. In this way, community policing is linked to real issues and problems faced by the organization.

It is critical that community policing be viewed not as the *end* or expected outcome of any change effort, but that it is the *means* or engine to becoming a more efficient and effective police agency. Unless the leader and various members of the agency can clearly identify how community policing can lead to "good things" (i.e., minimizing weaknesses, building on strengths, increasing opportunities, and minimizing threats) there will be no sense of urgency for the change effort. Unfortunately, many attempts to transform an agency to community policy begin with a bold vision, but lack any attempts to generate a real sense of urgency throughout the organization.

Planning for the Change: Creating a Powerful Guidance Team for Change

A second leadership challenge is how to set up a strategic planning process that allows for important input and involvement, but at the same time creates the momentum to move the change effort forward.

Kotter (1995) contends that a key outcome of the planning process must be the creation of a committed guidance team or coalition powerful enough to lead or drive the change effort.

In most change efforts for community policing, top leaders form a guidance team that cuts across organizational levels and departmental functions to define the vision for the transformation and to discuss how to implement the change process in the organization. Although a necessary step, Kotter (1995) stresses the importance of clearly specifying the goals of the team, gaining consensus that change is needed, and determining what power the team has to proceed within the existing organizational structure.

The leadership challenge that this poses for police agencies is to ensure that the guidance team has the goals, direction, and power to make change happen. All too often, police chiefs assume that high involvement means little direction. Thus, guidance teams are given some general goals to think about, but no real boundaries within which to operate. This lack of management of the change process can lead to two key problems. One problem is that the guidance team members may feel they are adrift. These feelings of role ambiguity can lead to much discussion, but little action. A second problem is that the team may plow ahead and suggest a bold plan for change, only to find out that the chief is uncomfortable with the direction the team is taking. This can lead the team to become frustrated with the change effort, and can reinforce the notion that involvement only works if the end result is what the chief wants.

Another tendency in police agencies is to assume that an *ad hoc* guidance team will somehow overcome or be more powerful than the existing hierarchical structure to drive the change process. This clearly underestimates the difficulties that the guidance team will face in trying to produce change. In a sense, without dealing with the issues of goals, commitment, and power, the leader is hoping against hope that the entrenched hierarchy will do things that they were not willing or able to do on their own. This is a recipe for failure.

Instead, leaders must recognize the indisputable fact that power, politics, and control are integral to understanding organizations. Politics involve activities taken to acquire, develop, and use power to obtain one's preferred outcomes in a situation in which there is uncertainty about choices. Though we often think of power and politics as negative, they are critical issues for changing organizations that must be understood and dealt with rather than ignored in the hopes that they will just go away. As one observer noted, "For change to occur in an organization, power must be exercised" (Burke, 1982).

From an OD perspective, the assumption is that collaboration, co-operation, and joint problem solving are better ways to get things done in organizations than relying solely on politics and control. This means that the guidance team needs to include key players in the organization, including union representation, administrators, record keepers, investigators, officers, firstline supervisors, and middle management, as well as the top leaders. Though the existing hierarchical structure maintains the administrative, day-to-day realities of policing, this new coalition of individuals must create a structure to deal with the changing realities that come with the move towards community policing. The agenda must include how the agency will conduct its work differently in the future, including changes to the hierarchical ordering or control that currently exists.

A good way to start such a group is to conduct an initial exercise called "hopes and fears." The members can identify what they see as their greatest hopes for this group and their greatest fears for this group. Typically, such an exercise will reveal many hopes that the transformation can occur, because individuals see the need for change. In addition, the exercise typically reveals a number of fears revolving around such issues as concerns about top management support, the feeling that we have tried this before and it failed, and the sense that the time spent in the team will not be productive or that the existing hierarchical system will not allow for any change to really occur. These fears are individual and collective realities that must be faced and addressed rather than ignored by the team. Only by facing these fears and discussing them can hopes become a reality.

Once hopes and fears are dealt with in the team, team members can then identify what it would take for the group to be successful in planning for and implementing a transformation effort such as the move to community policing. The guidance team must develop a sense that the team can do something worthwhile and that the transformation is a winner. The team can then be lead to discuss what power it needs to make change possible. How leaders respond to the fears and the need for the team to have the power to make change happen will be closely watched by the guidance team to see whether the initiative has a chance to succeed.

Implementing Change:
Creating Opportunities for Innovation

Transformational change requires a long-term commitment to challenging the *status quo*. This change will not occur unless individuals most affected by the change are given the resources and power to implement the plan in a way that best meets the needs of their customers. The move to community policing is an attempt to deal with long-standing problems. These types of problems often require creative and innovative solutions that require integrated and sustained actions. These notions of innovation, creativity, and sustained experimentation are at odds with the typical organizational push for standardization, conformity, and moving on quickly to the next crisis. Consequently, the third leadership challenge revolves around the need for creating a climate that supports creativity, innovation, and experimentation relevant to the change effort.

Developing new norms or a climate of innovation is not easy. Innovation requires new mechanisms for identifying problems, analyzing root causes, developing action steps, and generalizing or diffusing innovations developed in one part of the agency to other parts of the organizational system (Scholtes, Joiner, & Streibel, 1996). Thus, new structures and processes need to be developed to accumulate new ideas and knowledge, to support the development of new ways of doing things, and to disseminate the innovations so they can become institutionalized in the agency. For example, a group of sergeants may come up with an effective way of tracking community problems, assigning officers to those problems, and monitoring effective responses. These sergeants could then provide a mini–training program on their system and how to use it. After the training, support can be given to those trained to utilize their new skills.

A key step is for leaders to "model the new way" (Kouzes & Posner, 1990). Leaders must show a willingness to explore within the agency the issues surrounding innovation, creativity, and experimentation. It takes not only a clear statement that innovation will be supported, but also action by leaders to show that they mean it.

One way to show support is for leaders to facilitate what has been called *action learning* (Marguardt, 1997). The action-learning approach emphasizes that most innovation and creativity can occur by dealing directly with work-related issues during a formal training session. The focus in the training is on understanding and solving a complex real-world problem (e.g., dealing with vandalism of cars and properties in a particular sector of a city). The training experience can include "what if" scenarios, in which individuals across a number of functions and departments are brought together to work simultaneously on the problem. As trainees discuss how they might approach the problem, a trainer can introduce new situations and problems that must be addressed by the group. Once the scenario is completed, the trainees can discuss lessons learned and how suggestions from the group of trainees can be implemented to resolve the problem. What is encouraged during this exercise is the need to think creatively and for everyone to participate in the process of identifying the problem, the underlying root causes, and the steps necessary to resolve the problem. This learning can lead to solving specific organizational problems, as well as to developing expertise within the organization to apply this learning to other change initiatives. Conducting a number of these types of training sessions on a variety of outstanding issues and problems, with involvement by a number of police personnel, will show that the leaders are serious about approaching issues and problems in a way different from the traditional policing model.

Monitoring the Change Effort: Showing Constancy of Purpose

Most organizations are able to develop a vision or mission statement and to do some planning for the change process. Sustaining momentum for a transformation requires much more effort. Leaders need to communicate the vision repeatedly, encourage and manage the process of implementation, and deal with ongoing change dilemmas. Thus, once a transformational process is beginning to unfold, a key leadership challenge is to demonstrate constancy of purpose (Deming, 1986).

With many change efforts, leaders devote a large amount of time early in the process to building a shared vision and directing a guidance team on creating an implementation strategy. Once the plan for implementation is completed, however, top leaders often go back to the important work that could not be addressed while the change process was being initiated. As an analogy, often leaders feel that the rock of change has been rolled up to the top of the hill and is ready to roll down the hill of implementation. This is an understandable reaction as top leaders are faced with new issues and fires to fight. The leadership challenge is how to stay focused and show commitment to the transformation throughout the implementation process, especially given the harsh reality that their attention must be in multiple places at the same time.

The paradox of change is that the implementation of the transformational effort such as community policing requires even more time and energy than the initial planning steps. For example, time must be spent on understanding the changes the organizational systems are undergoing relevant to the change to community policing. This requires the development of accurate information and feedback.

In addition, the leaders must encourage and support midcourse corrections to maintain momentum. Without this hands-on approach, leaders will continue to feel that they roll the rock up the hill only to see it slide back down so they have to do it again. Over time, this will lead to frustration that progress is not being made, impatience with the pace of change, and, ultimately, abandonment of the change effort. A better analogy for leadership is to consider that the initial planning actually rolls the rock only to the base of the hill rather than thinking that the rock has been rolled up the hill. Only in this way can leaders contemplate what steps they can take to show constancy of purpose as the initiative is rolled out in the police agency.

Constancy of purpose is difficult to accomplish, because there are always other issues to distract a leader from full attention to the community-policing effort. In addition, there are clearly forces within and external to a police agency that are resistant to any change effort. Thus, leaders not only must show constancy of purpose relevant to guiding the efforts of the forces for change, but also must recognize, acknowledge, and continually address the forces that may be resistant to the change effort.

One useful technique for identifying and dealing with driving and resisting forces is through a force field analysis (Burke, 1994; Lewin, 1951). A force field analysis asks individuals to consider the key drivers for change that exist in the agency and for each driver to specify a counter resisting force. For each resisting force, one can ask how likely it is that the force can be influenced and what effect reducing that resisting force (large or small) can have on helping the driving forces moving the change effort forward. The analysis of a force field diagram helps to indicate which forces would be more worth influencing. Based on those priorities, one can decide on a manageable course of action that involves both encouraging the driving forces and redirecting the restraining forces. This force field analysis can be done at various points in the implementation process to keep attention focused on the steps that must be taken to keep the momentum going. The leader can show constancy of purpose by continually working with others to encourage drivers and to minimize resisting forces.

Institutionalizing the Change: Building on Successes

Successful change has occurred when the traditional police model is the "way we *used* to do things" around here. New behaviors become routinized, and there are new norms and shared values (French & Bell, 1995; Kotter, 1995). Thus, the move to community policing begins with a vision based on values that now have become reality in everyday life. Clearly, for change to last, leaders must manage a process that changes the core components (i.e., organizational structure, reward system, communication system, human resource system) of an organization (Conger & Benjamin, 1999). This institutionalization process will not occur just by changing the core components. The changes in those core components must then lead to changes in what individuals see as their roles and responsibilities as part of this new organization. Therefore, a final leadership challenge is how to build upon initial successes so that new behavior patterns, norms, and values become institutionalized across individuals within the police agency.

Effective leaders look for ways to encourage the heart while the change process is implemented (Kouzes & Posner, 1990). Encouraging the heart can come from recognizing small wins on the way to fully implementing community policing. This can come in the form of rewarding individual contributions and celebrating team accomplishments. The rewards and accomplishments can only be effectively recognized if there are clear performance and service level improvements. This calls for information systems that monitor success over time in areas that traditional policing may not have been monitoring (e.g., officers attending community meetings, solving long-standing problems in the community, aiding individual community members, or going out of their way to help victims get back on to their feet).

The celebration of small wins helps reinforce the notion that the transformation process is continuing and that the effort is not going to diminish. With changes in the way the agency is run and what is valued, personnel in the agency will begin to feel that the move to community policing is taking hold. Former resisters can become new drivers for the transformation process. Tracking changes in perceptions, then, is a viable way of examining if the transformation process is taking hold. Organizational surveys that focus on perceptions of officers regarding such issues as top management support for community policing, reward-system alignment with the goals of community policing, the support by first-line supervisors for community policing, and the commitment of officers to the goals of community policing, can be constructed and completed by police personnel. Completing the survey multiple times over the course of the transformation process allows for the monitoring of changes in perceptions and helps determine whether new norms and values are beginning to emerge. The feedback from the surveys can also be used to identify areas in which expected perceptual changes have not occurred. These areas can then become the focus of a new round of identifying causes and determining what needs to happen to change perceptions. This shows constancy of purpose and a systematic approach to change. It also shows that individual voices are being heard.

CONCLUSION

This chapter has discussed some fundamental issues in organizational change and their implication for a successful move towards community policing. I leave you with these final thoughts regarding effective transformation efforts:

1. Think systematically about organizational systems.

2. Transform resisting forces and turn them into drivers for success.

3. Involve those who are part of the problem as well as those who are part of the solution.

4. Think creatively about problems, and turn them into opportunities for success

5. Address underlying dilemmas of change rather than ignoring them or hoping that they will go away.

6. Focus attention on leadership challenges throughout the transformation process.

REFERENCES

Burke, W. (1982). *Organizational development: Principles and practices.* Boston: Little, Brown.

Burke, W. (1994). *Organizational development: A process of learning and changing.* Reading, MA: Addison-Wesley.

Coch, L., & French, J. R. P. (1948). Overcoming resistance to change. *Human Relations, 1,* 512–532.

Conger, J. A., & Benjamin, B. (1999). Building leaders: How successful companies develop the next generation. San Francisco: Jossey-Bass.

Cutcher-Gershenfeld & Associates. (1998). *Knowledge-driven work.* New York: Oxford University Press.

Deming, W. E. (1986). *Out of the crisis.* Cambridge, MA: Massachusetts Institute of Technology, Center for Advanced Engineering Study.

Ford, J. K. (1999). Organizational development. In D. G. Langdon, K. S. Whiteside, & M. M. McKenna (Eds.), *Intervention resource guide: 50 performance improvement tools.* San Francisco: Jossey-Bass.

Ford, J. K., & Fisher, S. (1994). The transfer of safety training in work organizations: A systems perspective to continuous learning. *Occupational Medicine: State of the Art Reviews, 9*(2), 241–259.

Ford, J. K., Boles, J. G., Plamondon, K. E., & White, J. P. (1999). Transformational leadership and community policing: A roadmap for change. *Police Chief, 66*(12), 14, 16, 18–22.

French, W., & Bell, C. (1995). *Organizational development* (5th ed.). Englewood Cliffs, NJ: Prentice Hall.

Geller, W. A. (1997). Suppose we were really serious about police departments becoming "learning organizations." *National Institute of Justice Journal, 234,* 2–8.

Gersick, C. J. (1991). Revolutionary change theories: A multivariate exploration of the punctuated equilibrium paradigm. *Academy of Management Review, 16*(1), 10–36.

Goldstein, J. (1990). Beyond Lewin's force field: A new model for organizational change interventions. In F. Massarik (Ed.), *Advances in organization development* (Vol. 3, pp. 72–88). Norwood, NJ: Ablex.

Katzenbach, J. R., & Smith, D. K. (1993). *The wisdom of teams: Creating the high performance organization.* Boston: Harvard Business School Press.

Kotter, J. P. (1990). *A force for change: How leadership differs from management.* New York: Free Press

Kotter, J. P. (1995). Leading change: Why transformation efforts fail. *Harvard Business Review, 73*(2), pp. 59–67.

Kouzes, J., & Posner, B. (1990). *The leadership challenge.* San Francisco: Jossey-Bass.

Lawler, E. E. (1992). *The ultimate advantage: Creating the high involvement organization.* San Francisco: Jossey-Bass.

Lewin, K. (1951). *Field theory in social science.* New York: Harper.

Marguardt, M. (1997). *Action learning.* Alexandria, VA: American Society for Training and Development.

Miller, D., & Friesen, P. H. (1982). Structural change and performance: Quantum versus piecemeal-incremental approaches. *Academy of Management Review, 4,* 867–892.

Mirvis, P. (1989). Organizational development: An evolutionary perspective. *Research in Organizational Change and Development, 2,* 1–57.

Ostroff, C., & Ford, J. K. (1989). Assessing training needs: Critical levels of analysis. In I. Goldstein (Ed.), *Training and development in work organizations* (pp. 25–62). San Francisco: Jossey-Bass.

Porras, J. I., & Robertson, P. J. (1992). Organizational development: Theory, practice, and research. In M. Dunnette & L. M. Hough (Eds.), *Handbook of industrial and organizational psychology* (2nd ed., pp. 760–797). Palo Alto, CA: Consulting Psychologists Press.

Rothwell, W. J., McLean, G. N., & Sullivan, R. (1995). *Practicing organizational development: A guide for consultants.* San Francisco: Jossey-Bass.

Schein, E. (1985). *Organizational culture and leadership.* San Francisco: Jossey-Bass.

Scholtes, P. R., Joiner, B. L., & Streibel, B. J. (1996). *The team handbook* (2nd ed.). Madison, WI: Joiner.

Senge, P. (1990). *The fifth discipline: The art and practice of the learning organization.* New York: Currency Doubleday.

Senge, P. (1994). *Moving forward, thinking strategically about building learning organizations: The fifth discipline fieldbook.* New York: Doubleday.

Sitkin, S., Sutcliffe, K., & Schroeder, R. (1994). Distinguishing control from learning in total quality management. *Academy of Management Review, 19*(3), 537–564.

Stewart, T. A. (1997). *Intellectual capital.* New York: Doubleday.

Tannenbaum, S. (1997). Enhancing continuous learning: Diagnostic findings from multiple companies. *Human Resource Management, 36*(4), 437–452.

Vail, P. B. (1989). *Managing as a performing art.* San Francisco: Jossey-Bass.

Wellins, R. S., Byham, W. C., & Wilson, J. M. (1991). *Empowered teams.* San Francisco: Jossey-Bass.

Zhao, J., Thurman, Q. C., & Lovrich, N. P. (1995). Community oriented policing across the U.S.: Facilitators and impediments to implementation. *American Journal of Police, 14*(1), 11–28.

Part III

*C*reating
*P*artnerships

CHAPTER 8

Focus on Internal Partnerships

A Framework for Implementing Community Policing in a Unionized Department

Michael J. Polzin
Julie L. Brockman

> Many police organizations are at a loss to move much further forward at this point in time beyond some incremental amount. Simply put, American police agencies do not appear to know what it is that they should be doing next
>
> *H. Greene (1993)*

> The simplistic "police and community working together" slogan has an appeal similar to that of "let's wage a war against drugs." Unfortunately, these two maxims suffer from the same weakness: the failure to address *how* to do it. Until proponents stop writing volumes on the community policing philosophy and develop clear strategies that are easily understood by both the police and the public, it will remain an unattainable goal
>
> *R. D. Hunter and T. Barker (1993)*

The above statements reflect a continuing concern about the feasibility of implementing community policing and actually transforming the practice of police work. Will or can community policing become a successful manifestation of the reinventing govern-

155

ment movement, or will it merely be a vehicle for agencies to tap into available federal funding while they do little to change the nature and delivery of police services (Gianakis & Davis, 1998)? Numerous factors, of course, can affect the ability of a law enforcement agency to define a course for its community-policing initiative and to implement it effectively. Resistance from patrol officers is one of them. Resistance can interrupt the agency's work, reduce acceptance and commitment to change, cause a focus on symptoms rather than causes of both internal and external problems, and impede necessary systemic changes.

Our experience in providing technical assistance and training reveals that police agencies encountering resistance from officers have not fully implemented three principles critical to the success of community policing: (a) developing a department-wide strategy with participation from all members of the agency; (b) integrating all divisions and individuals into the community-policing process; and (c) providing training to all department personnel regarding the philosophy, strategies, and duties associated with community policing (Breci & Erickson, 1998). In effect, agencies have not engaged their internal partners— patrol officers, staff, and command—in the process of change.

PARTNERSHIPS

Forming unlimited partnerships is one of the key elements that undergirds the framework of community policing. Forming partnerships with individuals and organizations in the community is essential, though not sufficient, to the success of community-policing initiatives. Partnerships help to build trust and break down the "us" versus "them" perceptions that can prevent a department from effectively connecting with the community and interacting with various service providers in addressing community needs and correlates of crime.

Many police and sheriff's departments apply the concept of forming partnerships more or less exclusively to constituents—schools, church groups, civic organizations, neighborhood groups, the media, businesses, and business organizations (Gianakis & Davis, 1998; Zhao, Thurman, & Lovrich, 1995). These groups are important players in a department's efforts to apply a community-policing strategy. Nonetheless, it also is essential to partner with the employees who will carry out the operational changes that a community-policing initiative will bring about, and whose acceptance of and commitment to change are vital to its effectiveness and success.

To a degree, it is understandable that the hand of partnership might not be extended to employees of police and sheriff's departments because of a perception that they were already partners in fighting crime. After all, employees signed onto the force to serve the public and follow the chain of command, and they continue to work in the department out of their own volition. One might expect that employees would continue to do as instructed; adhere to the same goals as management; maintain loyalty to their community, command staff, and profession; and willingly accept any changes desired by the agency leadership. Some of the literature targeting police chiefs and sheriffs has supported this perception by creating limited impressions that internal partnerships consist of top-down communication, employee buy-in to management-made decisions, and use of recruitment rather than organizational change to build acceptance of the concept of community policing within the department (Stipak, Immer, & Clavadetscher, 1994). For many police executives who did not anticipate resistance, it has come as a surprise that resistance does occur (Breci & Erickson, 1998; Polzin & Brockman, 1999b).

Much of the resistance police personnel have to community policing can be abated. Resistance occurs in reaction to decisions made and actions taken by people within the system. Consequently, people within the system can moderate the level of resistance by altering their decisions and actions. Thus, it is imperative that law enforcement agencies forge internal partnerships with employees—with patrol officers, supervisors, and support staff—and with the organizations that may represent them in collective bargaining to minimize resistance and achieve the greatest effectiveness in designing and implementing the changes most appropriate for the community.

Building and sustaining internal partnerships is challenging. Regardless of whether employees are represented in collective bargaining, the department must work carefully to assure that efforts to create and sustain partnerships do not isolate or favor some individuals or groups, but do invite a representative view of the current environment and utilize a process that facilitates all voices being heard. A unionized department presents additional challenges, which should not be construed as insurmountable barriers, but rather as factors that help to define the scope and boundaries of the change effort.

Discussions of unions as stakeholders or partners in community-policing initiatives are largely absent in the literature. However, unions represent a group without whom changes in operations cannot easily or effectively be implemented. Moreover, unionized departments constitute a sizable portion of the law enforcement agencies in the United States. The 1999 union density figures show that 61.1% of police and detectives are members of unions, with 64.8% covered by collective-bargaining agreements. Additionally, 39.3% of sheriffs, bailiffs, and other law enforcement officers are members of unions, and 44.2% of them are covered by collective-bargaining agreements (Hirsch & Macpherson, 2000).

WORKING WITH A UNIONIZED POLICE FORCE

In unionized police departments, community-policing initiatives meet with unique challenges and opportunities. The challenges result from collective-bargaining agreements that constrain management's ability to impose changes unilaterally. For example, if a chief or sheriff wishes to use grant funds to create a new Community Police Officer position, she or he has to make the selection and shift assignment in a manner consistent with language in the collective-bargaining agreement—or negotiate with the union to make an exception. This challenge is magnified when the union is told that, in order for community policing to be initiated and successful, the contract must be changed so that the chief or sheriff has the flexibility needed to meet the community's demands or expectations (Polzin & Brockman, 1999a, 1999b).Executive management often views collective-bargaining agreements as barriers to getting things done. What often goes unnoticed is that the existence of a collective-bargaining agreement provides a unique opportunity for a department to facilitate the change effort. The contract provides a structure that forces union and management to come together to resolve issues pertaining to wages, benefits, and working conditions. It also typically includes language that assures fairness and equity in dealing with employees and that minimizes favoritism in matters of discipline, assignment, and promotion. In effect, the contract can minimize conflict and allow employees and management to focus their time and energy on both providing effective services to their constituents and improving the quality of the work environment.

Four attributes of a collective bargaining unit contribute to the possibility that a union can positively affect change: the union (a) is democratic, (b) is representative, (c) articulates the collective voice of its membership, and (d) provides safeguards to employees to assure candor and honesty in internal discussions. The union structure provides all members with a vote, and assures them a right to speak during discussions on union and union-management matters. Thus, individual voices can be heard, at least within the union, on all organizational change efforts. (The qualifier *can* is used, because union members are not forced to participate in discussions, but the option is always present to them and reinforced by union bylaws.) Individual voices, however, may not directly be heard in union-management discussions, because union members elect representatives to speak and negotiate on their behalf. It is reasonable to assume that thoughts articulated by individual members, when capturing the interests and intent of a majority of members, can be heard in conversations carried out by union leaders. However, when the union leadership speaks for the union and/or reaches agreements with management, their thoughts represent the interests, ideas, values, and goals that are supported collectively by at least a majority of the membership. In addition, individuals who articulate points of view that are unpopular with management are protected from reprisal by the collective-bargaining agreement, which assures fair treatment of employees and backs that up with the legally mandated duty of fair representation.

Some police executives emphasize deviation from the ideal attributes of unions. They may wish to negotiate directly with a few selected employees about changes in which they wish them to participate. Some executives believe that the union leadership does not, at least at times, effectively represent the interests of a majority of union members, but represents only its own interests or those of a select few. They also may wish that the only points of view expressed be those that are consistent with their own, or that members' thoughts that differ from the points of view articulated by union leadership be expressed.

These seemingly negative attributes, however, can serve management interests and the process of change. It is unlikely that police chiefs or sheriffs would really want to negotiate separately with all of their employees. They might never have time to do anything else because of the sheer number of employees or because any time an employee received something the others did not have more rounds of negotiation would be demanded or there would be hard feelings festering among those who felt left behind. Unions hold elections of officers regularly: Leaders who run too far afield of members' interests and support face the threat of being voted out of office. Moreover, the process of change through partnership requires that participants, including individual union members serving with the sanction of the union, be able to speak freely, even if the views expressed are unpopular, so that problems can be fully understood and the best decisions reached.

Thus, the existence of union representation is not necessarily an impediment to change, and, in some situations, union representation and the corresponding collective-bargaining agreement provides a structure and process that facilitate building partnerships between police management and other employees. The union process can, in fact, minimize resistance to change and build commitment to the long-term success and effectiveness of the department's change to community policing.

CHAPTER FOCUS

We do not presume that the above arguments will be sufficient to convince law enforcement agency executives that forming partnerships with their unions is something that they need to consider in order to expand and enhance their community-policing efforts. Consequently, to inform partnership-exploration efforts, we place police union-management partnerships in a broader context, showing how community policing links with the movements towards quality-driven and customer-focused organizations that have been under way in both the public and private sectors of the United States for many years. Then, we present alternative visions of union-management partnerships that would fit different organizations. We also examine practices that management might consider employing to demonstrate its commitment to the partnership process.

Many law enforcement unions will not automatically step forward when the possibility of partnership is offered, and will require some convincing that the opportunity they are being offered is in the best interests of their members and the union organization. The suggestions that we offer are in response to issues and ideas generated in forums that we facilitated with participants from police union officials, police managers and executives, and union-management groups from police and sheriff's departments in Michigan. Finally, we set forth a model for creating and sustaining union-management partnerships in law enforcement agencies as they further attempt to implement community-policing initiatives.

THE CONTEXT FOR PARTNERSHIP

In 1992, Osborne and Gaebler published a book that described how the entrepreneurial spirit is transforming the public sector. In their book, *Reinventing Government,* they made the case that, to assure that citizen needs are met even as revenues decline, public sector organizations must become entrepreneurial; that is, they must use resources in new ways to maximize productivity and effectiveness. To do so, they must: fund outcomes rather than inputs; be driven by their mission and not by their rules; empower communities rather than deliver services; meet the needs of customers, not the bureaucracy; invest in prevention rather than cure; and employ participative, team-oriented management systems and results-oriented evaluative criteria. The book highlighted change efforts accomplished or under way in state and local governments across the country, and catalyzed additional public sector change initiatives in a wide range of locations and services.

Many public sector organizations have also been heavily influenced by quality concepts and employ quality-management approaches to their work. Developed principally by W. Edwards Deming, the quality-management approach helped to ignite the Japanese post–World War II economy by focusing on meeting or exceeding customer expectations through ongoing quality improvement. The management philosophy was slow to catch on in the United States, but as market share for U.S. manufactured products was lost in the late 1970s and early 1980s to Japanese-made products, U.S.-based corporations gave it increasing attention. By the late 1980s, an increasing number of quality-management applications could be found in the public sector. Many of the quality-management principles are incorporated into the reinventing government philosophy, which also includes attributes that reflect the particular characteristics of public sector organizations. Community policing is widely regarded as the law enforcement manifestation of the reinventing-government movement, even though it builds on previous innovations in policing (e.g., on problem-oriented policing and team policing) that predate the formal reinventing-government and U.S.-based Total Quality movements (Gianakis & Davis, 1998).

Understanding that community policing has some correlates provides ideas for implementing change strategies within law enforcement agencies. Certainly, from the quality approach, one can learn that, to be most effective, change requires that internal organizational concerns be an essential component of the effort. Deming's "14 Points for Management" encourages organizations to break down barriers between staff areas, drive out fear, remove barriers to pride in one's work, and institute a vigorous program of education and self-improvement (Walton, 1986)—all necessary conditions for building the partnerships essential for successful implementation of change. Scholtes (1988) defined "Quality Leadership" as managers identifying and removing barriers that keep employees from doing the best job possible, and encouraging workers to use the knowledge and insight they gained from their years working on the job. According to the reinventing-government approach, the work of the public agency is to catalyze and empower, to be competitive and mission-driven, and to fund outcomes and not inputs. The agency should also focus on the customer, be enterprising if not entrepreneurial, focus on prevention, and be both participatory and market oriented (Osborne & Gaebler, 1992).

The above analysis strongly suggests that there are conceptual links between community policing and the quality and reinventing-government movements, and that the changes introduced with community policing can have considerable breadth. Discussions of partnership, however, must also include emphasis on scope and boundaries. Not all partnerships will or should look or act the same. There is no prescription for how union-management partnerships should be structured, what the focus of their efforts should be, or the degree or focus of authority that should be delegated to the union-management partnership. Yet it is vital that law enforcement agencies consider and choose between alternative forms of partnership so that expectations are clear and potential sources of tension and conflict are removed from the partnership's interactions.

Union-Management Partnerships

The concept *union-management partnership* implies different things to different people. To some, it signals hope for a different, more effective future in which a collective employee voice will join with that of management in many discussions about the organization. To employees, it may surface fears that gains secured through collective bargaining will be eroded as employees and their unions agree to changes that undermine foundational elements of the contract. Managers may fear a loss of authority over things for which they will still be held accountable.

As a concept, union-management partnership is very simple. Within a partnership, both parties identify common goals or problems that they can work on together. The parties may have one or many goals in common, and may address a broad range of issues, including scheduling, making resource decisions, and strategic planning. In law enforcement agencies, the decision to attempt a change to community policing can be made in partnership, but, more typically, the chief, sheriff, or local government makes the decision, after which the union is enjoined to hammer out details about how the community-policing concept will be applied. Overall, the cooperative effort can take a wide variety of forms and structures, including *ad hoc* committees, problem-solving or continuous-improvement teams, self-managing work groups, and joint councils. The effort can take place at all levels of the organization.

The basic characteristic of partnership is that it provides a lens through which to examine how work should be accomplished and how decisions should be made within the organization. Partnership does not, by definition, imply codetermination, in which the union has equal say in all decisions affecting the organization. Nor does it, by definition, imply that unions merely be informed of and then acquiesce to management wishes. However, both of the above can be found at opposite ends of the spectrum of choices available to union-management groups when considering how decisions are to be made on various issues.

The purpose of union-management partnerships is to build a stronger relationship that supports involving workers in efforts to improve the quality of work processes and the work environment, manage changes effectively, and increase the overall effectiveness of the organization. This approach acknowledges that those closest to the work are the real experts in their jobs and are often able to find solutions that are not readily evident to other people.

The choice between different forms of partnership initiative that might be undertaken by police unions and management is influenced by the degree of trust between the parties, history with past initiatives, external challenges, and competitive needs. There is no single type of activity that is best for all organizations—the nature of a developing partnership should be determined by the needs of the parties. Several types of partnership change are described in Table 8.1. Not all of them directly enable unions and management to implement a community-policing initiative, yet they may be necessary to improve the union-management relationship to a point that instituting community policing is even possible.

TABLE 8.1 Alternative Types of Partnership Change

Types of Partnership Change

Collective bargaining and contract administration:
The focus is on improving the process and outcomes of collective bargaining, and continuing to strengthen the relationship between the union and management through more effective contract administration. The contract is recognized as belonging to both the union and the law enforcement agency, and both sides acknowledge and respect the responsibilities of the other. Any improvements obtained may or may not spill over in to other areas of operations and/or the relationship.

Improve on the status quo but maintain a traditional approach to the relationship:
The focus is on maintaining the existing structure of the labor-management relationship, but making it less "us" versus "them" and more effective. It may involve surfacing both current and long-standing tensions, acknowledging their impact on the relationship, and trying to address them and reduce them as barriers to improvement. At a minimum, the parties typically develop and utilize better ways to communicate with each other.

Issue initiative strategy: The focus is on application of a collaborative process to a specific project or issue, such as improving an attendance policy, developing a plan to augment youth activities in the community, or considering how to best implement neighborhood watch programs. An agency may focus on a project as a means to pilot joint labor- management approaches, with an evaluation component included in the pilot effort. Or, the organization may recognize that a joint approach is appropriate for a specific task or to address a specific issue, but not be inclined to apply the approach more widely at the time. Use of this strategy allows both union and management to explore how partnership might work for them and what issues they need to address and resolve if they are to expand use of this strategy to other areas.

Joint problem-solving strategy: The focus is on creating and maintaining an ongoing forum for addressing issues that affect both members of the bargaining unit and administration. Joint committee meetings might be held regularly with agendas and minutes. A systematic problem-solving process is often used along with a designated facilitator. Meeting guidelines are followed to keep the discussions on track and focused on issues, not personalities. Health and safety committees, labor-management committees, workers' compensation committees, and diversity committees are examples of this category of partnership activity.

Joint Labor-Management Committee (JLMC): The focus is on applying a labor-management lens to a wide range of contractual and organizational issues. This is, perhaps, the most expansive application of a union-management partnership process, because the parties look to the JLMC as a vehicle for achieving more productive operations and a higher quality of worklife, as well effective and enduring organizational change.

Characteristics of Effective Union-Management Partnerships

.A discussion of what a union-management partnership is must make note of some defining characteristics. For this discussion, we draw from Cohen-Rosenthal and Burton's book, *Mutual Gains* (1993).

Union-management partnership must support the fundamental respon-sibilities of both parties. In a cooperative venture, each party is clear about its interests and whom it represents. The parties work together because they believe it is in their best interest to do so. The cooperative effort must support each party's continuing ability to fulfill their respon-sibilities. Each party continues aggressively to represent their constitu-ents, though the tools that they use may lead to solutions that serve the interests of both parties without undermining the interests of either. Both parties support the collective-bargaining agreement.

Effective partnership requires conflict. In a union-management initia-tive, the parties will disagree. In fact, the diversity of thoughts that ema-nate from union-management groups is one key reason why partner-ships are desirable for implementing change. At times, the passions that certain topics or ideas generate may lead to conflict. Conflict brings out divergent opinions and perspectives, and sparks creativity and change. Conflict is not only inevitable, but also desirable; it marks the surfacing of tensions that, if left unattended, can fester until they taint thoughts, conversations, and relationships. Conflict will continue to exist in orga-nizations even after successful union-management cooperative efforts have been implemented. What is different is how the conflict is man-aged and how it is creatively channeled to achieve common goals.

A union-management partnership is an intentional relationship. It is joint, planned, deliberate, and structured. Cooperative practices require a great deal of effort and, often, training for both parties. Some require fa-cilitation by a third party to initiate a joint process or help move it along. Partnership requires ongoing maintenance, resources, and support.

A union-management partnership is a practical relationship. It is not a cozy, self-serving relationship that is counter to the interests of the par-ties' constituents. It is a practical relationship supporting the interests of both parties in making and implementing decisions that affect them without undermining the interests of either. It does not require either party to abdicate its traditional responsibilities.

Partnership will not solve all of an organization's problems. It is not a miracle cure for all of an organization's ills. The truth is that management is not always right and the union is not always right. However, if they work together, there is a better chance that they will craft appropriate solutions that best address the needs of each party.

A union-management partnership will help to build trust between the parties. The partnership does not require that the parties initially like or trust each other. Many union-management partnerships apply interest-based bargaining concepts to contract negotiations and administration, as well as to operational and relationship issues. In an interest-based process, the parties specify the needs or interests that must be addressed with any problem solution or decision. Presumably, if a party's needs were being met by a solution, it would clearly not be in their best interest to do anything that jeopardizes or sabotages implementation. Thus, willingness to support a decision does not have to be based on the degree of trust that exists between the parties. However, effective cooperation does require that parties approach the process with honesty and integrity. Hidden agendas may get one party a temporary advantage, but they will quickly scuttle cooperative efforts for a long time to come.

Scope of Authority of the Union-Management Partnership

Effective union-management partnerships require that both parties be clear about the degree of authority ascribed to the union-management group and the issues and concerns that can be considered. Differing expectations and understandings contribute significantly to breakdowns of trust that challenge the credibility of the process. Decision-making processes that are possible within a union-management partnership include *unilateral, consultative, delegated,* and *participative* processes (Vroom & Yetton, 1973). Again, there is no prescription as to which type of decision-making process is correct; it is situational. There are factors to consider when choosing a decision-making approach for a particular task.

A *unilateral* decision-making process is one in which the decision is made exclusively by management. Within a partnership effort, unilateral decisions might be made when time is a factor and/or when the group does not possess or know where to find the information necessary to make a good decision. Unilateral decisions can also be used when the group does not have the requisite abilities, skills, or motivation to make a good decision. If the group does not need to be convinced to accept the solution that is decided upon, management may also choose to make a particular decision unilaterally.

In a *consultative* decision-making process, the union-management group provides input to management on the matter at hand in limited form as shared information, perceptions, beliefs, interests, values, or needs, or in more comprehensive form as recommendations. Both parties need to know if they are to share their thoughts or offer recommendations. The consultative process might be used if there are few time constraints, the group's input can add value to the decision making process, acceptance of the decision by the group is important, or management is reluctant to commit up front to accepting the group's decision.

Delegated decisions are those in which management authorizes a designated party, in this case the union-management group, to make the decision on behalf of the organization. This type of decision making might be employed when the degree of acceptance of the decision is important; there is a high degree of trust between management and the group to which the decision has been delegated; time is not a significant factor; management wishes to facilitate development of an environment of empowerment; or management is willing to accept whatever decision is made. Some organizations delegate a range of decisions to employee groups, though there may be limits placed on the group's authority with respect to such things as spending money and involving other groups.

A *participative* decision-making process is one in which union and management agree that they will decide together on the most appropriate course of action. This strategy might be used when it is important that a high-quality decision be reached; there needs to be a high degree of acceptance of and commitment to the decision; the group has the requisite knowledge, skills, and motivation to make the decision, or management is willing to provide the necessary education and training; time is sufficient for such a process; and it is desirable to use the process to build or strengthen trust between the parties. Participative decisions in a union-management partnership are typically made by consensus.

Factors affecting the choice of decision-making strategy include time and resources available to make the decision; degree of trust between the parties; degree of acceptance of and commitment to the decision required; degree of quality required in the decision; knowledge, skills, and motivation of the group; management's willingness to share authority; and management's desire to build capability within the union-management group (Vroom & Yetton, 1973). It is not necessary (nor is it likely to be possible) to use the same decision-making strategy for all issues, even if the union and management have created a formalized, joint union-management partnership structure and process. What is important is that the parties clarify the decision-making strategy *before* beginning work on the task or problem.

Reducing Resistance

In some police departments, resistance to management initiatives has built up because of previous decisions and actions by either or both management and unions. Watson (1969) made several recommendations for reducing resistance, and these are listed in the left column of Table 8.2. In the right column, we provide data from union leaders, police administrators and executives, and police union-management groups that were collected during workshops, focus groups, and interviews conducted between 1998 and 1999. Unfortunately, our data reveal that practices employed in many law enforcement agencies run counter to Watson's recommendations.

The resulting resistance was revealed when many union leaders spoke disparagingly about the concept of community policing, though, when asked in a different way (e.g., "In what ways does your department need to improve police services and internal operations?"), they expressed ideas that clearly were consistent with community policing. Also, several police union leaders expressed a belief that community policing presented opportunities for them and their members. They envisioned that it could lead to a better work environment for their members, to more effective operations, and to increased recognition and support from the community. Some of them even wanted to see community policing integrated into the whole department and applied to all in their day-to-day work.

Union leaders also offered some clear indication of what they needed from departmental leadership to consider joining management in partnership to design and implement a change to community policing. For some departments, the insistence on clear and unwavering support for collective bargaining might even mean that the parties would agree that matters pertaining to the collective-bargaining agreement and process would be off-limits in discussions pertaining to community policing. In effect, the parties would agree to seek other solutions to issues rather than discuss changing the contract. This can be accomplished if interest-based bargaining applications are employed.

A FRAMEWORK FOR BUILDING A
UNION-MANAGEMENT PARTNERSHIP

Change occurs in response to a stimulus. External competitive challenges, need for improved quality, need to improve effectiveness of relationships, changes in the market, and new technologies are a few examples of stimuli that could compel unions and managers to contemplate making changes in their organizations. The critical issue is for influential individuals to recognize whether the current relationship and way of working does or does not allow the parties effectively to address the challenges facing the organization.

We describe a recommended process for building a union-management partnership to design and implement a change to community policing. Our process is atypical, to be sure, as most change processes within unionized law enforcement organizations are approached through a top-down organizational development strategy. Our strategy is deliberately different. It is different because it (a) acknowledges and takes advantage of the collective bargaining relationship, (b) intentionally attempts to focus on an internal application of the principles of community policing to coincide with the more customary external application, and (c) recognizes that the experience and knowledge of all employees are necessary and valuable to ensuring effective change.

The process proposed in this chapter does not assume that either the union leaders or the management leaders are more prepared than the others are to attempt a joint process. It takes into account the need for both parties to move beyond their shared history and establish a common vision and agenda for change within the scope and boundaries upon which they agree. It requires the parties to state clearly what it is that they need from each other to explore partnership and then commit to a cooperative working process to manage the change. It also requires that the boundaries and authority of the partnership be clearly defined, common ground rules and guiding principles for working together be established, goals and measurable objectives be formulated, and a working plan be developed through a process that leads to joint ownership and control of the initiative. It is through a process like this that an effective infrastructure for managing the change to community policing can be created.

There is no single prescription for the scope of work to be taken on through a joint labor-management process. The parties may decide to maintain the *status quo*, keep the *status quo* but improve upon it, focus on a specific issue, engage in problem solving on an ongoing basis,

TABLE 8.2 Recommendations to Reduce Resistance and Related Union
Officers' Comments Revealing Sources of Resistance to
Community Policing

Watson's (1969) Recommendations to Reduce Resistance	Union Officers' Comments Revealing Sources of Resistance to Community Policing
Source and sponsorship of the change	**Officers wanted**
• clear support from the leaders in the system, including union officials • those involved in or affected by the change must feel that the project is their own and not one devised by external forces	1. assurance that change would be supported by management and local government 2. input into decisions affecting their jobs **Officers reported** 1. They had not been involved in conversations about community policing or the ways to apply it in their communities.
Characteristics of the change being proposed	**Officers wanted**
• participants see the change as reducing rather than increasing their present burdens • the project is congruent with values and ideals that have long been acknowledged by participants • the change offers the kind of new experiences that interest participants • participants feel that their autonomy and their security is not threatened	1. staffing and resource issues addressed 2. authority to do their jobs supported 3. clear commitment to collective bargaining 4. clarity in expectations about their changing roles and training in performing those roles 5. fair and equal treatment for those performing community and traditional policing 6. assurance that high-quality traditional police services would be maintained 7. administrative practices realigned to support the work they were being asked to do 8. assistance in building a shared understanding with the public about community policing
Procedures to follow in instituting change	**Union leaders**
• jointly engage in diagnostic efforts that lead to shared understanding of what the problems are and their importance	1. requires from management a commitment to a real participatory process

TABLE 8.2 Continued

• affirm adoption of the change initiative by consensus • foster empathy between opponents and proponents • facilitate understanding of both parties' concerns and steps taken to relieve fears • opportunities for feedback of perceptions and further clarification as needed • facilitate tasks that can help build acceptance and trust between the parties • revise plan if experience dictates that changes would be desirable	2. did not insist on co-determination or decisions be made by consensus, but they did wish to be involved in all phases of the process 3. wanted their ideas and suggestions to receive serious consideration and be utilized when there was agreement that they were appropriate

engage in collaborative bargaining, create an ongoing joint labor-management committee and process, or some combination of the above. There is, however, a prescription that we suggest unionized departments follow so that unions and management can create change by developing a cooperative relationship within the context of organizational change. The prescribed method outlined below has four stages: (a) Getting Started, (b) Preparing to Change, (c) Working Cooperatively, and (d) Sustaining the Change.

Stage One: Getting Started

In stage one, the parties must prepare to explore change, meet to explore change, make informed choices about change, and create a constituency for change. It may be helpful if a third-party facilitator is present to assist the parties in moving through the initial difficulties often encountered by attempts to form new relationships or infrastructures.

Many change initiatives get off to a faulty start because they fail to lay the necessary foundation. Preparing to explore change is as much about the relationship between the parties as it is about the eventual change. Parties need to explore the scope of their cooperative relationship. The cooperative process is often initiated by management leaders, because managers, as part of their job responsibility, deliberate over potential change initiatives. It is necessary to gain the commitment of top union and management leaders to participate in a joint labor-management discussion about changing the parties' relationship and/or changing what they do jointly. This exploratory step does not require either party to commit to change. However, a prior agreement by the participants attending the session is needed. Generally, management and union leaders will each choose their own representatives. The size of the group participating in the initial meeting will vary according to the number of unions represented within the organization, the size of the organization, the task, and so forth. An agenda, including discussion of the meeting process and ground rules, also is prepared before to the first meeting. Another important agenda item (see Ongoing Concerns, below) is for the parties to determine if, when, and what to communicate with constituents.

When exploring change, management will typically decide on a plan before they identify the reasons for change. It is not sufficient that reasons have been identified by theorists or in other organizations, even if the organizational context is similar. For maximum commitment and support, everyone must know the reasons for considering a change to community policing, and unions and management must build this understanding together. As in the previous step (preparing to explore change), exploring change requires no long-term commitment from either party. The parties will explore the characteristics and possible forms of cooperation, and identify the demonstrations of commitment needed by the parties to move forward. They also will explore the desired outcomes of the change, surface potential dilemmas that might arise as a consequence of the desired changes, and discuss the implications of change for union and management leadership, their constituents, and stakeholders.

At this point in the process, if union and management wish to continue building a partnership, they are ready to make informed choices about change to begin defining the structure under which the parties will work together. The parties must decide on the forum for joint decision-making regarding the change and on how decisions will be made within that forum. For example, depending on the needs of the organization and the nature of the change effort, the parties may decide to form a joint union-management committee, which makes decisions by consensus, or they may decide to form joint problem-solving teams across departmental units to develop solutions using a consistent problem-solving method. In addition, the parties should develop principles to guide their behavior while working jointly, determine the scope of issues to be addressed by the partnership, and decide on the level of authority of the partnership. We would recommend that, unless already codified in the collective-bargaining agreement, all of the agreements and decisions made by the parties be set in writing as a reference for future decision-making purposes. The parties would not be legally bound by such a document, nor would it be unusual to change such a document as the parties move forward through the other stages.

The written document can also serve as a communication piece that begins the process of creating a constituency for change. The ultimate purpose of creating such a constituency is to gain acceptance of the change effort. Keeping constituents informed and involved in the process reduces resistance. Of course, this requires painstaking effort, constant attention, and no small amount of ingenuity. Constituents will have different perspectives from both their leaders and their coconstituents. We speak more about this in the section about ongoing concerns and communication.

Stage Two: Preparing to Change

In stage two, the parties must strategically plan the effort. The outcome of this stage is an action plan to be implemented in the third stage. Labor and management must both be involved in designing the key attributes of the new system. Questions to be asked and answered at this stage include the following: What will the new system look like? How will individual roles and responsibilities change? What will a day in the life of an employee, supervisor, or manager look like under the new system? Addressing these questions usually requires that a joint union-management committee agree on a set of dimensions within the boundaries of community policing and identify a range of options within each dimension. The group also assesses the degree to which the new attributes match the goals established for community policing in the department. Though guidelines may have been established by outside experts, the choices must be appropriate for the department and must be understood by all in order to be effectively carried out. Many police organizations must respond to multiple changes at one time—for example, to new technologies, legislatively mandated training, downsizing, and growth. Labor and management must determine whether these changes are likely to interfere with implementing community policing or *vice versa.* Unless the needs of all of the programs are reconciled, there is likely to be competition for scarce resources, including time, and a dissolution of energy and commitment as the attention needed to maintain focus and progress wears thin.

Stakeholders, individuals, and groups whose expertise or position can influence the change or who are likely to be affected by the change must be identified. The choices of the joint union-management committee must consider key stakeholder interests in community policing and its design in order to elicit their support and reduce the efforts to undermine planned change. Internal and external stakeholders, such as community groups and the local governance system, should be included in this analysis (see Table 8.1).

Top-level commitment from each of the key stakeholders is needed for the community-policing effort to succeed. Verbal commitment is an important first step, but is not sufficient over the long haul. If it is necessary to build or rebuild trust among labor and management, the leadership of each needs to give visible evidence of their commitment through changed behaviors and continuing efforts to remove barriers to implementing community policing. It may be useful for the union and management to identify actions that would demonstrate commitment to partnership and that would satisfy their constituents that this organizational change is different from resisted attempts that preceded it.

The group most often overlooked in any change effort is middle management, which includes mid- and first-level union leadership (see Chapter 6). This group is crucial, because they will oversee the operational transition to community policing. Their roles are likely to change in ways for which their previous experiences have not prepared them. Some may be concerned about their individual job security, or at least about how their career paths are likely to be affected. How their performance will be measured and rewarded, how community-policing functions will be integrated with traditional police functions, how they will be supported in their work, and other questions will need to be addressed. In addition, the group will require education in the forms of management and supervision that are integral to the new work system, and training in the actual skills that they will need to support the work of line staff.

Stage Three: Working Cooperatively

Exploring, designing, and implementing change is difficult when daily operations proceed at regular—that is, full—speed. Careful and comprehensive planning in stage two will facilitate a smoother implementation and evaluation in stage three.

A key question about implementing a change process is whether to do so throughout the entire organization at once, or to begin with a pilot project for a defined period of time, evaluate it, make adjustments, and then diffuse the change through the rest of the department. Several factors affect a department's answer to that question: Is there a portion of the organization that is more ready than the rest to take on the change? Would the department be better served by a pilot than by organization-wide implementation from the onset? What information or organizational learning would be generated by a pilot that would help overall implementation? How would a particular pilot help or hinder implementation department-wide? If a pilot is chosen, the pilot period should be of limited duration, usually three or four months, and an evaluation strategy should be built into the plan. Limiting the duration of the pilot keeps the department focused and on track to continue changing the entire organization. The pilot offers the department an opportunity to try out community policing on a small scale to smooth the process of diffusion. Nonetheless, managing the diffusion of the change throughout the department is likely to create heightened demands for limited resources, with one of the most significant being time. It is important to address issues about diffusion before beginning that process. How will the demands upon the organization for training be managed? What other initiatives or priorities create competing demands, and how will those be reconciled with the demands created by the change to community policing? Does the top-level commitment of labor and/or management need to be revisited to assure that the implementation process proceeds as smoothly as possible? The union-management partnership might also find it useful to cultivate in the organization an expectation that change is likely to be ongoing by developing mechanisms with which to continuously review, clarify, modify, and improve the effort.

Partners in a joint union-management committee must maintain close contact with their respective constituencies. It is also important to initiate a process of communication that begins to demonstrate that the department is embarking on a new era and elicits input into the change process from all members. Thus, mechanisms for communication and a plan for education and training are critical elements of the transformation process. It may not be necessary to have the plan for the transformation completed before taking it to the workforce. Indeed, doing so may have negative repercussions, because people may voice resentment for being left out of yet another process. It may also happen that, if information is not provided by the committee, people will be left to arrive at their own conclusions about what is and is not happening when union and management meet.

In the "Getting Started" and "Preparing to Change" stages, labor and management began the process of modifying or reengineering the department's internal systems and structures to support the change. It is likely, however, that the need for additional, unanticipated alterations will emerge as people acquire experience in the new work system. Mechanisms need to be in place to evaluate and monitor the progress and process of implementation, make adjustments to internal systems to assure that they are consistent with the goals of community policing, and improve internal processes that may be hindering achievement of individual and organizational goals.

Stage Four: Sustaining the Change

During stage four, the parties must plan to renew. A plan to renew requires that, within a predetermined time frame, the parties evaluate the change effort as it applies to the organization and reflect upon the changes that have taken place within the relationship between the parties. Both types of evaluation will highlight both newly acquired knowledge and skills and those needed for present and future activities.

In a step critical for sustaining and maintaining the change effort, after detailed discussion of the insights from their evaluation, the parties must set their energies to establishing new short- and long-term goals and objectives for the change effort and redefining their goals for the partnership. The outcome of establishing new goals and objectives is a new or updated plan for change, and a return to stage two of building a union-management partnership.

Ongoing Concerns

Collective bargaining issues are likely to surface at various points in the process of exploring, planning, and implementing community policing. How they are dealt with can significantly affect the trust built between labor and management, as well as labor and management's commitment to the joint process and to community policing, and strategic choices about the new work systems being developed. Joint union-management committees of many organizations direct that contractual issues are not permissible matters of discussion in the design process or within the work teams that might be created. Others respond that only when contractual issues are acceptable matters of discussion can the organization take on some of the seemingly intractable problems in the department and make deeper and more enduring progress.

Joint committees should not feel compelled to permit inclusion of contractual issues in their deliberations; this might be something that a joint committee takes on as trust between labor and management is strengthened, or it may not happen at all. The point to remember is that the manner in which the issues are addressed, by either labor or management, may affect both the degree of satisfaction that the parties have about their joint process and the outcomes of the change to community policing. Many departments make the mistake of claiming that only through contractual changes can significant progress be made toward community policing. Typically, this approach undermines the credibility of police management and the change effort itself.

Evaluating the change to community policing is also something that should be done on an ongoing basis—from the early stages of exploration, through implementation and beyond. Not only the expected outcomes, but also the process used to explore, design, and implement the change should be subject to review at each stage. But, what is to be measured? The union-management committee should identify the criteria for success for each stage and be sure that these criteria can be measured objectively. The committee should also think through how these measures will be packaged for review and how they will be used by the committee and by the workforce.

Effective communication among the union-management group, their constituents, and stakeholders is critical to the success of any change effort. Effective communication reduces and inhibits rumors, reduces psychological barriers to individual change, and alleviates fears associated with change. Communication is an ongoing concern because the union-management group must address it throughout the change effort. In fact, a common message to constituents regarding the purpose and outcomes of the very first meeting of the partnership group is a critical first step in setting an effective pattern and expectation for communication.

Creating a communication plan is a necessary activity to be completed within stage one of the change effort. Some questions the parties might want to consider before creating a communication plan are the following: Who are your constituents and stakeholders? What might they want to know about current and future change efforts? What are the interests of the constituents and stakeholders? How and when will they be communicated to? Keep in mind that each constituent group and each stakeholder group may have different interests and, therefore, different needs for what, when, and how information is communicated.

CONCLUSION

Adopting our recommended approach to organizational change is difficult, time-consuming, and costly, to be sure. In many cases, it requires putting aside the cynicism and hard feelings left over from previous failed initiatives and embarking on a journey over which one has little individual control. Most organizations have difficulty with this even when their leaders have the best of intentions. Most of us are not schooled or trained to act in a collaborative manner or to use data to solve problems. Indeed, leaders are typically expected to be strong and decisive, and are not rewarded for such things as inducing employee involvement in setting goals and developing strategies. In a command-and-control environment such as a police department, where the stakes are elevated by the potential for injury or worse, these expectations are intensified. Moreover, many police officers' role expectations are shaped by the command-and-control culture as well, thereby limiting the degree that they initially call for representation in these defining conversations.

Resistance to change can be overcome if those who are affected by it and called upon to carry it out are involved in making the change. Police officers and their unions have been quite clear that they want to have input into the process of applying community policing in their departments. They want strong leadership and direction from management so that the boundaries of rank-and-file involvement are clear and the degree of authority that they have to make decisions over a defined, yet expanded, set of issues is clearly specified. They want to engage in the change process without fear of hidden agendas so that they can throw the full force of their knowledge and experience into the task of making the department a better place to work and improving the effectiveness of services that are provided to the community. They also want the collective-bargaining process and agreement supported both to take advantage of the protections that it affords to individual members and to measure the degree to which management accepts and respects employees and the unions as worthy colleagues whose expertise and participation will add significant value to the change to community policing.

Certainly, changes in behavior are required by both parties for the transformation to community policing to be effective and enduring. We have focused on the issues of police unions, because we have found that their voice often is not heard in discussions about community policing, and, in fact, it often appears that police management and their union counterparts have difficulty talking to each other in a way that recognizes and supports the needs of both parties.

A systematic, cooperative approach to community policing taken on by a union-management partnership provides the greatest opportunity for a police organization effectively to design, plan, and implement an organizational change effort. As stated throughout this chapter, the most effective process of organizational change is one that has the commitment of and involvement from its key stakeholders—its employees. Unionized police departments have a unique opportunity to make the best use of the knowledge and expertise of the workforce through the collective voice of the union.

REFERENCES

Breci, M. G., & Erickson, T. E. (1998). Community policing: The process of transitional change. *FBI Law Enforcement Bulletin, 67*(6), 16–21.

Cohen-Rosenthal, E., & Burton, C. E. (1993). *Mutual gains: A guide to union-management cooperation.* Ithaca, NY: ILR Press.

Gianakis, G. A., & Davis, G. J., III. (1998). Reinventing or repackaging public service? The case of community-oriented policing. *Public Administration Review, 58*(6), 485–498.

Greene, H. (1993). Community oriented policing in Florida. *American Journal of Police, 12*(3), 141–155.

Hirsch, B. T., & Macpherson, D. A. (2000). *Union membership and earnings data book: Compilations from the current population survey.* Washington, DC: Bureau of National Affairs.

Hunter, R. D., & Barker, T. (1993). BS and buzzwords: The new police operational style. *American Journal of Police, 12,* 157–168.

Osborne, D., & Gaebler, T. (1992). *Reinventing government.* New York: Addison-Wesley.

Polzin, M. J., & Brockman, J. L. (1999a). A labor-management approach to community policing, *Journal of Community Policing, 1* (issue 1), 7–20.

Polzin, M. J., & Brockman, J. L. (1999b). What do police unions want? Observations about building an infrastructure for involving unions in community policing, *Journal of Community Policing, 1* (issue 2), 29–46.

Scholtes, P. R., (1988). *The team handbook: How to use teams to improve quality.* Madison, WI: Joiner.

Stipak, B., Immer, S., & Clavadetscher, M. (1994). Are you really doing community policing? *Police Chief, 61*(10), 115, 117–118, 120, 122–123.

Vroom, V. H., & Yetton, P. W. (1973). *Leadership and decision making.* Pittsburgh, PA: University of Pittsburgh Press.

Walton, M. (1986). *The Deming management method.* New York: Perigee.

Watson, G. (1969). Resistance to change. In W. G. Bennis, K. D. Benne, & R. Chin (Eds.), *The planning of change* (2nd ed.). New York: Holt, Rinehart & Winston.

Zhao, J., Thurman, Q. C., & Lovrich, N. P. (1995). Community-oriented policing across the U.S.: Facilitators and impediment to implementation. *American Journal of Police, 14*(1), 11–28.

CHAPTER 9

The Nexus of Community Policing and Domestic Violence

Merry Morash
Amanda L. Robinson

*A*t the federal level during the last decade, there has been considerable attention to improving the criminal justice system response to intimate partner violence, and to promoting the adoption and implementation of community-oriented policing. The establishment of the Violence Against Women Office (VAWO) and the Community Oriented Policing Services (COPS) Office, both within the U.S. Department of Justice, epitomizes federal acceptance and support of the two reform efforts. VAWO has emphasized, among other things, the need for better justice system response to women abused by their partners, the importance of coordination in response at the local level, and the necessity of advocacy and services for victims. COPS has emphasized a problem-solving approach to policing, in which police

---

AUTHORS' NOTE: This chapter focuses on intimate partner violence against women. It is recognized that some men are victimized by intimate partners, but women are more often victimized, particularly by severe forms of violence. Also, we use the term *domestic violence* because it is incorporated into the phrase "nexus of community policing and domestic violence." In doing this, we do not exclude other forms of intimate-partner violence.

and community (individual citizens, groups, and agencies) work together in partnership to identify crime and other problems, understand their causes, and effectively address the problems of most concern to citizens. VAWO has had an impact on resources and response to the victims of violence by a partner, and COPS has made major contributions to changes in the conceptualization and practice of policing.

This chapter explores the implications of the community-policing movement for police response to intimate partner violence. First, we set the stage with historical issues related to the police response to such violence, and we follow this with information on the contemporary police response and the related issue of how partner-violence victims are viewed within the police occupational culture. We also review efforts to develop a cooperative and effective nexus of community policing and domestic violence, and provide specific examples of community-policing strategies to combat partner violence. Finally, based on a presentation of our own process evaluation and the assessments of others, we offer several recommendations to victim advocates, concerned citizens, and law enforcement officials for how to build a partnership that enables an improved response to partner violence by drawing upon a philosophy of community policing.

AN EXAMINATION OF THE NEXUS

The philosophy of community-oriented policing, which originated during police reform efforts of the 1970s, is currently widespread and embraced by many citizens, police administrators, scholars, and local and federal politicians. The 1994 Crime Act authorized $8.8 billion for community-policing programs, and currently almost 90% of Americans are served by community police officers (U.S. Department of Justice, 1999a).

Federal Efforts

Most recently, federal efforts through the COPS office have sought to clarify and strengthen what they call the *nexus of community policing and domestic violence.* Beginning in 1998, COPS distributed over $12 million in grants to combat domestic violence.[1] This budget included $100,000 for each of 25 Regional Community Policing Institutes, which are funded by COPS to provide training and technical assistance in specific regions of the nation, to each convene a conference for citizens and law enforcement officials. Additional COPS initiatives have been a subcontract to the Federal Law Enforcement Training Center to develop curriculum relevant to the connection of community policing with domestic violence, and funding of ongoing training at selected Regional Community Policing Institutes. A look at the COPS Web site shows more than 15 resources for police departments interested in improving their response to domestic violence, including conference materials, handbooks, videos, and PowerPoint presentations. In a final example of federal activity to support a coming together of efforts to improve response to domestic violence and community policing, a recent U.S. Department of Justice report on innovative practices in the field identified three approaches used in contemporary responses to domestic violence:

1. Taking a comprehensive approach, for example by creating police-public partnerships or multidisciplinary task forces intent on improving the community-wide response to domestic violence.

2. Enhancing services to victims, for example with intensive follow-up contacts or special partnerships between police and victim advocates or social workers aimed at linking victims with additional resources in the community.

3. Using problem-solving techniques, for example analyzing crime data to identify particular areas of concern with regard to domestic violence, and implementing a specific plan of action to decrease domestic violence in the community (Sampson & Scott, 1999).

Sampson and Scott (1999) point out that each form of innovation reflects the three main tenants of the community-policing philosophy.

Community Policing and the Nexus With Domestic Violence

Community policing operates at two levels: within the interactions of individual police officers and other people, and as a pattern of activity by members of a police department occurring within the community over time. A connection of community policing and violence-against-women reforms can also be manifested at both levels. At the individual level, police interactions with abused women include informal conversations, for example with women seeking information, and formal police-citizen encounters when police have discretion or are legally required to make an arrest. At the community level, police might be part of a group attempting to coordinate responses to domestic violence, or they might be the focus of a community group that is critical of police practices.

The overlap of both individual and community-level policing activities with violence against women is not necessarily characterized by cooperation with the police. In fact, historically, the police-community relationship has been adversarial, with violence-against-women activists criticizing the police and demanding reform, and police resisting reform. Research conducted during the mid-20th century demonstrated that the criminal justice system's response to domestic violence was inadequate: Police often ignored or minimized the seriousness of violence between family members or intimates; difficulties in prosecuting batterers arose from legal requirements that the victim must serve as the complaining witness; and judges tended to give light sentences to batterers because of the financial support they might provide to the women and/or children whom they battered (Walker, 1985). Over the years, women abused by their partners have faced insensitivity from criminal justice system personnel, laws that did not protect them, decreased resources for victim services (including advocacy), and other hurdles blocking their access to justice (Walker, 1985). These problems reflect the long-standing cultural beliefs that a man's home is his castle, that family disputes and/or violence should be handled privately, and that preserving the family is more important than protecting women from physical abuse (Hirschel, Hutchison, Dean, & Mills, 1992; Okun, 1986; Pleck, 1987).

Until the 1970s, police officers were taught in training academies that domestic violence was a private, family concern and, as such, inappropriate business for the criminal justice system (Pleck, 1987). Violence among family members or intimates was defined as a disturbance call (along with public intoxication, for example) that required no specific actions of officers. Officers were trained to handle these calls with the main goal of settling the parties down and restoring order. Consequently, arrest was used only as a last resort, and was seen as a threat to continuation of the nuclear family as a unit.

Almost three decades ago, several events converged to begin the still continuing transformational process in the criminal justice response to domestic violence. In the 1970s, the women's movement called attention to the plight of battered women and the prevalence of domestic violence in American families. During this time, the first battered women's shelters were created, and National Organization of Women chapters across the United States formed task forces on spouse abuse (Okun, 1986). Finally, many segments of the public became critical of the criminal justice system's historical lack of involvement in prosecution of domestic violence cases.

POTENTIAL FOR COOPERATION AT THE NEXUS

The underlying premise of the community-policing philosophy is that the police, other agencies, and the public should work together to accomplish mutual goals, such as solving community problems and reducing crime to improve the quality of life. In other words, the police and the public ought to become "coproducers" of public safety, each contributing to the maintenance of law and order. Community-policing proponents purport that "together, police and public are more effective and more humane co-producers of safety and public order than are the police alone" (Skolnick & Bayley, 1988, p. 1). Partnerships between police and various individuals, agencies, or organizations can be used both to identify and to find means of addressing community problems in a holistic, long-term fashion that is impossible when policing is limited to response to calls for service and follow-up investigation. For community policing to work, it is vital, therefore, that the police and the public become coproducers of crime reduction by creating meaningful, working partnerships (Skolnick & Bayley, 1988).

The community-policing reform emphasizes a broad, social role for the police, with the goal of police becoming more responsive to citizen concerns. Also referred to as "personal service," and following the trend in the private sector of putting "customers first" or "listening to customers" (Skogan, 1998, p. 162), this philosophical dimension aims to build trust and positive interactions between the police and the community they serve (Cordner, 1998). A community-policing role, therefore, is a broadened police role that focuses attention on the process of policing for people, not just the outcome of providing policing to people (see Mastrofski, 1999). Not surprisingly, then, when police start to pay attention to citizens' concerns and needs, they must also start to pay attention to victims' (and their advocates') concerns and needs. A victim-centered policing style is part of an overall community-oriented style of policing.

Problem solving is another important element of the community-policing reform. Eck and Spelman (1987) developed the widely accepted and used SARA (Scanning, Analysis, Response, and Assessment) model of problem solving as a tool for police departments in their efforts to fight specific crimes with specific plans in a community-oriented policing context (Goldstein, 1990). SARA provides a template to facilitate problem solving by identifying four stages of the problem-solving process:

1. Scanning to collect information to identify a crime problem

2. Analysis to determine the nature and extent of the problem

3. Response through the creation of a specific strategy to address the problem

4. Assessment to determine whether the response alleviated the problem

Problem solving has been recognized as a central characteristic of community-policing departments because it uses community input to identify crime problems and determine the appropriate strategies to address them. In other words, "community policing without problem solving is not community policing" (Jolin & Moose, 1997, p. 291). There appears to be a fit between (a) the notion that community-oriented policing involves a process of analyzing patterns of crime and working with a community (which would include domestic violence service providers and victims) to prevent or reduce domestic violence, and (b) citizen and victim service providers' concerns about domestic violence and interest in a cross-community, coordinated response to violence against women.

Challenges to Cooperation

Despite the apparent fit between community-oriented policing and the violence-against-women movement, at the community level there often is not congruence. This is in part due to previously described historical tensions between police and advocates for women abused by their partners (see, e.g., Hilton, 1989). There also are theoretical tensions. The violence-against-women movement grew out of an ideology and related theory that laws and advocacy were necessary to counteract women's lesser power in families and in the justice system, and that their lack of power, and men's greater power, were a root cause of wife abuse in the first place. This ideology is unlikely to be shared by most police. In fact, a recent inquiry into the Los Angeles Police Department revealed that Los Angeles police officers arrested for domestic violence are typically treated leniently by their own department (Spillar & Harrington, 1997).

Moreover, police departments traditionally do not emphasize addressing broad inequities in society, but instead focus on enforcing the law in specific situations. Community-oriented policing is intended to identify problems at a neighborhood level, and does not consider society-wide, gender-related social location as the root cause of problems. In contrast, the violence-against-women movement locates the cause in gender-related social structure. When community-police–oriented officers talk about responding to domestic violence, most consider the victimization of men and women to be rooted in similar causes that do not involve power inequities between women and men.

Additionally, there is substantial variation in the tactics and strategies used by police departments as part of community policing, and they vary in their applicability and relevance to domestic violence. Researchers concluded from a study of community-policing programs in eight cities that there were more differences than similarities among the programs; some focused on aggressive street enforcement and drug crackdowns as part of community policing, and others involved community organizing and interagency cooperation (Grinc, 1994; Sadd & Grinc, 1994).[2] Clearly, the latter emphasis is most consistent with a coordinated community response to domestic violence that characterizes the current violence-against-women movement. It should be noted, however, that victim services and advocacy groups do not typically view the police as the natural leaders in the development of a coordinated community response, but rather as partners, and as often in need of education on appropriate response. Thus, for the recommended cooperative *nexus* to develop, COPS-sponsored programs and other training must provide police with skills in partnering, or there will be considerable resistance by the advocates who view themselves as having unique knowledge of victims' needs. Advocates typically try to listen to battered women, believe that the women are the best source of information on their own experiences and the danger they and any children are in, and support women's preferences for resolution of their problems. They respect women's decisions not to become involved with the justice system, agreeing with them that police and courts are not always trustworthy in providing protection from very real threats of violence.

A final area of incongruence between police and domestic advocates occurs if police departments equate community-oriented policing with officers' walking and driving within one or more neighborhoods and becoming very familiar with residents. The "neighborhood officer" conceptualization emphasizes the individual-level interactions of police officers. Many advocates fear that neighborhood officers, who are predominately men, will be on friendly terms with men in the neighborhood, and thus will take their side in domestic disputes. The fear is based on practical knowledge that abusive men can appear as very reasonable and charming outside of the family, while they are controlling and abusive inside.

At the individual level, the intersection of community-oriented policing and the violence-against-women movement is complicated by the introduction of mandatory or pro-arrest policies. Although initially supported by many victim advocates (Wanless, 1996), there is widespread criticism when such policies result in the arrest of women whom advocates claim are acting in self-defense (Buzawa & Buzawa, 1993; Walsh, 1995; Wanless, 1996). Some advocates have found that policies leading to arrest and prosecution *regardless* of the victim's preference are disempowering for women, and lead victims to avoid further contact with the justice system (Ferraro, 1989). Many argue that victims should be given the opportunity to "negotiate their own security," thus improving their chances of becoming empowered instead of being doubly victimized by a generic criminal justice process (Fagan & Browne, 1994, p. 109) that has recently been likened to a form of state violence in its disregard for victims' needs and desires (Mills, 1999). In particular, Lewis, Dobash, Dobash, and Cavanagh (1997) showed with their qualitative research that the most common purpose that abused women had for contacting the police was for immediate protection and/or to obtain rehabilitation for the abuser, not to have them arrested. Furthermore, despite generally high levels of public support for pro-arrest policies, recent research revealed that women who had been victimized themselves were less likely to support the policies (Robinson, 1999). This may be because arrest can have direct negative consequences on abused women, who may lose their source of financial support, need to pay for bail, be at greater risk for victimization by men enraged by the arrest, or feel they cannot call on the police in the future if they want something done other than arrest. As one critic noted, "When strategies born of broad feminist goals conflict with the interests of individual battered women, we must rethink the strategies" (Mills, 1999, p. 612).

The tension in how victims, their advocates, and police view the appropriate response to domestic violence is related to a larger issue in law enforcement:

> Unlike [other] interventions, the criminal justice system must also represent society's interests. Its desired outcomes are independent, and at times they may differ from, and even appear to conflict with, those of the people who have been abused. Legal interventions must take into account the issues of due process and concern for the rights of victims as well as those accused of wrongdoing, seeking a balance among interventions to enhance victim protection, facilitate the prosecution of offenders, and preserve the state's interest in fair procedures. (Chalk & King, 1998, p. 158)

Although the ideology of community-oriented policing, with the emphasis on meeting the needs and responding to the preferences of citizens as "customers," would seem to be consistent with the viewpoints of abused women and their advocates, at the level of police behavior on the street, there can be conflict between police officers' mandate to enforce the law and victims' and their advocates' objective of ensuring that the law addresses individual victim needs and preferences.

At the very time that some advocates are raising questions about the desirability of laws that encourage arrest with no exceptions in domestic violence situations, the vast majority of departments have adopted a pro-arrest policy (Klinger, 1995).[3] In the 1980s, federally supported research conducted in Minneapolis indicated that, in comparison to mediation or separation, for domestic violence, arrest produced the greatest deterrent effect (Sherman & Berk, 1984). Following dissemination of the research findings, many departments adopted pro-arrest policies (Sherman & Cohn, 1989), and on average, though not for every department, there was a dramatic, nationwide increase in arrests for domestic violence. Despite later studies that failed to substantiate the beneficial outcomes of arrest identified in the Minneapolis Domestic Violence Experiment (Berk, Campbell, Klap, & Western, 1992; Berk & Newton, 1985; Pate & Hamilton, 1992; Sherman, Smith, Schmidt, & Rogan, 1991), by the late 1980s, a majority of police departments (84%) had implemented either mandatory or preferred arrest policies for misdemeanor domestic violence cases (Monk, 1993). Consistent with the changed policies, though there are contradictory findings (Ferraro, 1989; Fyfe, Klinger, & Flavin, 1997), some studies have found that arrest is more likely for domestic than for other assaults (Connolly, Huzurbazar, & Routh-McGee, 2000; Eigenberg, Scarborough, & Kappeler, 1996; Feder, 1998; Oppenlander, 1982) or that the probability of arrest is equivalent (Klinger, 1995; Smith and Klein, 1984). Moreover, police concerns about liability if harm comes to a battered woman whose abuser was not arrested provide further impetus to arrest (Buzawa & Buzawa, 1993, p. 563).

Contemporary Police Practices and Domestic Violence

Traditionally, police have been unlikely to see domestic violence as a high priority. First, police have long been struggling with how responding to intimate partner violence fits into their perspective of what constitutes "real" police work. Historically, they have viewed domestic violence calls as best dealt with by social workers or marriage counselors, and, at worst, as a waste of their time. Additionally, despite evidence to the contrary (Garner & Clemmer, 1986), police training, experience, and legend frequently perpetuate the belief that domestic violence calls are very dangerous for the police officer, and thus something to be avoided or handled as quickly as possible.[4] Combined with traditional views of women, these types of police beliefs can produce "a significant absence of taking women battering seriously" (Belknap, 1995, p. 59), leading to victim blaming and inaction at the scene (Saunders & Size, 1986, p. 38; Sherman & Berk, 1984), as well as police viewing "police intervention as ineffective and beyond their legitimate role" (Feder, 1997, p. 88). The implication for community-policing efforts is that victim advocates and others may have a hard time getting domestic violence to the top of a problem-solving agenda.

Although some victims and victim advocates criticize the police for a uniformly pro-arrest policy, without regard for the victim's preferences, others emphasize that they also do not listen to victims who are requesting an arrest, even though there are many factors supporting a decision to arrest. Buzawa and Buzawa (1993) found that officers usually do not believe that victims give an accurate or entirely honest account of the situation, and therefore are skeptical of victims who desire arrest of the perpetrator. Belknap (1995) found that half of the officers responding to her survey thought victims "didn't mean it" when they requested arrest and that most felt few victims really know what they want to happen as a result of police intervention. Davis (1983) concluded that the police ideology that "it takes two to tango" frequently leads to their view that victims are uncooperative (i.e., that they will change their minds later, want to drop the charges, etc.) and therefore unworthy of help. Ferraro (1989) supports the notion that police often think arrest is a waste of time because most victims drop the charges anyway. Police officers may identify with the husband in abuse situations, themselves feel the "home is a man's castle," or be abusive in their own families (Jaffe, Hastings, Reitzel, & Austin, 1993; Stith, 1990; Websdale, 1995). Research also has documented that most male police officers believe abused women could voluntarily leave their abusers, but that they willingly elected to stay (Ferraro, 1989; Websdale, 1995). In short, beliefs that characterize the police culture, such as masculinity, cynicism, and solidarity (see Crank, 1998), continue to influence police views about the nature of domestic violence and its impact on women, and subsequently affect views of what constitutes the appropriate police response.

EFFORTS TO CREATE A COOPERATIVE NEXUS
OF COMMUNITY POLICING AND DOMESTIC VIOLENCE

Given the conflicting objectives, ideologies, and broader worldviews that might exist at the nexus of community policing and domestic violence in a particular location, how have police and their communities attempted to forge a positive alliance to confront domestic violence? There is limited written material or reported research on this area, but a review of what is available explores (a) the nature and amount of interaction that community police officers have with domestic violence victims and offenders, (b) police department attempts to forge a partnership with victim advocates and service providers, or (c) police application of problem-solving approaches to the crime of domestic violence.

Community Police Interacting With
Parties Involved in Domestic Violence

Miller's (1999) ethnographic research on one police department suggests that community-oriented policing may give women access to more types of assistance from police than is afforded when police come into contact with abused women primarily through calls for immediate help. Her study specifically sheds light on how Neighborhood Policing Officers (NPOs) respond to domestic violence given the apparent contradiction between community policing (which stresses innovation, creativity, informality, and discretion) and mandatory arrest laws (which remove discretion and flexibility to try and produce uniform and formal police responses). Miller documented one of the differences between NPOs and traditional patrol officers in their response to domestic violence:

> The nature of the neighborhood position encouraged officers to become actively involved with the community they served: in prevention programs, case follow-ups, working on continuing problems, and acting as liaisons with residents, businesses, city services, and the criminal justice system. (p. 183)

Some of the results were that, compared with traditional patrol officers, NPOs more often had the information about the community that they needed to make referrals, they informally monitored the offender, and they offered continuing advice to the offender about ways to address underlying problems (e.g., drug or alcohol abuse) and to the victim about using the criminal justice process to stop the violence. Officers said that their experience as NPOs reduced their resistance to handling domestic violence incidents, because there was some level of trust between them and both the offender and the victim. NPOs also felt they were the "conscience of the community," serving as reminders of appropriate behavior. Additionally, NPOs used a more informal style of policing and, despite mandatory arrest laws, were more likely than patrol officers were to use mediation. One officer quoted by Miller said, "I know who is lying, everyone's history, prior conflicts, everything going on in their houses. I know the 'real' story to begin with, so I am able to mediate with more knowledge and to a better end" (p. 183). This police officers' perspective and action would be welcomed by victims and victim service providers who view mandatory arrest as contradicting the mediation or other informal responses that many victims prefer when the police are called. However, it would raise concern among those who suspect that police will be misled by "charming" offenders and/or take the side of abusive men. In fact, at least one officer whom Miller interviewed indicated that it was easier to make the decision to arrest an abuser after returning to regular patrol, where he did not know the people involved. However, overall, NPOs did not think they actually made fewer arrests than did traditional patrol officers, and they emphasized that NPOs followed up with victims, for instance making sure that restraining orders were enforced. In one case, a NPO who worked with an immigrant population that tended to tolerate abuse provided public education regarding U.S. laws.

Similar to Miller's findings, a study conducted in Great Britain concluded that domestic violence units using the community-policing style were successful because victims were able to explain their individual needs and officers were given the discretion necessary to address the unique aspects of each case (Sheptycki, 1991). In the United States, Davis and Taylor (1997) found that specialized units (police officer–social worker teams) increased victim willingness to report violence; the authors suggested that this may be attributed to improved confidence of victims in police operating with a community-policing philosophy. Community policing appears to support repeated and informal interactions with police and victims, sometimes in teams with other professionals, resulting in more individualized services to the victim, and to services beyond the traditional law enforcement response. Martin (1997) found that most domestic violence victims rated the police response in a community-policing department positively, and the most important predictor of victim satisfaction was the level of assistance offered by officers. This evidence led her to assert that "the quality of the immediate interaction" (p. 145), rather than the long-term outcome of police intervention, was of the greatest importance to victims, controlling for other factors. In conclusion, she found that at the individual level, community policing can play an important role in getting officers to comply with policies, providing help during police-citizen interactions, and treating victims with the respect they deserve and desire.

Problem Solving Applied to Domestic Violence

The SARA model described earlier provides a method for police departments to determine the scope of the domestic violence problem in their community, implement a specific response, and evaluate the effectiveness of that responses. Case studies of selected departments suggest that police knowledge of the SARA model or similar problem-solving approaches has led them to view domestic violence as a serious problem, and to develop either internal procedures or partnerships that effectively address domestic violence.

After analyzing calls for service and discovering that a significant proportion of repeat calls were due to domestic violence, and that the seriousness of incidents escalated over time, a Fremont, California, police sergeant established a new domestic violence protocol for his department. The protocol mandated that officers complete reports for every domestic incident, make personal contact with the victim within seven days of the initial contact, and again 28 days later. The purpose of these follow-up visits was to provide victims with information, ascertain whether additional violence had occurred, and refer victims to social service providers in the community. Reflecting a community-policing orientation, the department took a proactive approach, with the goal of preventing new violence from occurring. Assessing whether this new police response was effective, the sergeant analyzed additional crime data and found that calls for service decreased 57% from 1996 to 1997 in the locations that had received three or more calls for service in previous years (Sampson & Scott, 1999).

Other police departments have also had success using problem-solving techniques to reduce the incidence of domestic violence. For example, a COPS brief on a special domestic violence unit operating in Sonoma County, California, (where specially trained officers and detectives respond to calls, which are then assigned to YWCA victim advocates) reported that domestic violence incidents decreased 19% in 1998, and the number of recidivist couples was reduced by 39% (U.S. Department of Justice, 1999b).

A police department studied by Robinson and Chandek (2000) provides a third example of how police used a problem-solving orientation as an impetus to creating a community partnerships with the district attorney, health department, various advocate groups, and referral services. Because less than one fifth of domestic violence complaints resulted in a warrant being issued against the suspect, the police identified low levels of victim participation as a problem. To help victims successfully navigate the criminal justice system, and thereby encourage their participation in case prosecution, the Domestic Abuse Response Team (DART) was created. This group of detectives made contact with all victims, and provided support and information. For example, DART detectives established a positive working relationship with a court advocate so victims who wanted to obtain a Personal Protection Order (PPO) could do so easily. Research, however, demonstrated that victim participation did not increase to a statistically significant extent due to the implementation of DART.

Robinson and Chandek's (2000) finding of no increase in victim participation in case prosecution brings attention to the potential for difference between police and victim or victim advocate perceptions of problems and solutions. The police goal of more prosecutions is not necessarily the goal of victims and their advocates, who might instead emphasize the cessation of violence or keeping the family intact. Increased prosecution is not necessarily related to the outcomes of victim satisfaction, sense of safety, or empowerment. Police application of problem-solving approaches to the crime of domestic violence can result in some positive outcomes for victims. However, success is defined according to police interest in clearing cases and increasing prosecutions and convictions. Outcomes valued by violence-against-women activists are those that give women power to escape violence, but not necessarily by increased involvement in the justice system. It appears that the DART example is based on a limited definition of partnership, with police identifying the goal of increased prosecution, and then obtaining cooperation and support from other "partners." Ideal forms of community-oriented research, as well as action research, would require that stakeholders participate together in identifying key indicators of success; such a process would contribute to their having at least a recognition of multiple standpoints when data are scored, analyzed, and presented as information to stimulate actions.

Police-Public Partnerships

Theoretically, community-oriented policing can promote the formation of partnerships in which police and others work together to identify problems in response to domestic violence, and develop shared goals and strategies to address these problems. Research conducted by Jolin and Moose (1997) documents how a community-policing response to domestic violence was in fact implemented in Portland, Oregon. Community representatives and criminal justice officials worked together to develop a plan to reduce domestic violence. The Domestic Violence Reduction Unit (DVRU) began operation in 1993, with the goal of proactively serving domestic violence victims in the context of a community-wide coordinated effort, including social service, criminal justice, and treatment agencies. Collaboratively agreed on goals were (a) increasing negative consequences for batterers and (b) empowering victims. Agreement on goals by multiple stakeholders typically is achieved with considerable effort during face-to-face meetings to understand alternative points of view, and then to reach some agreement about shared goals. The efforts did result in lower levels of victims' self-reported exposure to domestic violence by increasing victims' empowerment as well as batterers' experiences of arrest, prosecution, conviction, and sanctions (Jolin, Feyerherm, Fountain, & Friedman, 1998). Different from a community police officer's use of problem solving in isolation from an actual partnership with violence-against-women activists, there was, at least explicitly, evidence that police and advocates shared the goal of empowering women.

Research on the Portland, Oregon, project provides an important insight into the process of establishing community-police partnerships. The police were participants in a coordinated community response, not leaders, and the objectives of the project (empowerment of women and increased sanctions for abusive men) reflected not only the purposes of individual police officers or the police department, but of victim services providers. As a result, information on impact could be used either to reinforce continuation of efforts that resulted in positive impact, or to cause rethinking of efforts that fell short.

A fourth example of an effort to stimulate development of positive overlap between community policing and domestic violence is a model for workshops sponsored by the Michigan Regional Community Policing Institute (RCPI). The workshop was designed to improve the communities' capability to develop a coordinated community response to domestic violence and to provide SARA as a tool that participants in such a response could use for joint planning. The three-day program took place in 1999, and was funded by COPS to provide a setting where victim advocates, police, court personnel, and citizens concerned about crime could jointly learn how forming a partnership could reduce domestic violence in their communities, and to build necessary partnerships.

The conference was planned at a meeting of key domestic violence advocates and personnel from law enforcement agencies that had worked successfully with victim advocates. The primary goal of the conference was to deliver a realistic, skill-building experience that demonstrated the integration of community-policing principles and service-provider delivery systems to address domestic violence. As shown in Table 9.1, nine conference objectives and six learning objectives were used to organize the conference

Notable features of the program included equal attention to the community-policing and the advocacy response to domestic violence, promotion of a common understanding of both the dynamics of domestic violence and the law and police policies, and efforts to stimulate dialogue and relationships so that conference participants could increase their social capital. Empirical research on Social Capital Theory (Newton, 1997) was the basis for emphasizing program activities that

TABLE 9.1 Conference and Learning Objectives

Conference Objectives	Learning Objectives
• To provide a basic overview of community-policing (CP) principles and philosophy. • To provide a basic overview of domestic violence (DV), family safety, and related issues. • To discuss the religious, ethical, and cultural issues that must be considered when determining appropriate responses to DV. • To present the service provider and the advocacy response to DV. • To identify ways that law enforcement, service providers, and the advocacy community can integrate CP principles with DV prevention efforts. • To provide a forum for dialogue, resource sharing, and information exchange between law enforcement, service providers, and the community. • To present successful approaches, programs, and lessons learned in working police-advocate-community partnerships. • To begin developing partnerships, solutions, and action plans among attendees.	• Learn the philosophy and principles of CP. • Present legal updates regarding police responses to DV. • Understand DV and related issues. • Apply the principles and philosophy of CP in addressing DV. • Begin to think outside the box in identifying partners, actions, and solutions to DV. • Understand the importance of developing partnerships with different segments of the criminal justice, medical, and social service delivery systems in order to affect DV in their communities. • Identify potential traditional and nontraditional partners in their communities to address problems.

would increase participants' power and influence with each other (i.e., their social capital). Relationships high in trust, understanding, cooperation, empathy, and mutual influence constitute social capital, an important resource for collective efforts to accomplish change (Portes, 1998), including establishing or improving a coordinated community response to domestic violence.

For the workshop, 23 speakers and 7 facilitators, representing police, court, advocacy, and community segments, presented information and led discussions. The format consisted of panel discussions, practitioner and academic presentations, skill-building sessions involving case studies, and analyses of best practices in the field. An entire day was devoted to the SARA problem-solving model of policing and how it specifically applies to the problem of domestic violence. Fifteen teams, organized by county/regional areas to include representatives of police, court, domestic violence service providers, and citizens concerned with crime worked to apply the SARA model to case studies of community domestic violence problems.

A follow-up survey revealed that participants of each type felt that, as a result of the conference, they had gained knowledge about the dynamics of domestic violence, methods for increasing victim safety, the meaning of community policing, the meaning of coordinated community response to domestic violence, and the SARA model and its applicability to addressing domestic violence. A majority of police and smaller numbers of other participants reported that after attending the conference, they were more likely to think that community policing would be helpful in addressing domestic violence in their communities. Police also felt that in their relationships with other participants, there was greater trust when working on domestic violence issues, better understanding of and empathy with each other regarding domestic violence, and increased cooperation with and influence regarding domestic violence.

CONCLUSIONS AND RECOMMENDATIONS

We have provided several examples of police practices and activities that might be used to develop cooperation at the complicated nexus of community policing and domestic violence. A few of the examples follow the approach, which is frequently described in the community-policing literature, of singular efforts by one or more police officers to identify factors contributing to a pattern of crime. Citizens or other agencies may be involved in providing information on the nature of the problem and possible solutions, but it is clear that the individual police officer is the "problem describer" and the "solution selector." Hearing or reading of the fence that was erected to keep schoolchildren from crossing a dangerous highway, the teen center that opened to draw youth from a retail district, or installation of lighting on park pathways hardly conjures up a picture of a dynamic community-police partnership that will continue over time to address difficult, even controversial issues, such as patterns of violence against women.

The Portland and Michigan conceptualizations of community policing and domestic violence emphasize partnership. Because partnership is a dynamic interaction involving ongoing communication and exchange, the Michigan conference is being followed up by intensive work with 15 partnerships at the community level.[5] The follow-up activities include technical assistance to help departments and communities in further building their relationships, for example through facilitated group interactions or common training. The conference also was designed to increase levels of social capital, because trust, understanding, cooperation, empathy, and mutual influence are necessary for increasing successful and long-lasting police-public partnerships.

Given the likelihood of disparate objectives and for conflicting perceptions of the nature and causes of violence against women, it would be naïve to ignore the developmental work that is necessary for partnerships to form to address the issue of domestic violence. Police are likely to be trying to develop partnerships with groups that they do not completely understand or agree with, and with whom they have little social capital. Other stakeholders find themselves in a similar position. Thus, a variety of stakeholder individuals and groups may need skills to work effectively in such situations, and may also need to recognize that they are at best equal partners rather than organizers and leaders in a coordinated effort. For instance, some police departments would need to address police culture and department priority issues, provide incentives for spending time on addressing domestic violence, and remove other barriers to partnership before or through interacting with people from other agencies and groups or citizens at large.

However, it would be a mistake to accept a deterministic view of police beliefs, norms, or organization as an invariant and uniform barrier to improving the situation for abused women. In fact, at the individual level, police referrals often serve as a critical link between the victim and other social services that enable women to escape abuse (Belknap & McCall, 1994; Ferraro, 1989). Miller's (1999) ethnographic study of one department, for example, reveals ways in which this capacity to link women to services can be increased through community-policing activities.

Several factors would increase the potential for police and other elements in the community to improve response to abused women at the community level:

1. A true partnership, with sharing of influence, would involve such entities as police and fire departments, courts, battered women's shelters, hospitals, schools, and the media. Through interacting with each other, these groups could build the social capital neces-

sary to address the problem of adequately responding to domestic violence.

2. The groups would develop some agreement on what will help victims and what takes power from them. Legal constraints on the police, and the emphasis by victim assistance providers on victim choices need to be reconciled; and the partnership needs to involve people whose organizations do not demand or reward a sole objective of meeting organizational demands—for example, to clear cases through arrest.

3. Problem-solving approaches can be one-time, police-initiated, and police-led "fixes" to an immediate problem, but they will have a more positive impact if they include police as equal partners with others. Partnership for problem solving involves multiple parties developing a reasonably congruent conceptualization of the problem and its causes.

Our prior research (Robinson & Morash, 2000) to evaluate the outcome of a one-week intensive program for professionals who work with crime victims was based on curriculum objectives similarly identified by a joint group of law enforcement personnel and violence-against-women activists. This research did demonstrate that participants with increased social capital were able to improve coordination of response within their communities. Specifically, stakeholders came together to share information, identify common goals, and act to achieve these goals. In both the Portland and the Michigan efforts to build an effective connection of community policing and domestic violence, it is clear that organizations, their agents, and other individuals are engaged in a multistep process in varying and complex environments. The central theme is partnership, and research at both of these sites has identified essential ingredients—for example increasing social capital and the formation of shared objectives and perspectives on the cause of crime—for building an effective nexus.

Community-policing efforts to take effective action against domestic violence require a recognition and exploration of the tensions and contradictions between law enforcement agencies and groups that provide domestic violence services. To maximize the chances of positive outcomes, any coming-together of community-oriented policing and domestic violence services would need to be proceeded by a well-designed process to clarify differences and similarities in the meaning of success, and to arrive at some understanding of shared criteria for judging success, as well as a plan to achieve it. Technical assistance from outside or resources within the community will be necessary both to ensure that the process of building a partnership occurs and to generate useful research information for the potential or actual members of the partnership. Individuals and groups will need to know whether they agree on desired outcomes of the partnerships' actions and on whether they have the requisite relationships and resources to work together.

NOTES

1. More broadly, since its inception in 1995, the Violence Against Women Office at the U.S. Department of Justice (created under the Violence Against Women Act, Title IV of the Violent Crime Control and Law Enforcement Act of 1994) has distributed over $270 million *per year* in grants to communities to help them implement more effective criminal justice system responses to domestic violence.

2. Critics also note that police may use the ambiguous and ill-defined nature of the term *community policing* to further their own (often traditional) police goals (Bayley, 1994; Lyons, 1999; Manning, 1984).

3. Some research on police beliefs suggests that police themselves may be sympathetic to views that uniform arrest policies are undesirable. Smith (1987) found that many police officers believed that "no set of organizational rules or guidelines could capture the complexity of human problems which police confront" (p. 768), and thus would reject the notion that they should always make an arrest when there is probable cause that domestic violence has occurred.

4. There had been early published research reports that family disputes were the most frequent cause of death of officers (Jaffe et al., 1993).

5. The Michigan RCPI additionally emphasizes the need for organizational change within the police department so police can participate in such a partnership. Such change would require a shift from a police culture that accepts domestic violence, to the extent that such a culture persists in any particular department.

REFERENCES

Bayley, D. H. (1994). *Police for the future.* New York: Oxford University Press.

Belknap, J. (1995). Law enforcement officers' attitudes about the appropriate response to woman battering. *International Review of Victimology, 4,* 47–62.

Belknap, J., & McCall, K. (1994). Women battering and police referrals. *Journal of Criminal Justice, 22*(3), 223–236.

Berk, R. A., Campbell, A., Klap, R., & Western, B. (1992). The deterrent effects of arrest in incidents of domestic violence: A Bayesian analysis of four field experiments. *American Sociological Review, 57,* 698–708.

Berk, R. A., & Newton, P. J. (1985). Does arrest really deter wife battery? An effort to replicate the findings of the Minneapolis spouse abuse experiment. *American Sociological Review, 50,* 253–262.

Buzawa, E. S., & Buzawa, C. G. (1993). Opening the doors: The changing police response to domestic violence. In R. G. Dunham & G. P. Alpert (Eds.), *Critical issues in policing*. Prospect Heights, IL: Waveland.

Chalk, R., & King, P. A. (1998). *Violence in families: Assessing prevention and treatment programs*. Washington, DC: National Academy Press.

Connolly, C., Huzurbazar, S, & Routh-McGee, T. (2000). Multiple parties in domestic violence situations and arrest. *Journal of Criminal Justice, 28*(3), 181–188.

Cordner, G. W. (1998). Community policing: Elements and effects. In G. P. Alpert & A. Piquero (Eds.), *Community policing: Contemporary readings* (pp. 45–62). Prospect Heights, IL: Waveland.

Crank, J. P. (1998). *Understanding police culture*. Cincinnati, OH: Anderson.

Davis, P. W. (1983). Restoring the semblance of order: Police strategies in the domestic disturbance. *Symbolic Interaction, 6*(2), 261–278.

Davis, R. C., & Taylor, B. G. (1997). A proactive response to family violence: The results of a randomized experiment. *Criminology, 35*, 307–33.

Eck, J. E., & Spelman, W. (with Hill, D., Stephens, D. W., Stedman, J. R., & Murphy, G. R.). (1987). *Problem solving: Problem-oriented policing in Newport News*. Washington, DC: Police Executive Research Forum.

Eigenberg, H. M., Scarborough, K. E., & Kappeler, V. E. (1996). Contributory factors affecting arrest in domestic and non-domestic assaults. *American Journal of Police, 15*(4), 27–54.

Fagan, J., & Browne, A. (1994). Violence between spouses and intimates: Physical aggression between women and men in intimate relationships. In A. J. Reiss & J. A. Roth (Eds.), *Understanding and Preventing Violence* (Vol. 3, pp. 115–292). Washington DC: National Research Council.

Feder, L. (1997). Domestic violence and police response in a pro-arrest jurisdiction. *Women & Criminal Justice, 8*(4), 79–98.

Feder, L. (1998). Police handling of domestic and non-domestic assault calls: Is there a case for discrimination? *Journal of Research in Crime & Delinquency, 44*(2), 335–349.

Ferraro, K. J. (1989). Policing woman battering. *Social Problems, 36*(1), 61–74.

Fyfe, J. J., Klinger, D. A., & Flavin, J. (1997). Differential police treatment of male-on-female spousal violence. *Criminology, 35*(3), 455–474.

Garner, J., & E. Clemmer. (1986, November). *Danger to police in domestic disturbances: A new look*. Washington, DC: U.S. Department of Justice, Office of Justice Programs, National Institute of Justice.

Goldstein, H. (1990). *Problem-oriented policing*. New York: McGraw-Hill.

Grinc, R. M. (1994). "Angels in marble": Problems in stimulating community involvement in community policing. *Crime & Delinquency, 40*(3), 437–468.

Hilton, N. (1989). One in ten: The struggle and disempowerment of the battered women's movement. *Canadian Journal of Family Law, 7*, 315–335.

Hirschel, J. D., Hutchison, I. W., Dean, C. W., & Mills, A. (1992). Review essay on the law enforcement response to spouse abuse: Past, present, and future. *Justice Quarterly, 9*(2), 247–279.

Jaffe, P. G., Hastings, E., Reitzel, D., & Austin, G. W. (1993). The impact of police laying charges. In N. Z. Hilton (Ed.), *Legal response to wife assault: Current trends and evaluation* (pp. 62–95). Newbury Park, CA: Sage.

Jolin, A., Feyerherm, W., Fountain, R., & Friedman, S. (1998). *Beyond arrest: The Portland, Oregon, domestic violence experiment* [Final Report]. Washington, DC: U.S. Department of Justice, Office of Justice Programs, National Institute of Justice.

Jolin, A., & Moose, C. A. (1997). Evaluating a domestic violence program in a community policing environment: Research implementation issues. *Journal of Research in Crime & Delinquency, 43*(3), 279–297.

Klinger, D. A. (1995). Policing spousal assault. *Journal of Research in Crime and Delinquency, 32*(3), 308–324.

Lewis, R., Dobash, R. P., Dobash, R. E., & Cavanagh, K. (1997, November). *Protection, prevention, rehabilitation, or justice? Women using the law to challenge domestic violence.* Paper presented at the American Society of Criminology Meetings, San Diego, CA.

Lyons, W. (1999). *The politics of community policing: Rearranging the power to punish.* Ann Arbor, MI: University of Michigan Press.

Manning, P. K. (1984). Community policing. *American Journal of Police, 3*(2), 205–227.

Martin, M. E. (1997). Policy promise: Community policing and domestic violence victim satisfaction. *Policing: An International Journal of Police Strategies and Management, 20*(3), 519–531.

Mastrofski, S. D. (1999). *Policing for people.* Washington, DC: Police Foundation.

Miller, S. L. (1999). *Gender and community policing: Walking the talk.* Boston: Northeastern University Press.

Mills, L. G. (1999). Killing her softly: Intimate abuse and the violence of state intervention. *Harvard Law Review, 113*(2), 551–613.

Monk, R. C. (1993). *Taking sides: Clashing views on controversial subjects in crime and criminology.* Guilford, CT: Dushkin.

Newton, K. (1997). Social capital and democracy. *American Behavioral Scientist, 40,* 575–586.

Okun, L. E. (1986). *Woman abuse: Facts replacing myths.* Albany, NY: SUNY Press.

Oppenlander, N. (1982). Coping or copping out: Police service delivery in domestic disputes. *Criminology, 20,* 449–465.

Pate, A. M., & Hamilton, E. E. (1992). Formal and informal deterrents to domestic violence: The Dade County spouse assault experiment. *American Sociological Review, 57,* 691–697.

Pleck, E. (1987). *Domestic tyranny.* New York: Oxford University Press.

Portes, A. (1998). Social capital: Its origins and applications in modern sociology. *Annual Review of Sociology, 24,* 1–24.

Robinson, A. L. (1999). Conflicting consensus: Public reaction to a domestic violence pro-arrest policy. *Women & Criminal Justice, 10*(3), 95–120.

Robinson, A. L., & Chandek, M. S. (2000). Philosophy into practice? Community policing units and domestic violence victim participation. *Policing: An International Journal of Police Strategies and Management, 23*(3), 280–302.

Robinson, A. L., & Morash, M. (2000). Use of the social capital framework for assessment of a training and education program for people working with crime victims. *Justice Professional, 13,* 307–341.

Sadd, S., & Grinc, R. M. (1994). *Innovative neighborhood-oriented policing: Descriptions of programs in eight cities.* New York: Vera Institute of Justice.

Sampson, R., & Scott, M. S. (1999). *Tackling crime and other public-safety problems: Case studies in problem-solving.* Washington, DC: U.S. Department of Justice, Office of Community Oriented Policing Services.

Saunders, D. G., & Size, P. B. (1986). Attitudes about woman abuse among police officers, victims, and victim advocates. *Journal of Interpersonal Violence, 1,* 25–42.

Sheptycki, J. W. E. (1991). Using the state to change society: The example of domestic violence. *Journal of Human Justice, 3,* 47–66.

Sherman, L. W., & Berk, R. A. (1984). The specific deterrent effects of arrest for domestic assault. *American Sociological Review, 49*(2), 261–272.

Sherman, L. W., & Cohn, E. G. (1989). The impact of research on legal policy: The Minneapolis domestic violence experiment. *Law and Society Review, 23*(1), 117–144.

Sherman, L. W., Smith, D. A., Schmidt, J. D., & Rogan, D. P. (1991). *Ghetto poverty, crime and punishment: Legal and informal control of domestic violence*. Washington, DC: Crime Control Institute.

Skogan, W. G. (1998). Community policing in Chicago. In G. P. Alpert & A. Piquero (Eds.), *Community policing: Contemporary readings* (pp. 159–174). Prospect Heights, IL: Waveland.

Skolnick, J. H., & Bayley, D. H. (1988). Theme and variation in community policing. In M. Tonry & N. Morris (Eds.), *Crime and justice: A review of research* (Vol. 10, pp. 1–37). Chicago: University of Chicago Press.

Smith, D. A. (1987). Police response to interpersonal violence: Defining the parameters of legal control. *Social Forces, 65*(3), 767–782.

Smith, D. A., & Klein, J. (1984). Police control of interpersonal disputes. *Social Problems, 31*(4), 468–481.

Spillar, K., & Harrington, P. (1997, May 16). The verdict on male bias: Guilty. Two reports confirm systemic mistreatment of women cops and cover-up of domestic violence in the ranks [Commentary]. *Los Angeles Times*.

Stith, S. (1990). Police response to domestic violence: The influence of individual and familial factors. *Violence and Victims, 5*(1), 37–49.

U.S. Department of Justice. (1999a). *The Clinton administration's law enforcement strategy: Combating crime with community policing and community prosecution*. Washington, DC: Author.

U.S. Department of Justice. (1999b). *COPS in action: Sonoma County, California*. Washington, DC: Author.

Walker, L. E. (1985). Psychological impact of the criminalization of domestic violence on victims. *Victimology, 10*, 281–300.

Walsh, K. (1995). The mandatory arrest law: Police reaction. *Pace Law Review , 16*(1), 97–108.

Wanless, M. (1996). Mandatory arrest: A step toward eradicating domestic violence, but is it enough? *University of Illinois Law Review 2*, 533–587.

Websdale, N. (1995). An ethnographic assessment of the policing of domestic violence in rural Eastern Kentucky. *Social Justice, 5*, 869–897.

CHAPTER 10

Action Research for Community-Oriented Policing and Comprehensive School Safety Planning

Audrey Z. Martini
Monique Fields
Tracey Goss McGinley
Amanda L. Robinson
Merry Morash

*T*he *1999 Annual Report on School Safety,* produced by the U.S. Departments of Education and Justice, notes that when all types of violence are considered, (e.g., simple assaults, aggravated assaults, and threats), the amount of violence in schools has decreased in recent years. Additionally, theft has been the most common crime in schools for many years. However, the particularly heinous offense of multiple-victim homicide has increased. According to the report, since the 1992–1993 school year, there has been at least one multiple-victim homicide event each year (except for the 1993–1994 school year). The number increased from two multiple homicide events in 1992–1993 to five events in 1997–1998. The number is even higher in the most recent years. Typically, these homicides have involved a student in high school acting on a plan to bring firearms and other lethal weapons into the school, and purposefully killing teachers and/or other students.

In response to extreme incidents of school violence, many communities have made efforts to reduce school crime and violence by adopting comprehensive, integrated, community-wide plans that include many different components, ranging from physical security within the schools to proactive efforts to promote a positive school climate. This type of comprehensive plan has been recommended in the *1999 Annual Report on School Safety* that the U.S. Departments of Education and Justice produced. A comprehensive plan prepares schools, along with their school districts and communities, to prevent, respond to, and deal with the aftermath of threats to school safety.

Before school shootings became the focus of national and local news reports, the Michigan Regional Community Policing Institute (RCPI) brought together people throughout the state from schools, communities, and police departments to encourage local problem solving relative to school violence. The Columbine tragedy, which involved high school students harming several people at their school, swelled the ranks of the group and shifted the focus somewhat. Members of what came to be called the Michigan Safe Schools Initiative continued to include Michigan RCPI staff in the facilitator role, and included federal, state, and local law enforcement officials, representatives from school administrator groups and the state department of education, individuals from parent groups, risk management and insurance specialists, school security service providers, and university faculty. The core purpose of the group was to coordinate and disseminate knowledge of best practices in school safety planning for local districts and to provide an organized voice for sustaining local effort. The group also served to link representatives of local communities (including police and schools) with federal and state organizations relevant to school safety, for example the FBI and the Michigan Department of Education.

Concomitant with the organization of the Michigan Safe Schools Initiative, federal funding was authorized to encourage police involvement in promoting school safety. The school grant program was designed to help local law enforcement agencies fund the hiring of community-policing officers to work in schools. By providing grants to hire specialized police officers in local communities, the program provided an incentive for law enforcement agencies to build working relationships with schools and to use community policing to combat school violence. In addition, the Federal School-Based Partnerships program brought community-policing and problem-solving strategies into the schools by giving grants to encourage long-term relationships between police agencies and their communities.

During 2000, to further promote local effort and with support and staff input from the Safe Schools Initiative, the Michigan RCPI and Michigan State Police partnered to invite and coordinate individuals from schools, police, and other entities relevant to school safety into county *school safety summit* meetings. Groups in 39 of Michigan's 83 counties requested and received assistance in organizing and holding the summits, and data considered in this chapter were available for 26 of the counties. Participants from some of the 26 counties were from low-population counties that were proximate to each other and that took part in combined summits. Furthermore, in one case, a school district serving a fairly large city had a separate meeting. Thus, data collected during 17 summits were analyzed for this chapter.

The totals across the 26 counties for each job type included in the summits were as follows: 16 schoolteachers, 107 school-level administrators, 32 district- or state-level administrators, 66 police, 7 emergency medical services personnel, 22 fire fighting personnel, 8 local emergency coordinators, 3 court personnel, 4 hospital employees, and 3 people representing parent groups. Another 59 people were in some other category not specified on the survey instrument, including parents who were not affiliated with any parent group and small numbers of individuals from other groups, such as the Red Cross, the local YMCA, or 911 dispatchers. Despite efforts to obtain more variation in the people attending each summit, participants were predominantly school administrators from local or higher levels, or they were police. As will be discussed in more detail below, many communities would benefit from assistance in organizing a greater range of stakeholders into a group to ensure the effectiveness of school safety planning.

RESEARCH METHODOLOGY

This research was designed to give police and other community members concerned with school safety the information that would be useful in identifying next steps for working in partnership to develop and implement a comprehensive plan. This information included community members' perceptions of the importance of various components of a comprehensive plan to promote school safety, the degree to which these components were in place, and the need for assistance from outside of local communities to put each component in place.

Identifying the Components of a Safety Plan

Components of a comprehensive plan, which are listed below, were identified from the literature (e.g., see Stephens, 1998) and with input from members of the Michigan Safe Schools Initiative. They are as follows:

- Physical security of grounds and facilities

- Positive school climate (e.g., the absence of bullying and alienation, as well as a promotion of healthy emotional development)

- Identification of youth at risk for perpetrating violence

- Identification of youth at risk for being victimized at school

- Procedures and programs responsive to youth at risk for perpetrating violence

- Procedures and programs responsive to youth at risk for victimization at school

- School-based prevention programs, such as DARE (Drug Abuse Resistance Education), GREAT (Gang Resistance Education And Training), health education, and mediation programs

- Coordinated planning in schools regarding school safety issues

- Coordinated planning between schools and others in the community about school safety

Consistent with the philosophy of community-oriented policing, unlimited partnerships are a key to identifying specific problems relevant to school safety (e.g., patterns of incidents, lack of preventive efforts, lack of preparation for crisis situations) and then effectively addressing these problems. Thus, the survey also collected information on the nature of relationships that each summit participant had with several types of people relevant to ensuring school safety. These include people inside of the school, specifically school- and district-level administrators, members of Parent-Teacher Association (PTA) and other parent groups, schoolteachers, and students. They also include police, fire fighters, the media, protective services workers, emergency medical service providers, local emergency management coordinators, prosecutors and judges, medical personnel, mental health professionals, and other human service providers.

When people have a network of relationships that are characterized by frequent contact and high levels of trust, understanding, cooperation, and empathy between the parties, we say that they have *social capital* (see Chapter 9 for further information), and thus they have some level of solidarity, influence, and control with each other. In order to work on school safety issues effectively, the various stakeholders or resource providers relevant to school safety must have interactions that create social capital. It is particularly important that the relationship characteristics (e.g., contact, trust, understanding, and cooperation) that influence social capital are present between police and members of the school community, and between each of these two groups and various other relevant entities, in order for community-oriented police to be effective in their partnerships with schools. If there is social capital in a network of relationships, there will be a degree of social solidarity, influence, and access to information, all of which are needed for effective problem solving to occur (Sandefur & Laumann, 1998).

Action Research

To collect information useful to summit participants about the conditions necessary to improve or maintain school safety in their communities, a two-page, structured *School Safety Summit Survey* was administered (see the Appendix for the survey). This type of study would be described as *action research,* because "creating a positive social change" is the predominant driving force (Berg, 2001, p. 178). As such, the results were intended to be used by the summit participants as they solved problems in relation to the school safety plan in their own locations. It was also intended to be used by Michigan Safe Schools Initiative members as they sought how best to meet needs of and support local efforts.

Summit participants were asked to rate each of the several components of a school safety plan described above on three dimensions:

- Importance of promoting school safety in respondent's community

- Degree to which the respondent's community is currently successful in this aspect of the plan

- Community need for outside assistance to accomplish this aspect of the plan

Questions also covered respondents' place of work and role (e.g., parent, school administrator, fire emergency specialist). A primary purpose of the survey was to identify parts of a school safety plan that were considered important, but for which there was a lack of needed information or resources at the local level. Such information would be helpful at the county level in efforts to improve local school safety plans, and at the state level to the Michigan Safe Schools Initiative as the group identified how it could bring information and other resources to the local level.

The survey also asked summit participants to report on their relationships with other stakeholders or resource providers essential to developing and acting on a comprehensive school safety plan. Consistent with the literature on social capital, the relationship dimensions that were assessed were contact frequency, trust, empathy, understanding, and cooperation.

Surveys were voluntarily completed at the beginning of each summit, and this experience was used to sensitize respondents to the variety of components that might be included in a comprehensive school safety plan, and to encourage them to think both about their view of the availability of information and resources at the local level to put a plan into effect and about the quality of interrelationships (i.e., the social capital) among people who would need to be involved in comprehensive planning for school safety. Summit participants therefore had a sense of the initial steps they would need to take to develop their community ties and resources, and they could consider this knowledge along with specialized information on how to put a safety play together and existing information an protocols they might adapt and build. For counties in which an adequate number of people (18 or more) were present at the summit, we also later provided summary feedback specific to the county. Thus, the surveys were used to enhance the summit meeting, and results were later provided back to communities and the Michigan School Safety Initiative to assist them in identify steps to take in the planning and implementation effort to improve school safety at both the state and community levels.

SURVEY RESULTS

The numbers of individuals filling out their surveys in each of the summits varied considerably, and ranged from just 4 responses in a summit
for three rural communities to 79 for a midsize county summit. A
broad range of participants from several different groups were sought,
but local interest, availability, and existing networks pertinent to
school safety had considerable impact on the number and types of people who actually attended each county-level summit.

Administrators based in schools were the largest number of participants (32.7%, or 107 of those responding to this survey item), followed
by police (20.2%, or 66 respondents), district or state level school administrators (9.8%, or 32 respondents), fire fighters (6.7%, or 22 respondents), and schoolteachers (4.9%, or 16 respondents). Less than
3% of respondents fell into each of the following categories: court personnel, parent groups, hospital personnel, emergency medical service
staff, and local emergency coordinators. An additional 18.0% (59) of
survey respondents either did not indicate their affiliation or did not
answer this question.

Importance of Key Aspects of a
Comprehensive School Safety Plan

The results for data aggregated over all of participating counties
showed that 90% or more of the respondents either agreed or strongly
agreed that each component of a school safety plan is important. The
respondents most strongly agreed that school safety depended on a positive school climate, a comprehensive planning effort, and the physical
security of the school (see Table 10.1).

The proportion of summit participants disagreeing that the
schools in their area had achieved each part of a comprehensive school
safety plan was taken as an indicator of the perception that there were
problems with a part of the plan; and the proportion indicating a need
for outside assistance in each area provided an indicator of the roles
that the Michigan School Safety Initiative could usefully play. Results
indicated that schools were viewed as least successful in providing procedures and programs aimed at youth most at risk for either victimization or perpetration of violence, with fully one quarter of respondents
feeling the schools were not successful in these areas. Sizeable minori-
ties (about 15%) of participants also felt that there were problems in

TABLE 10.1 Perceptions of Success and Need for Outside Assistance With Various Aspects of School Safety Planning

School Safety Plan Components	Disagree About Accomplishment	Agree About Need for Outside Assistance
Physical security of grounds and facilities	10.0%	50.8%
Positive school climate	12.3%	48.9%
Identification of youth at risk for perpetrating violence	15.8%	55.3%
Identification of youth at risk for being victimized at school	14.3%	57.3%
Procedures/programs for youth at risk for perpetrating violence	24.5%	56.7%
Procedures/programs for youth at risk for victimization	24.3%	55.0%
School-based prevention programs	12.5%	47.4%
Coordinated planning in schools regarding school safety issues	11.4%	56.5%
Coordinated planning involving community	15.3%	58.8%

identification of both of these at-risk groups, or that there were shortcomings in efforts to coordinate planning between school personnel and other community entities.

Close to 50% or more of respondents agreed that outside expertise was needed to address every component of school safety included in the survey. The area in which the largest proportion of people felt this way was in coordinated planning that would involve not just the schools or the school department, but also other groups and organizations in the community.

The survey results provided additional evidence of interest in outside assistance with school safety. Out of the 336 respondents, 46.4% (156) felt that there was a high probability, and 40.5% (136) felt there was some probability, that they would draw on the resources of a central place in Michigan that maintained information and materials on school violence prevention. Less than 10% (9.8%, or 33 respondents) did not know whether they would use such a resource or answered that they would not use it. Regarding the need for evaluation of their own community's school safety program, 39.5% of respondents indicated high need, 44.1% some need, and only 15.8% indicated no need or that they were uncertain about the need. About one third of summit participants (34.8%, or 117 respondents) indicated a high need for information on best practices, 50.9% some need, and 11.9% either little or no need, or uncertainty about need. Finally, 22.9% felt that there was a high level of need for assistance in working across agencies and groups to promote safe schools, 46.7% that there was some need, and 16.7% that there was little or no need. An additional 11.0% indicated they were uncertain about need for this type of help.

Based on classifications used by the Federal Office of Management and Budget as of June 30, 1999, 7 of the counties where summits were held were classified as urban, and 19 were classified as rural. Whether a county was classified as urban or rural had little effect on survey responses. School safety planning is viewed similarly, regardless of whether schools are located in rural or urban areas.

Social Capital to Promote School Safety

An assessment of the relationships of both school department personnel and police with the range of people needed for developing and implementing a comprehensive school safety plan suggests that, at least in some communities, there are major limitations imposed by the nature of interconnections. Notably, as shown in Table 10.2, there is very little social capital involving the media. In addition, only the police indicate relationships with the courts that create positive social capital. Although not as dramatic, the police tend to generate social capital through their interactions with emergency medical services personnel, and school officials do not. Overall, police appear to be closely tied to school personnel and several other entities in the community. Thus, school-police partnership would seem to be a very promising approach to stimulating the quality of interactions among all of the stakeholders in school safety, with the exception of the media. Because several experts on school safety have emphasized the importance of involving the media in planning, particularly for an event of violence and the aftermath, local partnerships of other community entities would need to develop a strategy for their inclusion in some aspects of the partnership.

County-Specific Results

One objective of the survey was to provide county-specific analysis that would inform summit participants of problems they need to ad-

TABLE 10.2 Social Capital Through Relationships That Educational and Police Personnel Have With Others Relevant to School Safety

	State/District Administrators	School Administrators	Teachers	Police
State/district school administrators		22.5	17.6	20.4
School-level administrators	23.7		20.8	22.5
Teachers	22.4	22.7		21.3
Parent groups, PTA	20.2	20.3	18.7	17.2
Students	19.6	22.7	23.0	19.1
Police	20.6	21.9	18.9	
Fire	18.3	20.1	18.8	21.1
Emergency medical services	18.0	19.1	17.6	21.8
Emergency medical coordinators	18.2	18.7	14.2	19.8
Hospitals	17.0	18.0	17.3	18.6
Child protection services	17.4	17.8	17.6	18.0
Mental health/social work	17.9	19.5	19.2	16.2
Courts	16.2	17.9	14.0	21.0
Media	15.6	13.9	12.0	15.9

dress to move towards a comprehensive school safety plan. Each county received three types of county-specific information. First, individuals in the county received information on a lack of consensus about whether the community was accomplishing a particular type of activity that is part of a school safety plan—for example, maintaining security of school grounds and facilities or providing school-based prevention programs. Participants from a particular county could follow up by gathering concrete information on specific areas, through discussion aimed at understanding alternative viewpoints, or by using the information as a basis for evaluation and assessment efforts leading to results that could be fed back to the group.

Second, county-level information was provided when a high proportion (ranging from one to two thirds of respondents) did not know whether the community had the information or resources, or felt the need for outside assistance, to accomplish different parts of the school safety plan. For many parts of the plan, respondents indicated they were "neutral" in response to questions about information and resources available in the community and for questions about the need for outside assistance. Follow-up activities in such a county could include presentations, written material, or discussion that would supply information of this type to participants.

Third, information was fed back to communities when there was consensus or a sizeable minority that felt that schools were failing in one or more dimensions of a school safety plan, and/or consensus that the community needed outside assistance to succeed. Future meetings among summit participants would need to address the questions of whether school safety plan components were effective and/or whether external assistance is available or should be established.

In addition to use of the survey information at the county levels, the information is being shared with people involved in the state-level Michigan Safe Schools Initiative and, through these people, with their groups or organizations. Moreover, involvement of Michigan State University, which houses the Michigan RCPI and has a land-grant mission of meeting state and local needs in such areas as school safety, opens the door to collaborative efforts involving the university in the dissemination of information or training through its statewide extension service.

CONCLUSION

In the opening chapter of their book *Violence in American Schools*, Elliott, Hamburg, and Williams (1998) decried the emphasis on increased punishment as the primary response to school violence, and called for "new intervention strategies for making our schools safer places of learning" (p. 3). The U.S. Departments of Education, Health and Human Services, and Justice are jointly administering a program that promotes comprehensive, integrated community-wide strategies for school safety and healthy child development across the country. The state group, the Michigan Safe Schools Initiative, and the linked county-level summits on school safety provide a model that responds to the need for alternatives to punitive response and that offers assistance to communities working towards a comprehensive school safety plan.

An important next step is additional assessment of the quality of the implemented components of school safety plans in each school district. For example, school climate information is being collected; this can provide more in-depth information to the developing local groups working on the comprehensive school safety plan and can fill gaps in knowledge indicated by the school safety survey.

Our research has shown that individuals and organizations in many communities want and need facilitative intervention in identifying their strengths and weaknesses in promoting school safety and in building the social capital necessary to move ahead on comprehensive plans. As Stephens (1998) noted, "Although state and federal policy makers are beginning to recognize the need for and require schools to design safe school plans, many educators and community leaders are at a loss as to where to begin" (p. 254). There appears to be an important role for some centralized source of information on best practices and evaluation expertise, particularly in the area of identifying and programming for youth at high risk for violent offending and victimization through violence. There also is a need for technical assistance to communities in working across the many entities pertinent to a school safety plan. Police-community partnerships, which stimulate the use of information to understand fully the need for change in order to improve safety, can bring a critical resource to stimulating safe schools planning. The provision of action research in the initial phase of developing a group to engage in formulating, assessing, and improving the local safety plan is a useful input into the process.

APPENDIX

School Safety Summit Survey

Thank you in advance for providing us with information to help guide the direction of future School Safety Summits and to help us understand the needs that individuals and communities have for training, information and technical assistance.

Please indicate your agreement with the following statements regarding school safety in your community.

	Strongly Disagree	Disagree	Neutral	Agree	Strongly Agree	N/A
Security of School Grounds and Facilities						
This is important for promoting school safety in my community.	☐	☐	☐	☐	☐	☐
My community is currently accomplishing this objective.	☐	☐	☐	☐	☐	☐
My community has the information/resources to accomplish this.	☐	☐	☐	☐	☐	☐
My community needs outside assistance to accomplish this.	☐	☐	☐	☐	☐	☐
Positive School Climate (e.g., reducing bullying and alienation, promoting healthy emotional development)						
This is important for promoting school safety in my community.	☐	☐	☐	☐	☐	☐
My community is currently accomplishing this objective.	☐	☐	☐	☐	☐	☐
My community has the information/resources to accomplish this.	☐	☐	☐	☐	☐	☐
My community needs outside assistance to accomplish this.	☐	☐	☐	☐	☐	☐
Identification of Youth at Risk for Perpetrating Violence						
This is important for promoting school safety in my community.	☐	☐	☐	☐	☐	☐
My community is currently accomplishing this objective.	☐	☐	☐	☐	☐	☐

My community has the informa-
tion/resources to accomplish this.
☐ ☐ ☐ ☐ ☐ ☐

My community needs outside assistance to accomplish this.
☐ ☐ ☐ ☐ ☐ ☐

Identification of Youth at Risk for Being Victimized in School

This is important for promoting
school safety in my community.
☐ ☐ ☐ ☐ ☐ ☐

My community is currently accomplishing this objective.
☐ ☐ ☐ ☐ ☐ ☐

My community has the informa-
tion/resources to accomplish this.
☐ ☐ ☐ ☐ ☐ ☐

My community needs outside assistance to accomplish this.
☐ ☐ ☐ ☐ ☐ ☐

Procedures and Programs Responsive to Youth at Risk for Perpetrating Violence

This is important for promoting
school safety in my community.
☐ ☐ ☐ ☐ ☐ ☐

My community is currently accomplishing this objective.
☐ ☐ ☐ ☐ ☐ ☐

My community has the informa-
tion/resources to accomplish this.
☐ ☐ ☐ ☐ ☐ ☐

My community needs outside assistance to accomplish this.
☐ ☐ ☐ ☐ ☐ ☐

Procedures and Programs Responsive to Youth at Risk for Victimization at School

This is important for promoting
school safety in my community.
☐ ☐ ☐ ☐ ☐ ☐

My community is currently accomplishing this objective.
☐ ☐ ☐ ☐ ☐ ☐

My community has the informa-
tion/resources to accomplish this.
☐ ☐ ☐ ☐ ☐ ☐

My community needs outside assistance to accomplish this.
☐ ☐ ☐ ☐ ☐ ☐

School-Based Prevention Programs (e.g., anti-gang, DARE, GREAT, substance abuse, etc.)

This is important for promoting
school safety in my community.
☐ ☐ ☐ ☐ ☐ ☐

My community is currently accomplishing this objective.
☐ ☐ ☐ ☐ ☐ ☐

My community has the informa-
tion/resources to accomplish this.
☐ ☐ ☐ ☐ ☐ ☐

My community needs outside assistance to accomplish this.
☐ ☐ ☐ ☐ ☐ ☐

Coordinated Planning in Schools Regarding School Safety Issues

This is important for promoting school safety in my community.	☐	☐	☐	☐	☐	☐
My community is currently accomplishing this objective.	☐	☐	☐	☐	☐	☐
My community has the information/resources to accomplish this.	☐	☐	☐	☐	☐	☐
My community needs outside assistance to accomplish this.	☐	☐	☐	☐	☐	☐

Coordinated Planning Between Schools and Other Relevant Community Groups Regarding School Safety

This is important for promoting school safety in my community.	☐	☐	☐	☐	☐	☐
My community is currently accomplishing this objective.	☐	☐	☐	☐	☐	☐
My community has the information/resources to accomplish this.	☐	☐	☐	☐	☐	☐
My community needs outside assistance to accomplish this.	☐	☐	☐	☐	☐	☐

Capacity for Schools and Other Relevant Community Groups to Respond to Threats to Safety at Schools

This is important for promoting school safety in my community.	☐	☐	☐	☐	☐	☐
My community is currently accomplishing this objective.	☐	☐	☐	☐	☐	☐
My community has the information/resources to accomplish this.	☐	☐	☐	☐	☐	☐
My community needs outside assistance to accomplish this.	☐	☐	☐	☐	☐	☐

Please consider your relationships with representatives of the following groups and on a scale of 1 (low) to 5 (high), rate each relationship on the following dimensions:

Students

	1	2	3	4	5	n/a
Contact	☐	☐	☐	☐	☐	☐
Trust	☐	☐	☐	☐	☐	☐
Understanding	☐	☐	☐	☐	☐	☐
Cooperation	☐	☐	☐	☐	☐	☐
Empathy	☐	☐	☐	☐	☐	☐

School Teachers

	1	2	3	4	5
Contact	☐	☐	☐	☐	☐
Trust	☐	☐	☐	☐	☐
Understanding	☐	☐	☐	☐	☐
Cooperation	☐	☐	☐	☐	☐
Empathy	☐	☐	☐	☐	☐

School-Level Administrators
(principals, counselors)

	1	2	3	4	5	n/a
Contact	☐	☐	☐	☐	☐	☐
Trust	☐	☐	☐	☐	☐	☐
Understanding	☐	☐	☐	☐	☐	☐
Cooperation	☐	☐	☐	☐	☐	☐
Empathy	☐	☐	☐	☐	☐	☐

District-Level School Administrators

	1	2	3	4	5
Contact	☐	☐	☐	☐	☐
Trust	☐	☐	☐	☐	☐
Understanding	☐	☐	☐	☐	☐
Cooperation	☐	☐	☐	☐	☐
Empathy	☐	☐	☐	☐	☐

Police (city, sheriff, 911-dispatch)

	1	2	3	4	5	n/a
Contact	☐	☐	☐	☐	☐	☐
Trust	☐	☐	☐	☐	☐	☐
Understanding	☐	☐	☐	☐	☐	☐
Cooperation	☐	☐	☐	☐	☐	☐
Empathy	☐	☐	☐	☐	☐	☐

Emergency Medical Services
(nurses, EMTs)

	1	2	3	4	5
Contact	☐	☐	☐	☐	☐
Trust	☐	☐	☐	☐	☐
Understanding	☐	☐	☐	☐	☐
Cooperation	☐	☐	☐	☐	☐
Empathy	☐	☐	☐	☐	☐

Fire

	1	2	3	4	5	n/a
Contact	☐	☐	☐	☐	☐	☐
Trust	☐	☐	☐	☐	☐	☐
Understanding	☐	☐	☐	☐	☐	☐
Cooperation	☐	☐	☐	☐	☐	☐
Empathy	☐	☐	☐	☐	☐	☐

Local Emergency Management Coordinator

	1	2	3	4	5
Contact	☐	☐	☐	☐	☐
Trust	☐	☐	☐	☐	☐
Understanding	☐	☐	☐	☐	☐
Cooperation	☐	☐	☐	☐	☐
Empathy	☐	☐	☐	☐	☐

PTA & Parent Groups

	1	2	3	4	5	n/a
Contact	☐	☐	☐	☐	☐	☐
Trust	☐	☐	☐	☐	☐	☐
Understanding	☐	☐	☐	☐	☐	☐
Cooperation	☐	☐	☐	☐	☐	☐
Empathy	☐	☐	☐	☐	☐	☐

Court (prosecutors, judges)

	1	2	3	4	5
Contact	☐	☐	☐	☐	☐
Trust	☐	☐	☐	☐	☐
Understanding	☐	☐	☐	☐	☐
Cooperation	☐	☐	☐	☐	☐
Empathy	☐	☐	☐	☐	☐

Media (newspaper, television journalists)

	1	2	3	4	5	n/a
Contact	☐	☐	☐	☐	☐	☐
Trust	☐	☐	☐	☐	☐	☐
Understanding	☐	☐	☐	☐	☐	☐
Cooperation	☐	☐	☐	☐	☐	☐
Empathy	☐	☐	☐	☐	☐	☐

Hospital / Medical Centers

	1	2	3	4	5
Contact	☐	☐	☐	☐	☐
Trust	☐	☐	☐	☐	☐
Understanding	☐	☐	☐	☐	☐
Cooperation	☐	☐	☐	☐	☐
Empathy	☐	☐	☐	☐	☐

Protective Services Workers (FIA)	1	2	3	4	5	n/a
Contact	□	□	□	□	□	□
Trust	□	□	□	□	□	□
Understanding	□	□	□	□	□	□
Cooperation	□	□	□	□	□	□
Empathy	□	□	□	□	□	□

Mental Health Professionals / Social Workers	1	2	3	4	5
Contact	□	□	□	□	□
Trust	□	□	□	□	□
Understanding	□	□	□	□	□
Cooperation	□	□	□	□	□
Empathy	□	□	□	□	□

Would you yourself draw on the resources of a central place in Michigan that maintains information and materials on school violence prevention?

__ High probability I would   __Some probability I would   __Don't know   __Unlikely I would   __Definitely would not

Do you see a need for an evaluation of the school safety program in your community?

__High need   __Some need   __Don't know   __Little need   __No need

Do you have a need for information regarding best practices in creating safe and effective schools?

__High need   __Some need   __Don't know   __Little need   __No need

Does your community need help in working across agencies to address school safety issues?

__High need   __Some need   __Don't know   __Little need   __No need

Finally, please provide us with some information about yourself. Your responses will enable us to better understand school safety issues in your community. All of your responses will be kept confidential. Also, you may refuse to answer any question, or may decline to participate altogether.

Job (You are here representing what group) (check one):

___School Teacher

___School-Level Administrator

___District or State School Administrator

___Police
___EMS
___Fire
___Local Coordinator
___Court
___Media
___Hospital
___Protective Services Worker
___Parent Group (PTA, etc.)
___Student
___Other: [Please Write In]

As part of your job, do you participate in a school safety planning or response team? [Check all that apply]

___With people in the schools or school administration
___With other agencies/organizations in the community

Years at Job: _____

Gender: Male   ☐   Highest level of education: High School   ☐
             Female ☐   Bachelor's Degree ☐
                                                           Some College   ☐
                                                           Master's   ☐
                                                           Associate's   ☐
                                                           Ph.D.   ☐

May we contact you if we have any additional questions?   Yes ☐   No ☐

Are you interested in receiving a 1-page summary
of the findings?   Yes ☐   No ☐

Name and mailing address:_____   [Name]

_____   [Street]

_____   [City, State, ZIP]

_____   [E-mail address]

Thank you for completing this survey

REFERENCES

Berg, B. L. (2001). *Qualitative research methods for the social sciences.* Boston: Allyn & Bacon.

Elliott, D. S., Hamburg, B., & Williams, K. R. (1998). Violence in American schools: An overview. In D. S. Elliott, B. A. Hamburg, & K. R. Williams (Eds.), *Violence in American schools* (pp. 3–28). New York: Cambridge University Press.

Sandefur, R. L., & Laumann, E. O. (1998). A paradigm for social capital. *Rationality and Society, 10*(4), 481–501.

Stephens, R. D. (1998). Safe school planning. In D. S. Elliott, B. A. Hamburg, & K. R. Williams (Eds.), *Violence in American schools* (pp. 253–289). New York: Cambridge University Press.

U.S. Department of Education & U.S. Department of Justice. (1999). *The 1999 Annual Report on school safety.* Washington, DC: Government Printing Office.

CHAPTER 11

Social Capital, Collective Action, and Community Policing
A Case Study in Sioux City, Iowa

Mark E. Correia

*I*n the Sioux City, Iowa, area (population 80,500), economic decline, increased diversity (Bureau of the Census, 1990; McCormick, 1997), and physical deterioration of the inner city have lead to an erosion of neighborhood identity and heightened fear of crime (Maas, 1996; McCormick, 1997). In an effort to increase citizen participation in public safety promotions, reduce the fear of crime, and improve the overall quality of life of the community, the Sioux City Police Department implemented the COPS-inspired Community Action Support Team (CAST) in 1994.

Research conducted over the past decade has contributed greatly to the theoretical and practical understanding of community policing (Goldstein, 1990; Sadd & Grinc, 1994; Skolnick & Bayley, 1986; Trojanowicz, Kappeler, Gaines, & Bucqueroux, 1998; Wycoff & Skogan, 1994; Zhao, Thurman, & Lovrich, 1995). At the same time, however, few studies have focused upon the impact of *neighborhood* social norms and networks on citizen participation in community-policing programs. The importance of such an analysis is supported by members of the National Institute of Justice Policing Research Institute,

who argue for a better understanding of the "political, cultural, and social realities of communities," and contend that we have to "build from
the neighborhood up" (Brady, 1996, p. 4; see also Sampson, 1995;
Sampson & Groves, 1989).

In an effort to develop a better understanding of these characteristics and to assess their relationship to community-policing programs,
this chapter focuses on the effect that social norms and networks (e.g.,
social capital) have on collective activities, in particular on activities related to community policing.

OVERVIEW OF RECENT SIOUX CITY HISTORY

The move to community policing in Sioux City, Iowa, must be placed
in the context of the changing demographics and economic base in the
city. In addition, a change in command led to the acceleration of the
community-policing philosophy.

Changing Demographics and Economic Base

Between 1980 and 1990, the Sioux City area experienced tremendous shifts in population. Historically, the area's minority population
was composed of substantial groups of Native Americans and African
Americans. According to the 1990 census, and in line with observational accounts, a major shift in the manufacturing sector of the city
occurred during the late 1980s, which resulted in an influx of people of
Hispanic and Southeast Asian cultural backgrounds (McCormick,
1997). Unfamiliar with these ethnic groups, many city service providers, especially the police, had a difficult time dealing with the cultural
change (McCormick, 1997).

Changes also came from the proliferation of verified gang members
coming from larger cities across the United States (e.g., Chicago),
which further complicated relations among citizens and between citizens groups and police. The migration of these new arrivals into an already fractured community resulted in a marked increase of gang-re-
lated behavior, as well as increased citizen fear of crime (McCormick,
1997).

In addition to these broader structural changes, in 1993, the loss of
two of the city's major employers resulted in substantial economic
change. Combined, these two manufacturers accounted for nearly

1,500 jobs. Sergeant Mike McCormick, a 15-year veteran of the police department and coordinator of the CAST program, contended that community relations became very strained at this time.[1] The economic adversity faced by the city heightened tensions between residents and, in several incidents, police had to intervene in confrontations between people from different ethnic groups.

The fraying of the city's social fabric, evidenced by the increasing social and physical deterioration of its historical areas, further escalated tensions. These, in combination with the economic challenges and the increasing fear of crime, propelled the Sioux City Police Department leadership to adopt an untried community-policing philosophy.

Policing in Sioux City: An Example of Community Policing

Before the adoption of a community-policing philosophy, Sergeant McCormick described the department's philosophy as traditional, hierarchical, and focused on solving violent and major property crimes. The main goal of the department was to increase its presence in the community, control crime, and make as many arrests as possible.

Ten years in the detective division led Sergeant McCormick to believe that "citizens were most concerned with rape, murder, and assault," not with quality-of-life issues. "Our primary focus was on making arrests, not solving citizen problems," he says, voicing a perspective similar to those held by police officers across the country (Zhao, 1996). Six years later, however, Sergeant McCormick and the other CAST officers sounded very different.

A major influence on the adoption of CAST was the new chief, Gary Maas, hired in 1991. Over the years, the Sioux City Police Department had demonstrated an unwillingness to adapt to a changing public service environment (Trojanowicz et al., 1998; Zhao, 1996). In response to the structural and social changes occurring in the city, city leaders agreed to hire an outside candidate for chief of police who brought a strong record of innovation and a devotion to community policing (McCormick, 1997).

Immediate changes in the department included rewriting the mission statement, marked decentralization of services, and use of a community survey to gain a broader perspective on citizen concerns. The results of the community survey were quite unexpected, and, according to Sergeant McCormick, "opened the eyes of the department" to citizen concerns. Instead of citizens expressing their fears about rape, murder, and assaults, their responses focused primarily on *quality-of-life issues* (e.g., barking dogs, noisy neighbors, and litter; McCormick, 1997). Using the survey results as a basis for change, the department applied for and received a federal grant for the CAST program.[2]

Implementation of CAST occurred over three years. Initially, two officers and one sergeant were appointed; later, seven officers were added.[3] Each officer was assigned to a geographical area identified as being at the tipping point—that is, having characteristics of physical deterioration and high levels of physical disorder, unemployment, transience, and calls for service (Maas, 1996; McCormick, 1997).

Each of the current nine CAST areas is heterogeneous, composed of both single- and multifamily housing and some businesses, and covers between 24 and 36 square blocks (Maas, 1996). The CAST objective was to work with citizens to develop solutions for their problems, not to impose change upon the community. As stated by former Chief of Police Maas (1996),

> Just as a physician places a cast on an injured limb, the department places a CAST Officer in each of the targeted neighborhoods. However, like a physician's cast, the Officers are not there to heal the neighborhood; they are there to support the neighborhood while it heals itself (p. 3).

In general, support for the CAST program appears to be widespread throughout Sioux City. Within local government, the city council and mayor are strong proponents of the community-policing philosophy. Private industry has also been highly supportive of CAST, and has given substantial sums of money and in-kind contributions to ensure the continuation of the program.[4] Further support has come from the print media, which reports on CAST events several times a month. Most important, however, was the support provided by the citizens. The following statements highlight this support (see Schoenherr, 1996):

> We worry that if the neighborhood gets cleaned up too much, we won't have a CAST officer anymore. We'd loose the personal touch with police officers and probably loose ground.

> I was ready to move, and then they started these [CAST] meetings.

Support from these various groups is important to the long-term programmatic success of citizen-police collaboration.

CAST: SUCCESSES AND PROBLEMS

The most notable success of the program has been in cleaning up the neighborhoods where CAST has been implemented. For example, in an area that had chronic drug problems and was experiencing increased rates of petty theft, as well as showing signs of substantial physical deterioration, citizens expressed their dismay that the police were unable to stop the spiraling decay of their neighborhood (see Kelling & Coles, 1996; Skogan, 1990; Wilson & Kelling, 1982). Working with landlords, the narcotics division, various city-level departments, and residents of the area, the CAST officer was able to act as a catalyst in solving the problems caused by drugs (McCormick, 1997).

Coupled with these practical successes, however, is the persistent problem of obtaining and sustaining community participation. Levels of citizen commitment and participation in CAST-sponsored activities have been sporadic and unequal, with areas varying from quite high to very limited participation. Because of the importance of citizen involvement, CAST officers worry that those areas where citizens are not becoming involved will continue to deteriorate (CAST, personal communication, 1997).

Low levels of citizen participation in collaborative efforts is not unique to Sioux City (Kelling & Coles, 1996), but little is known about the differences between those areas with high rates and those with low rates of participation. Hence, an analysis of the social norms and networks that contribute to participation in the CAST areas could provide important information related to this variation. Understanding these social processes will enable policing agencies to tailor their efforts to a particular area. It may be the case that citizens in some areas are unwilling to collaborate with the police, whereas others are much more willing. Further, it may be that some areas merely require preliminary efforts before effective collaboration can occur. In any case, these alternative possibilities require different policing efforts.

Collective Action

An important component of effective community policing is the willingness of citizens to engage in public activities. Accordingly, strong community-policing efforts are dependent upon the ability of citizens to come together to solve their problems. This type of social behavior is termed *collective action*, and has been defined as "activities which produce collective or public goods, that is, goods with the non-excludability property that their provision to some members of a group means that they cannot be withheld from others in the group" (Oliver, 1984, p. 602).

The most common examples of collective goods include commodities, such as national defense and use of public lands (e.g., water or grazing rights). Properly reconceptualized, neighborhood safety and social order can also be defined as a collective good. Problems of physical and social disorder, as well as crime, are collective action problems—problems that affect all the individuals in the area and require a collective response in order to be alleviated.

Effective community policing is built upon the collaborative efforts of police, community-based organizations, and citizens. Within the community-policing literature, academics and researchers have suggested that effectiveness is contingent upon the broad-based participation of individuals (Skolnick & Bayley, 1986; Trojanowicz et al., 1998). In fact, a consistent finding among researchers has been that citizens' low levels of participation are detrimental to the programmatic efforts of police departments (Sadd & Grinc, 1994).

Complicating the matter of collective action are the different types of communal structures that may exist—strong communal bonds, larger and heterogeneous community composition, weak communal bonds, pockets of "community" within a larger community, and lack of any type of communal bonds are all possible contexts for collective action efforts (Taylor & Singleton, 1993, p. 202). Each of these variations in community structure may affect the manner in which individuals seek to solve their problems collectively.

A second factor complicating collective action is an individual's perceived sense of safety, which numerous researchers have suggested effects one's attachment to the community (Perkins, Florin, Rich, Wandersman, & Chavis, 1990; Slovak, 1986; Taylor, Gottfredson, & Brower, 1984). Perceptions of safety are related to the incidence of incivilities and disorder within a neighborhood or community (Covington & Taylor, 1991; Skogan, 1990; Skogan & Maxfield, 1981). These reductions can lead to physical and/or psychological withdrawal from public spaces and to isolation from neighbors, depletion in the stocks of social capital, and minimal levels of collective action (Miethe, 1995; Skogan, 1987, 1990; Taylor & Hall, 1986).

The importance of understanding collective action phenomena for assessing the potentialities and limitations of community policing is clear inasmuch a working partnership between members of the community, the police, other governmental agencies, and institutions to solve chronic problems of crime and disorder within the community constitute the core elements of community policing. As articulated by Friedman and Clark (1997),

> The importance of organizing and organization cannot be overemphasized. The community needs to be organized because it is the most effective way to work with a highly organized partner like the police and against often well-organized and frightening adversaries. (p. 12)

Though some appreciation of the importance of collective action exists among law enforcement and community-policing reformers, community policing is still plagued by the inability to sustain citizen participation in community-policing programs in many settings where it is being attempted. The following section will focus on those characteristics of social networks that have been identified as most responsible for initiating and sustaining collective action for the production of public goods.

Social Capital

Social capital theory suggests that social relationships influence collective action, including collaboration between the community and police. Coleman (1990) defined social capital as a variety of different entities having two characteristics in common: They all consist of some aspect of a social structure, and they facilitate certain actions of individuals who are within the structure (p. 302). The two most important entities are *trustworthiness* and *obligations,* both of which vary according to the social environment and relations within that environment.[5]

Building on Coleman's (1988, 1990) definition, Putnam (1993, 1995a, 1995b, 2000) explained that social capital reflects how embedded individuals are in their communal and governmental affairs. The more embedded a person is, the higher the level of trust among and between citizens and their governmental institutions. More specifically, social capital can be defined as the reserves of *trust* and *engagement* found in a community. Social capital is important because "it constitutes a force that helps to bind society together by transforming individuals from self-seeking and egocentric calculators with little social conscious or sense of mutual obligations, into members of a community with shared interests" (Newton, 1997, p. 576).

The importance of social capital is further evident in the wealth of research conducted at different levels of social aggregation (i.e., family, community, and society). For example, Hagan and his colleagues (Hagan, MacMillan, & Wheaton, 1996) found that family social capital is an important mediating variable between family dislocation and educational attainment (p. 376), and Parcel and Menaghan (1993) indicate that it can reduce behavioral problems in children.

At the community level, Putnam (1995a, 1995b) concluded that significant declines in social capital, as evidenced by the decreasing participation in civic organizations, have resulted in many social problems within American communities (see also Ladd, 1996). In fact, in analysis of statewide murder rates between 1980 and 1995, Putnam (2000) found a linear relationship between social capital and rates of murder. Specifically, Putnam found that states with high levels of social capital had low rates of murder.[6] As this body of research indicates, social capital plays an important role at all levels of society.

Social Capital and Social Responsibility

Accounting for the different types of social relationships, Putnam (1995a) suggested that there are two distinct levels of social capital—local social capital and public social capital. The first and most basic form of social capital, local social capital, is found among members of the family and between citizens within a community. At this level, trust and reciprocity among individuals is key. Another important aspect is informal responsibility, which is inherent to trust and reciprocity. Informal responsibility pertains to obligations felt to those informal groups that immediately surround the individual—for example, family and friends—and relies upon the ability of the neighborhood and/or friendship networks to enforce informal rules of social conduct through social disapproval (Bursik & Grasmick, 1993; see also Greenberg & Rohe, 1986).

The second level of social capital, public social capital, consists of those social networks tying the individual to broader community institutions, such as churches, schools, civic and voluntary organizations, and various levels of government (Yankelovich, 1994). These informal associations with other citizens help build familiarity and trust among individuals, and keep individuals engaged in communal affairs; such engagement is a necessary component to facilitating collective activities and resisting the spiral effect of social disorder (Skogan, 1990; Wilson & Kelling, 1982). Putnam (1993) suggests that these associational networks are important, because members of associations are much more likely than nonmembers to participate in politics, to spend time with neighbors, to express trust, and so on (p. 36).

In terms of linking individuals to local government, an important consideration is the perception of access and influence an individual has to public officials and their institutions. Collectively, the ability of citizens to secure necessary assistance from broader government agencies relies on the capacity of citizens to gain access to government officials, effectively lobby them, and influence the official agencies through a mobilization of citizen concern. Researchers have found evidence of a strong relationship between public dialogue and higher levels of collective activities (Yankelovich, 1994), effective community-based criminal justice policies (Donziger, 1996), lower levels of physical disorder (Skogan, 1990), and larger stocks of social capital (Putnam, 1995b).

Both local and public social capital may influence collaboration between citizens and the police. Communities holding high levels of local social capital may need limited efforts of the police, whereas those with lower levels may need increased police efforts. Likewise, those communities better able to build strong relationships with social institutions will have more resources to draw upon in their fight against criminal activity. As Putnam (2000) stated, "Social capital makes us smarter, healthier, richer and better able to govern a just and stable democracy" (p. 290).

RESEARCH FOCUS

As the literature above suggests, the variation in rates of citizen participation in community-policing programs are likely a result of forces outside policing organizations, primarily of characteristics found in social norms and networks. Hence, the primary interest of this study was the exploration of those elements that characterize the community and that affect citizen participation and, therefore, the implementation and ultimate effectiveness of community policing.

Data Collection and Methods

All nine CAST areas were classified as having either low or high rates of citizen participation.[7] Low-participation areas had an average of 3 to 5 citizens attending meetings, while high-participation areas had an average of 25 or more attending. From these categories, two low-participation (Areas 1 and 2) and two high-participation areas (Areas 3 and 4) were selected for these analyses.

During the spring of 1997, surveys were sent to households selected for the study. Addresses were obtained from the CAST officers in the selected areas, for a total of nearly 4,100 households. The survey was to assess the strength of social cohesion in the CAST area. A random selection of 150 households from each sample area was taken, which provided an overall sample of 600 households. Because of the exploratory nature of this study, only one wave of data collection was completed, which yielded an overall response rate of nearly 38%.[8]

The respondents' personal characteristics for the low-participation CAST areas indicate that the majority are Caucasian, female, and over 50 years old, and tended to hold at least a high school degree and have an income of under $19,999 per year. Those respondents in the high-participation CAST areas tended to be Caucasian, female, and over 36 years old, having taken some college courses and making between $20,000 and $49,999 per year. Comparatively, individuals from the high-participation CAST areas tended to be slightly younger, have slightly higher incomes, and be more educated than those individuals in the low-participation CAST areas.

To assess the importance and influence of those variables described in the Methods section below, several statistical methods were utilized. First, Kendall's rank-ordered correlation coefficient analysis was conducted. This coefficient is similar to, but a more conservative estimate than, Spearman's rho (Miller & Whitehead, 1996). Secondly, a means comparison test was employed to assess the differences between the areas. For this analysis, the two low-participation areas were compared with the two high-participation areas. Lastly, regression analyses were used to assess the influence of the independent variables on three different models.

Measurement

Several variables and additive scales were incorporated to assess the relationships among underlying social processes, community policing, and collective action. In terms of the independent variables, the survey items tapped into issues of the level of (a) familiarity or connection among neighbors, (b) perceived incivilities in the neighborhood, (c) participation in civic organizations, and (d) perceived ability of individuals to employ informal social control mechanisms. In addition, one scale measured the individual's perceived level of safety during the day, whereas another measured one's perceived level of safety during the evening. The reliabilities for each scale were adequate, ranging from 0.71 to 0.87. These scales measure behavior thought to influence the likelihood of participation in collective activities. Lastly, several control variables were also included—age, education, and income.

Three dependent variables were used in the analyses. First, a measure for *collective action* was constructed. In order to create a measure representing Putnam's (1995b) conceptualization of local and public social capital, many additive scales were combined to create a more reliable measure. Local social capital is constituted of the following variables: *sense of community, informal social control,* and *trust*. Public social capital, on the other hand, is composed of *public dialogue* and *public trust*.

Analysis of Community Cohesion

Kendall's Rank Order. The overall data are reported in Table 11.1. For the four CAST areas, the data were transformed into rank order from lowest to highest levels of collective action. Included in this analysis are those aggregate community-level variables thought to be related to collective action. Kendall's tau statistic was used as a measure of the degree of association between the measure of collective action and the other measures of hypothesized significance to social cohesion. The results reported suggest that two significant correlations occur.

First, it appears that a significant association occurs between levels of public social capital and collective action. This association suggests that those areas most likely to engage in collective action activities (e.g., solving complex social problems) are also more likely to trust public officials. This is especially important in determining the willingness of an area to work with the police. Second, the significant association between citizen participation and collective action suggests that those areas with higher levels of participation also have higher levels of perceived ability of neighbors to solve problems facing the community.

Means Test. The results were further analyzed to identify differences between high- and low-participation CAST areas. As expected, the high-participation CAST areas had significantly higher levels of informal social control ($p < 0.05$), local social capital ($p < 0.01$), and public social capital ($p < 0.01$). These findings are similar to findings in previous research. These social "mechanisms" provide the foundation for sustained levels of engagement in civic matters (Putnam, 2000).

Importantly, the high-participation CAST areas had greater levels of perceived safety during the day and evening when compared to the low-participation CAST areas ($p < 0.001$). Similarly, the high-participation CAST areas also had lower levels of incivilities. These findings are important, because previous research has identified the influential nature of perceived safety and social incivilities.

Regression. As previously discussed, three models were constructed to measure the effect of various neighborhood-level predictors of local social capital (Model 1), public social capital (Model 2), and collective action (Model 3). For this particular analysis, the four CAST areas were combined. The results are presented in Table 11.2.

The results for the local social capital model (Model 1), reported in Table 11.2, reveal that three indicators were significant. First, it showed that higher levels of neighboring behavior increases levels of local social capital, a finding consistent with the literature ($p < 0.001$). In fact, a key ingredient of local social capital is the level of trust and reciprocity among neighbors (Unger & Wandersman, 1982). These appear to be built through familiarity with and positive interactions among neighbors (Putnam, 2000; Unger & Wandersman, 1985; Wandersman, Florin, Rich, Friedman, & Meier, 1987). Another significant finding was that increases in a perceived sense of safety during the day was related to increased levels of local social capital ($p < 0.05$). This is an important finding, because previous research indicates that low levels of perceived safety can affect people's trust in their neighbors and, in turn, affect their ability to engage in collective activities. A somewhat unexpected finding was the significant influence of age ($p < 0.05$). Research does indicate, however, that as individual's become older, they tend to move less and to participate in communal activities more often, which leads to the development of networks of trust and reciprocity (Putnam, 2000).

As Table 11.2 indicates, only two indicators were significant for the public social capital model (Model 2). As expected, increases in levels of sense of community increased levels of public social capital ($p < 0.05$). Another finding consistent with the literature was the significant influence of higher levels of education ($p < 0.01$). Putnam (2000) indicates that individuals with higher levels of education are more likely to be familiar with and hold an interest in local government affairs. There-

TABLE 11.1 Mean Scores of Community Variables Representing Community Cohesion

	Informal Social Control	Neighboring	Civic	Incivilities	Safety (Day)	Safety (Night)	Local	Public*	Citizen Participation*
Cast 1	11.84	5.42	20.33	23.64	2.36	3.63	29.28	23.56	1
Cast 2	12.65	5.79	21.14	24.04	2.41	3.42	30.73	24.50	2
Cast 3	15.00	6.44	20.84	25.86	1.65	2.48	37.14	26.52	3
Cast 4	13.79	6.15	22.36	24.40	1.80	2.71	34.65	26.60	4

*$p < 0.5$

TABLE 11.2 Summary of Results of Regression for All CAST Areas

	Model 1: Local Social Capital b(t ratio)	Model 2: Public Social Capital b(t ratio)	Model 3: Collective Action b(t ratio)
Income	0.043(0.504)	0.139(1.426)	0.109(1.107)
Age	0.190(2.284)*	0.095(1.174)	0.068(0.692)
Education	0.078(0.857)	0.285(2.600)*	−0.092(−0.799)
Neighborly behavior	0.361(4.297)***		0.100(0.969)
Incivilities	0.103(1.123)		−0.037(−0.359)
Civic behavior		−0.017(0.164)	0.231(2.253)*
Sense of community		0.303(3.422)*	
Safety during day	0.222(2.158)*		0.015(0.129)
Safety during evening	0.143(1.308)		0.030(0.237)
Local social capital			0.135(1.209)
Public social capital			0.326(3.401)***
N	112	112	112
R^2	0.399	0.280	0.262
Durban Watson	2.02	2.13	2.15

*$p < 0.5$; **$p < 0.01$; ***$p < 0.000$

fore, they tend, as this research indicates, to feel they have greater levels of access to and influence over local officials.

For those policing agencies that have adopted a community-policing philosophy, the ability of citizens in a neighborhood to work collectively is a vital indicator of success. As the data reported in Table 11.2 show, the significant indicators of collective action–type behaviors are civic behavior ($p < 0.05$) and public social capital ($p < 0.001$). These findings support the contention that those with high levels of civic behavior are more likely to be engaged in other aspects of the community, collective activities being among them (Putnam, 1993, 1995a, 1995b).

Unexpected was that neither measure of perceived safety was a significant indicator of collective action. It may be that the relationship between collective activities and one's perceived level of safety is more complex than anticipated.

DISCUSSION

The present analysis helps provide clarity to the understanding of the underlying social processes taking place in the neighborhood context. Through the consideration of social capital and other socially embedded phenomena, we are better able to understand those factors that may be responsible for successful community-policing initiatives.

Though exploratory, this analysis also highlights the importance of conducting neighborhood-level research, as well as the role community context ought to play in social science research. In terms of community policing, Kelling and Coles (1996) note the importance of this area of study in their statement that "context adds meaning to an act and is a key element in police officer decisions" (p. 32). Despite the relevance of this area of research, few researchers have studied social capital at the neighborhood level (for exceptions, see Hagan et al., 1996; Hagan, Merkens, & Boehnke, 1995; Schneider, Teske, Marschall, Mintrom, & Roch, 1997).

The most significant finding reported here is the differences observed in dynamics characterizing the CAST areas, with the high-participation areas possessing stronger and more consistent social processes than the low-participation areas. The comparison of the two types of areas reported here suggests that residents in the low-participation CAST areas differed significantly from their counterparts in the high-participation areas in terms of perceived safety, local and public social capital, and informal social control (see Table 11.2). This finding lends empirical support to the theoretical hypothesis that social capital may be a prerequisite to citizen engagement in community level efforts (Putnam, 1993, 1995a, 1995b).

Levels of public social capital proved to be a correlate of collective activity. Hence, the ability to hold trust in local officials and the level of perceived access to government agencies and politicians increases the likelihood that an individual is going to engage in collective activities. However, the theoretical assumption that a citizen's level of collective activity is reliant upon bridging local and public social capital is not supported by this study (Evans, 1996).

Oliver (1984) claims that individuals with the greatest sense of collective identity and strongest informal social processes are the least likely to get together with others to solve their problems. Instead, individuals that are less well connected and have lower neighboring activities are more likely to engage themselves. This "paradox of community life" is not supported by the current analysis. In fact, quite the opposite was found—those areas with a stronger sense of collective identity were more likely to "incur the costs of community activism" (Oliver, 1984, p. 609). In fact, it appears that these social norms and networks provide the mechanisms necessary to deal with collective action problems more effectively (Putnam, 2000).

This finding holds crucial implications for community-policing efforts. First and foremost, this analysis indicates that before community-policing efforts are initiated, it is wise to have a firm understanding of the social norms and networks present throughout the various parts of the community. Second, community police officers will have to work harder to engage citizens in those areas lacking strong informal social networks, and must realize they may not be as successful as their colleagues working in other areas of their agency's jurisdiction. Last, community-policing efforts may be most successful in those areas that have strong, preexisting informal social ties, where such external efforts may not be as necessary.

Given the results of the present research, the inability of community-policing programs consistently to sustain citizen participation may not be a problem inherent to policing. Indeed, it appears that social norms and networks latent in the community may be the determining factors of success for community-policing efforts in cities across America.

NOTES

1. Sergeant Mike McCormick, of the Sioux City, Iowa, Police Department was interviewed for research in April, 1997.

2. The grant received by the Sioux City Police Department was to provide for the supplemental hiring of officers. Unfortunately, the grant did not require any formal eval-

uation; consequently, the department has not conducted any type of systematic, formal evaluation of the CAST program.

3. In order to recruit the officers for the program, Sergeant McCormick and the chief sent out letters to each officer in the department asking for volunteers. They received only nine responses out of 275 officers. All nine of these individuals tended to be younger than the average officer is, and to be within their first 5 years of service.

4. The department has received high levels of support from many area businesses. The largest contributions have come from the Gateway Computer Company, which recently donated $365,000 to keep the program operating for another 3–5 years. Previously, the company held a golf tournament to benefit the CAST program.

5. *Trustworthiness* refers to the level of trust that citizens within a community have for one another as well as for their public institutions. *Obligations* can be likened as "credit slips" held between individuals. For example, if John does something for Jane and trusts that Jane will reciprocate in the future, there is an expectation of John and an obligation held by Jane to keep the trust (Coleman, 1988).

6. For additional research on the effects of social capital, see Brehm and Rahn (1997), Lappe and Du Bois (1997), and Potapchuck, Crocker, and Schecter (1997).

7. Because official records have not been collected concerning citizen participation, I have relied upon police officer perceptions, which were confirmed by Sergeant McCormick.

8. Although this appears to be a relatively low response rate, a much higher rate could have been achieved with two more waves of data collection. Champion (1993) reports that research projects using mail surveys typically yield an average response rate of 30% for three waves of data collection. In addition, bad addresses were not considered in the final total, consequently the total sample for each area is actually somewhat fewer than 150 households. Incidentally, the lower participation areas held the lowest response rates (28% and 37%), while the higher participation areas had higher response rates (40% and 44%).

REFERENCES

Brady, T. (1996). *Measuring what matters, part one: Measures of crime, fear, and disorder.* Washington, DC: U.S. Department of Justice, Office of Justice Programs, National Institute of Justice.

Brehm, J., & Rahn, W. (1997). Individual-level evidence for the causes and consequences of social capital. *American Journal of Political Science, 41*(3), 999–1023.

Bureau of the Census. (1990). *Social and Economic Characteristics: Iowa.* Washington, DC: U.S. Department of Commerce, Economics, and Statistics Administration, Bureau of the Census.

Bursik, R., & Grasmick, H. (1993). *Neighborhoods and crime: The dimensions of effective community control.* New York: Lexington Books.

Champion, D. (1993). *Research methods for criminal justice and criminology.* Englewood Cliffs, NJ: Prentice Hall.

Coleman, J. (1988). Social capital in the creation of human capital. *American Journal of Sociology, 94*(Suppl.), s95–s120.

Coleman, J. (1990). *Foundations of social theory.* Cambridge, MA: Belknap.

Covington, J., & Taylor, R. (1991). Fear of crime in urban residential neighborhoods: Implications of between-and within-neighborhood sources for current models. *Sociological Quarterly, 32,* 231–249.

Donziger, S. (1996). *The real war on crime: The report of the National Criminal Justice Commission.* New York: HarperCollins.

Evans, P. (1996). Government action, social capital and development: Reviewing the evidence on synergy. *World Development, 24,* 1119–1132.

Friedman, W., & Clark, M. (1997). Measuring what matters, part two: Developing measures of what the police can do. Washington, DC: U.S. Department of Justice, Office of Justice Programs, National Institute of Justice.

Goldstein, H. (1990). *Problem-oriented policing.* New York: McGraw-Hill.

Greenberg, S., & Rohe, W. (1986). Informal social control and crime prevention in modern urban neighborhoods. In R. Taylor (Ed.), *Urban neighborhoods: Research and policy* (pp. 79–122). Westport, CT: Praeger.

Hagan, J., MacMillan, R., & Wheaton, B. (1996). The new kid in town: Social capital and the life course effects of family migration on children. *American Sociological Review, 61,* 368–385.

Hagan, J., Merkens, H., & Boehnke, K. (1995). Delinquency and disdain: Social capital and the control of right-wing extremism among East and West Berlin youth. *American Journal of Sociology, 100*(4), 1028–1052.

Kelling, G. L., & Coles, C. M. (1996). *Fixing broken windows: Restoring order and reducing crime in our communities.* New York: Free Press.

Ladd, E. (1996). The data just don't show erosion of American social capital. *Public Perspective, 7*(4), 1, 5–6.

Lappe, F., & Du Bois, P. (1997). Building social capital without looking backward. *National Civic Review, 86,* 119–128.

Maas, G. (1996, November/December). CAST helps neighborhoods heal. *Community Policing Strategies,* p. 3.

McCormick, Sergeant Mike. (1997, April). Interview by Mark E. Correia.

Miethe, T. (1995). Fear and withdrawal from urban life. *Annals of the American Academy of Political and Social Science, 539,* 14–27

Miller, L., & Whitehead, J. (1996). *Introduction to criminal justice research and statistics.* Cincinnati, OH: Anderson.

Newton, K. (1997). Social capital and democracy. *American Behavioral Scientist, 40,* 575–587.

Oliver, P. (1984). If you don't do it, nobody will: Active and token contributors to local collective action. *American Sociological Review, 49,* 601–610.

Parcel, T., & Menaghan, E. (1993). Family social capital and children's behavior problems. *Social Psychology Quarterly, 56,* 120–135.

Perkins, D. D., Florin, P., Rich, R., Wandersman, A., & Chavis, D. (1990). Participation and the social and physical environment of residential blocks: Crime and community context. *American Journal of Community Psychology, 18,* 83–115.

Potapchuck, W. R., Crocker, J., & Schechter, W. (1997). Building community with social capital: Chits and chums or chats with change. *National Civic Review, 86,* 129–140

Putnam, R. (1993). The prosperous community: Social capital and public life. *American Prospect, 4*(13), 35–42.

Putnam. R. (1995a). Bowling alone: America's declining social capital. *Journal of Democracy, 6*(1), 65–78.

Putnam, R. (1995b, December). Tuning in, tuning out: The strange disappearance of social capital in America. *PS: Political Science and Politics, 28*(4), 664–683.

Putnam, R. (2000). *Bowling alone: The collapse and revival of American community.* New York,: Simon & Schuster.

Sadd, S., & Grinc, R. (1994). Innovative neighborhood orienting policing: An evaluation of community policing programs in eight cities. In D. P. Rosenbaum (Ed.), *The challenge of community policing: Testing the promises* (pp. 27–52). Thousand Oaks, CA: Sage.

Sampson, R. (1995). The community. In J. Wilson & J. Petersilia (Eds.), *Crime* (pp. 193–216). San Francisco: ICS.

Sampson, R., & Groves, B. (1989). Community structure and crime: Testing social-disorganization theory. *American Journal of Sociology, 94*(4), 774–802.

Schneider, M., Teske, P., Marschall, M., Mintrom, M., & Roch, C. (1997). Institutional arrangements and the creation of social capital: The effects of public school choice. *American Political Science Review, 91*, 82–93.

Schoenherr, J. (1996, July 15). Citizens applaud CAST's results. *Sioux City Journal,* pp. A1, A10.

Skogan, W. (1987). The impact of victimization on fear. *Journal of Crime and Delinquency, 33*(1), 135–154.

Skogan, W. (1990). *Disorder and decline: Crime and the spiral of decay in American neighborhoods.* Berkeley, CA: University of California Press.

Skogan, W., & Maxfield, M. (1981). *Coping with crime: Individual and neighborhood reactions.* Beverly Hills, CA: Sage.

Skolnick, J. H., & Bayley, D. H. (1986). *The new blue line: Police innovations in six American cities.* New York: Free Press.

Slovak, J. (1986). Attachments in the nested community: Evidence from a case study. *Urban Affairs Quarterly, 21*, 575–597.

Taylor, R. B., Gottfredson, S. D, & Brower, S. (1984). Block crime and fear: Defensible space, local social ties, and territorial functioning. *Journal of Crime and Delinquency, 21*, 303–331

Taylor, R. B., & Hall, M. (1986). Testing alternative models of fear of crime. *Journal of Criminal Law and Criminology, 77*(1), 151–189.

Taylor, M., & Singleton, S. (1993). The communal resource: Transaction costs and the solution of collective action problems. *Politics and Society, 21*, 195–214.

Trojanowicz, R. C., Kappeler, V. E., Gaines, L. K., Bucqueroux, B. (1998). *Community policing: A contemporary perspective* (2nd ed.). Cincinnati, OH: Anderson.

Unger, D., & Wandersman, A. (1982). Neighboring in an urban environment. *American Journal of Community Psychology, 10*, 493–509.

Unger, D., & Wandersman, A. (1985). The importance of neighbors: The social, cognitive, and affective components of neighboring. *American Journal of Community Psychology, 13*, 139–169.

Wandersman, A., Florin, P., Rich, R., Friedman, R., & Meier, R. (1987). Who participates, who does not, and why? An analysis of voluntary neighborhood organizations in the United States and Israel. *Sociological Forum, 3*, 534–557.

Wilson, J. Q., & Kelling, G. (1982, March). Broken windows: The police and neighborhood safety. *Atlantic Monthly,* pp. 29–38.

Wycoff, M. A., & Skogan, W. G. (1994). Community policing in Madison: An analysis of implementation and impact. In D. P. Rosenbaum (Ed.), *The challenge of community policing: Testing the promises* (pp. 75–91). Thousand Oaks, CA: Sage.

Yankelovich, D. (1994). A conversation about public priorities. *National Civic Review, 83*, 389–399.

Zhao, J. (1996). *Why police organizations change: A study of community oriented policing.* Washington, DC: Police Executive Research Forum.

Zhao, J., Thurman, Q. C., & Lovrich, N. P. (1995). Community-oriented policing across the U.S.: Facilitators and impediments to implementation. *American Journal of Police, 14*(1), 11–28.

Part IV

Dealing With Ongoing Challenges

CHAPTER 12

The Challenge of Effective Organizational Change
Lessons Learned in Community-Policing Implementation

Joseph A. Schafer

> Community policing . . . incorporates a new philosophy that
> broadens the police mission from a narrow focus on crime to a
> mandate that encourages the police to explore creative solutions
> for a host of community concerns, including crime, fear of crime,
> disorder, and neighborhood conditions. Community policing in
> its ideal form, is not merely a means to address community
> concerns, but it is a philosophy that turns traditional policing on
> its head by empowering the community. . . . In this sense
> policing derives it[s] role and agenda from the community rather
> than dictating to the community.
>
> *Trojanowicz, Kappeler, Gaines, & Bucqueroux (1998)*

Over the course of the past decade, commu-
nity policing has been one of the most dominant innovations in American policing. From our nation's largest police force (the New York City
Police Department [NYPD]) to rural forces employing one or two offi-

AUTHOR'S NOTE: This project was supported under award number 95-IJ-CX-0093
(S-1) from the National Institute of Justice, Office of Justice Programs, U.S. Department
of Justice. Points of view in this document are those of the author and do not necessarily
represent the official position of the U.S. Department of Justice.

cers, agencies across the country have attempted to embrace this new philosophy of policing. The subject of thousands of media accounts, hundreds of research studies, and millions of federal grant dollars, it has redefined the expectations many citizens have of their local police.

As Trojanowicz, Kappeler, Gaines, & Bucqueroux (1998) indicate in one of the seminal texts on the subject, community policing is more than just a program. In its idealized form, community policing fundamentally transforms how police officers and organizations operate. It should not be a mere program, but rather a philosophy that influences all aspects of policing. Many American police departments have attempted to implement some form of community policing. Federal grants have enabled departments across the country to hire additional officers to support community-policing efforts. Some organizations have even attempted to embrace community policing fully as a philosophy by requiring that all employees involve themselves in community-policing activities.

The transition away from traditional policing operations and strategies is not an easy process. This chapter first explores the challenges of bringing about change in organizations, with a specific focus on police agencies. It then focuses on the attempt made by a medium-size police organization seeking to make the transition from a specialized to a generalized model of community policing. The barriers encountered by this agency are presented in the form of lessons learned, to serve as a tool for other police organizations seeking to implement community policing. Based upon this agency's experiences, it is possible to identify certain key issues that agencies must understand, clarify, and overcome in order to improve the success of their innovations.

IMPEDIMENTS TO ORGANIZATIONAL CHANGE

Two categories of factors impede planned change within organizations in general: organizational issues and human issues. Organizational issues (planning, clarity, resources, etc.) are those factors that impede successful change because of the way in which such change was planned and/or implemented. Human issues (culture, politics, employee-management tension, etc.) are factors that involve the actual employees of an organization. These human factors may impede organizational change regardless of how the change is implemented and independently of the nature and form of the change. Failure to realize a change in a structure, a program, or a policy within a police agency is most likely the result of some combination of human and organizational factors. Having a basic understanding of their core elements helps explain why the change process is difficult in organizations of all shapes, sizes, and forms. The following discussion provides a brief introduction to selected core organizational and human issues that are related to change.

Organizational Issues

Community policing alters how police agencies are structured, how officers perform their duties, and how police employees relate with one another. This departure from the traditional manner in which agencies functioned may result in confusion and uncertainty among those most affected by change. If police leaders and planners expect to achieve success in implementing community policing, they must first identify, clarify, and overcome such problems. Of course, failing to address and resolve these issues will not automatically result in a failed implementation effort. Conversely, even if organizations do attempt to address these issues, they may still impede the successful implementation of community policing.

Planning and Clarity. Police agencies have assigned varying operational definitions to the term *community policing.* Consequently, police officers may be unsure exactly what it means to do community policing. The loose definition of community policing is an asset, because it allows agencies to determine how best to apply this concept within their organizational and community context (Trojanowicz et al., 1998). The amorphous nature of the philosophy does, however, create an additional burden that must not be overlooked by police leaders. In making the transition away from traditional policing, agencies must be explicit in defining what community policing means within their organization and describing how officers would perform their duties in a manner consistent with this philosophy.

When an administrator announces that a department is adopting community policing, employees in that organization may be uncertain what such an adoption entails and how they will need to alter the way in which they perform their duties. It is also frequently the case that, throughout transitional periods for organizations, police at all levels lack a clear understanding of the new role called for by community policing (Skogan & Hartnett, 1997). Officers working in community-policing environments are often critical of the organization for failing to clarify the mission, goals, and objectives of innovation. Officers consistently reflect little understanding of the goals and means associated with community-policing innovations; this lack of understanding may result in resistance as officers struggle to understand exactly what they are supposed to be doing (Sadd & Grinc, 1994). Confusion over new goals and means is common in the context of a changing organization (Trojanowicz et al., 1998); problems arise when goals and means are not ultimately clarified.

Research literature from the past 15 years is replete with anecdotal examples of successful organizational change in police agencies in major American cities (Eck & Spelman, 1987; Skogan & Hartnett, 1997; Skolnick & Bayley, 1986; Wycoff & Skogan, 1994). Despite these successes, it would seem that they are the exception, not the rule, in implementing community policing. Many attempts at implementing community policing have been characterized by poor planning, unclear goals and objectives, internal resistance to change, and inadequate financial resources (see, generally, Greene & Mastrofski, 1988; Rosenbaum, 1994). A common complaint heard from patrol officers in agencies attempting to implement some form of community policing is that their organization had not been sufficiently clear about the nature of their new job, how they would be evaluated, to whom they were accountable, and how they would carry out their duties (Sadd & Grinc, 1994). If agencies fail to be explicitly clear on these core issues, an attempt to implement community policing runs the risk of failing in its infancy.

Accountability, Evaluations, and Performance Measures. As public employees, police officers have always been accountable for what they do and what they produce. The traditional bureaucratic model of police organizations removed accountability from political influence and vested it within the police agency (Walker, 1977). Under this former hierarchical structure, each employee was held accountable to his or her immediate supervisor; for the average patrol officer, accountability started with the patrol sergeant. Employee evaluations were based on measures that could be computed quickly and easily. Typically, officers were given numerical ratings that assessed their quantitative performance (e.g., citations issued, arrests made, calls for service handled), their demeanor and appearance, their ability to follow orders, and their compliance with policies and procedures.

Organizations implementing community policing will find that traditional accountability patterns and evaluation techniques are no longer sufficient to meet their changing needs. Because it requires community partnership, accountability under community policing is more complex than it has traditionally been in policing (Trojanowicz et al., 1998). Community policing requires that police officers and organizations take on a level of accountability to the public; greater consideration is given to incorporating the community in the process of formulating policy and plans of action (More, 1998). This dual accountability to the organization and the community presents a challenge as agencies attempt to identify broader performance measures to assess productivity of their officers.

Agencies adopting community policing must refine their performance measures and develop ways to reward officers who are performing in a manner consistent with the organization's new goals. Redesigning performance measures not only involves rethinking what matters within an organization, but also involves various legal and contractual issues (Skogan & Hartnett, 1997). Well-designed performance evaluations may be critical to the success of community-policing programs, because they help guide employees toward a better understanding of the new organizational goals (Moore & Stephens, 1991). In the absence of a performance evaluation system linked to these new goals, agencies cannot expect to achieve widespread success with community-policing programs.

Community Policing as a Specialist Versus a Generalist Function. In planning the transition to community policing, police administrators must resolve whether community policing will be performed as a specialist or generalist function. There are advantages and disadvantages to each approach. As a specialist function, a select group of employees within the organization carry out community policing; as a generalized function, all employees are expected to adopt an organization's community-policing philosophy. When community policing is a specialist function, it may be easier to monitor designated officers and to ensure accountability for problems in particular areas. Specialization may also serve as a stepping stone as organizations make the transition from traditional to community policing. Alternatively, specialization reduces communication and removes officers from the rest of the organization. This, in turn, may lead to an us-versus-them mentality or to the perception that only specialists need to solve problems, listen to the community, and think proactively (Eck, 1992; Sadd & Grinc, 1994).

Community policing as a general responsibility is more congruent with the notion that community policing is a philosophy (performed by all), not a program (performed by a few) (Gaines, 1994; Trojanowicz et al., 1998). The greatest challenge agencies face in generalized community policing are balancing traditional demands (i.e., calls for service) with new demands (i.e., problem solving and community obligations; Kennedy, 1993), ensuring accountability and responsibility, determining how to structure and deploy officers, and providing sufficient training and resources. Generalization of community-policing responsibilities can also result in problems as agencies try to teach an old dog new tricks by attempting to train traditional law-and-order followers to become innovative free thinkers.

Balancing Demands and Obligations. Change often results in new demands on resources (e.g., money, equipment, and personnel) and new obligations that an organization must fulfill; the transition to community policing is not an exception to this rule. In many situations, an organization may initiate a change in the form of a new program or service that it is offering. It would be common for such a change to be made without a significant adjustment to the organization's budget or level of resources. The problem with this scenario, as Lipsky (1980) notes, is that demand often rises to meet availability. Lipsky illustrates this point by using an example from the history of the NYPD. When the NYPD introduced its 911 system, the organization soon found that consumer demand was greater than the department's ability to receive and handle calls for service from the public.

Following Lipsky's (1980) example, it is conceivable that adopting community policing would *increase* the demands placed on police agencies. As ties between the police and the public are strengthened, community residents may be more likely to call the police to resolve minor problems. With an increase in the frequency of their contact with the police, citizens have more opportunities to report their concerns. As community policing spreads in a neighborhood, the police assume responsibility for a broader range of services and duties. In the end, even though crime may decline and quality of life increase, the police may still find that they are doing more "stuff" than they had done prior to adopting a community-policing philosophy.

Unions. Though police unionization is not universal, where unions are present, they pose a significant force that organizations must deal with when planning change. As noted by Polzin and Brockman (Chapter 8), police unions have a tremendous impact on the efficacy of organizational change. One way to ensure program failure is to exclude unions from the planning process and to give no attention to whether or not a proposed change is consistent with the union contract (Skogan & Hartnett, 1997). Unions are adamantly opposed to certain forms of change. For example, communities attempting to implement civilian review boards often face tough opposition from the local police union (Swanson, Territo, & Taylor, 1998). In contrast, when they are involved in the planning process, police unions can be a driving force assisting organizations in initiating change and securing officer support (Skogan & Hartnett, 1997).

By taking a joint labor-management approach to the development of organizational change, it is possible for police agencies to achieve greater success (Polzin, 1998). Unfortunately, labor-management relations are more often characterized by distrust and hostility (Guyot, 1991; More, 1998). As noted by Polzin (1998) in an earlier paper,

> Community policing is a process of organizational change that is most effective when it has the commitment and involvement of its key stakeholders. Employees are the stakeholder group most critical to the initiative's success. Unionized police departments have a unique opportunity to make the use of the workforce's knowledge and expertise through the collective voice of the union. A joint labor-management committee using a systematic approach . . . offers the greatest opportunity for community policing success.

Working closely with unions allows police executives to develop good relationships, to implement their policies, and to create organizational change (Hewitt, 1978).

Human Issues

Agencies seeking to bring about organizational change must do more than simply modify their policies, procedures, structures, and operations. Implementation planning must also incorporate the needs and motivations of those employees who will be affected by a change. Ignoring the human factor in the change process is to risk failure. In implementing community policing, planners and administrators must be aware of issues related to the needs, perceptions, and desires of their employees, and how these factors might ameliorate new initiatives.

Employee Attitude. Some scholars feel that employee attitudes and the organizational culture are the greatest obstacle to police innovation

(Sparrow, Moore, & Kennedy, 1990). Police officers tend to view organizational change with a healthy dose of skepticism. Management strategies, organizational structures, and department philosophies seem to come and go like the tides; officers with more tenure are likely to have picked up on such trends. It is common for officers to label community policing as the "management reorganization of the week" (Sadd & Grinc, 1994, p. 39). Given this labeling, many officers see community policing as another phase that management is going through and that will pass with time; its implementation is not taken seriously.

Because of the structure of community-policing units, the distribution of community-policing responsibilities, and the lack of understanding over community-policing goals, it is common for officers to view these programs with distrust. When community policing is conducted through a specialized unit, such units are seen as elite and as engaging in tasks other than real police work (Eck, 1992). Specialized units often grant officers the ability to flex their work hours, select their days off, and work at their own direction without being interrupted by routine calls for service (Wilkinson & Rosenbaum, 1994). Given this arrangement, officers perceive community policing as a "fluff" assignment; the units are viewed with disdain or even with jealousy by other officers within the organizations.

Perception of Change as a Threat. It is a common human reaction to seek the preservation of the *status quo.* We attempt to avoid that which we believe might alter how we are used to living our lives, doing our jobs, and relating with others. Although there is a constant state of flux in some organizations, it is typical for employees to make attempts at preserving this *status quo.* Employees might fear and avoid potential change, whether it is for better or worse (Barkdoll, 1998). In the context of community policing, experience has shown that officers tend to dislike this innovation and avoid altering their behavior.

This resistance to change is separate from employee attitudes and perceptions of the proposed alterations; it is not just that officers tend to resist the principals of community policing (which some do), but some officers resist any change to traditional policing (Sadd & Grinc, 1994). The nature of community policing might lead an organization to flatten its hierarchy and to decrease specialized assignments. Thus, some officers view the transition to community policing as a threat to their future prospects for promotion (Weisel & Eck, 1994) and/or special duty assignments. Research on the efficacy of team policing indicated that one reason for the failure of such programs was that supervisory and middle-level managers felt that team policing reduced their power and control; as a result, passive and active sabotage efforts were not uncommon (Gaines, 1994; Walker, 1993; also, see Chapter 6). Analogous situations may arise in agencies implementing community policing if employees believe that this innovation may hinder their power and control.

Tension Between Labor and Management. Currently, a key objective of most organizational innovations is to reduce tension between managers and line-level employees (Moorhead & Griffin, 1998). Such innovations seek to improve relationships, to foster a sense of teamwork, and to solicit line-level input for upper-level decision making. Police departments have historically been characterized by a chasm between street cops and management cops (Reuss-Ianni & Ianni, 1983). This chasm can lead to several problems as departments seek to implement community policing.

First, line officers may automatically view any management innovation, program, or plan with distrust simply because of its source. Second, community policing requires that power be shared within an organization as officers, managers, and citizens work cooperatively to set the police agenda (Trojanowicz et al., 1998), turning the traditional officer-supervisor relationship on its head. Third, unless supervisors are willing to close the chasm and remit some of their power to ensure this relationship, the attempted implementation may fail prematurely. These problems illuminate how community policing may challenge the traditional way in which both supervisors and officers have understood their responsibilities, their relationships, and their positions within the organizations.

A CASE STUDY OF COMMUNITY POLICING IN MOTOR CITY

This section focuses on an actual case example of a police department moving to a transformational change to community policing. The history behind the move is presented, followed by an analysis of what happened within the department and community during one phase of the change. Lessons learned from observing the department are then presented.

Historical Perspective

The Motor City Police Department (MCPD) began its community-policing initiative in October of 1990.[1] At that time, a number of inner-city neighborhoods were experiencing problems with crack cocaine. The selling of crack took place largely from open-air markets that had a disruptive and disturbing effect on community residents. Top MCPD leaders determined that it would deploy officers to work directly with community residents in developing and implementing solutions to this problem. These efforts were initially tested in two small beats. After experiencing early success, the program was expanded as a specialized unit. The size of the unit grew to 7 officers and a sergeant in 1991, then to 12 officers, a sergeant, and a lieutenant in 1992.

Officers in the community policing unit were assigned to work in small subsectors of patrol beats. The department funded some Community Policing Officers (CPOs) at its own expense and some with a grant. The original purpose of this unit was reflected in the department's 1992 Annual Report: From an examination of the MCPD Annual Reports and from interviews with police personnel, it was clear that

> the unit's short term goal of disrupting and reducing street-level drug dealing and criminal offenses, along with the long-term goal of making neighborhoods and communities safer and more crime resistant, continue to be it's primary focus. In addition to these goals, officers act as facilitators for bringing a variety of other services into the neighborhoods for the purpose of improving citizen knowledge and accessibility to those services.

By late 1992, the community was becoming increasingly aware of the efforts of the community policing unit. The department experienced an increased demand for the assignment of CPOs into additional neighborhoods.

After four years of pursuing this specialized approach to community policing, it became apparent to department administrators that many changes were needed. There was also a growing split between the patrol division and the community policing unit. Typical of departments the size of Motor City's, the agency was organized around a central police headquarters, from which all activities were directed. Communication patterns were up and down the chain of command;

requests for information went through formal channels. Decision making was highly centralized and formalized. Motor City citizens and top police leaders felt the department was too far removed from the community it served.

Department and city leaders were committed to a community-policing strategy, and believed that all personnel should be engaged in these activities. The department had anecdotal evidence that the CPOs were effective and efficient in cleaning up their assigned neighborhoods. At the same time, problems were migrating out of CPO neighborhoods and into neighborhoods that had previously been safe and quiet. In addition, the specialized nature of community policing in the agency isolated CPOs from the remainder of the officers. The department's administration began to realize that community policing could not just be delegated to specialists if it was to be an effective way to address problems of crime and order.

In response to this realization, the chief launched an effort to reorganize the department and to redefine the role of MCPD officers in the community. A Reorganization Committee, consisting of officers and supervisors below the rank of lieutenant, was formed to develop a plan for realigning the agency so that all officers were working together to target community problems. Efforts were made to keep the committee's activities in the spotlight, and representatives of the patrol officer's union and civilian staff were committee members. Based upon the committee's recommendations, the chief ultimately selected a plan to give patrol officers temporal and geographic responsibilities, and to strengthen ties between the detectives bureau and the patrol division.

The strategy gave all patrol officers responsibilities as problem-solving generalists, though some officers continued to serve as CPO specialists. Patrol officers would still have responsibilities for handling calls in an assigned geographic area during their shift, but they were also expected to solve long-term neighborhood problems in this area. These solutions were the collective effort of a team of the patrol officers and detectives who policed a given area around the clock.[2] In other words, officers handled the immediate problems that occurred in their area during their shift (temporal responsibilities) while working to address long-term problems that might occur in this area at any time of the day (geographic responsibilities).

The purpose of MCPD's reorganization was to remove structural obstacles to the effective and complete implementation of a community-oriented policing philosophy. The reorganization plan was based upon a new strategy of taking a team approach to community policing.

The plan specified that the department was to be divided into two precincts, North and South, each covering approximately half of the city. Each of the precincts were further subdivided into 10 patrol districts, or team areas, for a total of 20 team areas citywide (previously, the city had been divided into 14 such patrol districts).

Each patrol district was placed under the direction of a sergeant from the patrol division. The sergeant oversaw a team of four to seven officers from the patrol, traffic, and K-9 divisions. Some teams also included CPOs who were assigned to a small section of the team area. Patrol officers were responsible for providing primary law enforcement services for their team areas during their hours of duty. Under the supervision of their sergeant, each team identified and targeted team-specific problems that needed to be solved. Officers worked closely with neighborhood organizations and tried to attend their regular meetings to facilitate communication and understanding. Each sergeant had a small annual allotment of overtime to allow team members to work on problems outside of their regular duty hours. All other problem solving had to take place within the restrictions of an officer's routine shift.

The reorganization plan represented a major shift in the approach the MCPD was taking toward community policing. Problem-solving activities were no longer limited to those officers holding CPO assignments and the small areas they policed, but were department- and citywide. Top department leaders hoped that the team approach would capitalize on the strengths of task specialization (e.g., strong bonds with the community) without costs, such as the alienation of generalists from specialists and the marginalization of specialists from the core functions of policing. Other aims were to provide better service to the community and to improve work experiences for police officers. Management believed that the MCPD's success in integrating specialists (CPOs) with generalists (patrol officers) depended upon convincing personnel in all units of the interrelatedness and interdependency of specialized and generalized operations.

Evaluating the MCPD Model

In the early phases of the reorganization, an ongoing research partnership was established between the MCPD and the School of Criminal Justice (SCJ) at Michigan State University. A project team was formed consisting of four SCJ faculty members, selected managers from the patrol division, and a graduate research assistant. The department would be able to capitalize on the knowledge and experiences of the SCJ faculty. The SCJ was intrigued by the department's new direction, and wished to explore the experiences and opinions of those most affected by the change (i.e., rank-and-file officers and firstline supervisors).

The aim of the collaboration was to provide insights into how officers experienced the transition to a generalized approach to community policing. A corollary goal was to develop a better understanding of how police organizations might more effectively plan for and implement this alternative policing philosophy. The project team spent two years assessing the status of the reorganization as it progressed. The team was able to develop a rapport with department personnel, and team members were generally viewed as being unthreatening. Ultimately, the project team conducted dozens of interviews and focus groups, surveyed all officers and firstline supervisors in the patrol division, surveyed over 2,000 community residents, and conducted several hundreds of hours of systematic field observations. These research findings provide a comprehensive picture of how the change process was experienced in this organization.

This evaluative study clearly indicated that the steps the department had taken to study, plan for, and implement a new organizational structure and philosophy were insufficient to bring about the desired changes in officers' attitudes and behaviors. For a variety of reasons, restructuring the agency did not dramatically alter how officers performed their duties. The department did not begin their reorganization with clearly articulated goals, making it difficult accurately to assess whether the change effort was successful. Early in the evaluation process, department leaders conceded that their efforts were not achieving their desired outcomes. Given this situation, the evaluation team did not focus on evaluating how the organizational change affected crime or order in Motor City. Instead, they attempted to understand how the change process was experienced by patrol officers and what this experience might tell the department about how to alter their efforts in order to realize successful change in the future.

Despite the good intentions of department leaders and planners, the change to a generalized model of community policing was not well received in the organization. In both interviews and survey data, officers indicated dissatisfaction with their general work environment and their relationship with their supervisors. Officers felt the department had not done enough to clarify how they were to function under the reorganized structure and how the change altered the agency's values and goals. They felt that they no longer knew what mattered within the organization and were not clear on what behaviors were valued by the organization. The temporal and geographic nature of the new structure created competing demands that were difficult for officers and supervisors to resolve.

A key point of contention among survey respondents related to the resources available to team officers under the reorganized structure. It was commonly believed that there were not enough officers to provide even basic policing services in the community, making extracurricular team-based problem solving nearly impossible. Analysis of data collected through both interviews and observations showed that, in fact, officers spent much of their on-duty time handling calls for service outside of their assigned beat. The lack of funding to pay officers to engage in problem solving during their off-duty time, coupled with the small amount of on-duty free time at their disposal, made it difficult for the teams to pursue problem-solving objectives. In addition, there was a strong concern that officers lacked the resources, skills, and training to be effective in bringing about positive long-term change in their assigned team area.

Officers held mixed views about community policing as a philosophy. During interviews, officers typically claimed that they supported the *philosophy* of community policing, but were concerned with how it was instituted in Motor City. There were, however, a number of officers who disliked community policing as a whole; one third of the officers felt that the department should not be engaged in any form of community policing. Despite this strong resistance, most officers did believe there were merits to community policing, but maintained it should be a specialized rather than a generalized function. Input from community residents reflected a very high degree of support for tenets of community policing, supporting the department's decision to pursue the reorganization and its associated objectives.

Further analysis of the evaluation data revealed the beliefs, perceptions, and attitudes of those officers most affected by the reorganization (Schafer, 2000). Though overall support for community policing was weak, survey data indicated that female officers, supervisors, or those who had experience as a CPO held more positive attitudes about this philosophy than others did. Those who expressed more positive attitudes toward labor-management relations in the department tended to be more supportive of the reorganization efforts. In addition, officers who supported the overall philosophy of community policing believed the department should continue to use a generalized approach. In addition to findings from the quantitative analysis, qualitative research findings also offer critical insights into why Motor City's reorganization efforts were not entirely successful during the research period. The balance of this chapter discusses these research findings in the context of lessons learned about creating generalized community policing within a medium-size police organization.

Lessons Learned

The Motor City experience provides several important lessons for agencies seeking to implement community policing, particularly in a generalized form. The following is not meant to be an exhaustive list of challenges to be overcome and obstacles to be cleared; rather, it serves as a starting point for agencies seeking to implement some form of community policing.

Lesson 1: Clarity. Despite all of the planning and training invested in the reorganization process, the MCPD still failed to clarify how officers were to operate under the reorganized structure. Perhaps more than any other factor, the lack of clarity posed a problem for those affected by the change. Although some employees understood what was expected of them under the generalized community-policing initiative, even at the end of the research project most officers lacked a clear understanding of the department's new goals, objectives, means, and structure. Though some administrators believed that sufficient clarity had been provided, frontline personnel and supervisors did not share this view. In the absence of a collective understanding of what the reorganization meant, the department was unable to garner strong support for the new structure from the rank and file.

Lesson 2: Officer Accountability. Department planners considered how generalized community policing would change the department, but officer accountability was not adjusted. Despite the fact that officers were expected to perform certain duties for the sake of their team areas, there was no system for evaluating such conduct. A few officers actively resisted the reorganization by refusing to communicate with their team members (voice mail was a common mode of communication within the teams) and avoiding any work involving other members of their team. In the absence of any accountability measures, team sergeants lacked the means to bring these officers on board with the reorganization. Evaluation forms still graded officers in terms of traditional police performance measures. Under a community-policing philosophy, officers are expected to engage in a variety of duties, only some of which are captured with more traditional evaluation tools.

Lesson 3: Supervisor Accountability. In the Motor City experience, there was an accountability gap between precinct captains and patrol officers. Though sergeants were assigned to supervise a designated team (as well as supervising officers on their assigned shift), they were only minimally accountable for improving the quality of life in this geographic area. Lieutenants had some powers to maintain accountability, but their position had been made largely administrative by the reorganization. The net result was wide variation in how teams operated. Some teams were very proactive and involved in quality-of-life issues in their neighborhoods; others were not. In virtually every case, the sergeant set the tone for the productivity of a team. The process of planning and implementing generalized community policing overlooked how sergeants acted as a linchpin between administration and the frontline officers. They remained an untapped resource with the capacity to help the department achieve greater success in the reorganization.

Lesson 4: Training. Despite administrative protestations that sufficient training had been provided, most officers felt they lacked the skills necessary to solve community problems. Half of the officers reported having received no formal training in problem identification and resolution. The department had a tremendous wealth of internal knowledge in the form of patrol officers and sergeants who had served as some of the early CPOs. These former CPOs had experienced strong success in their early endeavors, but were never given the opportunity to pass their knowledge on to other officers. In addition, the department was undergoing a significant shift as Vietnam-era personnel retired; an influx of new personnel had little knowledge of the department's prior efforts. The majority of the officers lacked current training on problem-solving techniques and community-policing strategies. Lacking skills to perform their duties in a community-policing context officers tend to revert to familiar policing tactics (i.e., traditional approaches). In Motor City, this reversion minimized the amount of community-policing activities that were actually occurring in the community.

Lesson 5: Resources. The high retirement rate resulted in a long-term staffing shortage as the department struggled to hire, train, and retain new officers. At the same time, whenever a new unit was created within the organization, there was a long-standing practice of taking the personnel for the unit from the patrol division, resulting in a patrol division that was permanently 15 to 25 officers below its staffing level. Consequently, patrol officers often spent much of their time responding to calls throughout their precinct rather than focusing their undirected patrol time within their team area. Officers routinely spent only one third to one half of their shift in their assigned team area. Officers had a great deal of difficulty finding time to engage in problem solving or other team business during their routine working hours.

Lesson 6: Balancing Responsibilities. Under the reorganization plan, patrol officers and patrol sergeants were left in a precarious position. They had to struggle to balance their obligations to their team (i.e., geographic responsibilities) with their obligations to their designated shift (i.e., temporal responsibilities). In light of the aforementioned resource limitations, officers were torn between pleasing their shift sergeants by promptly handling calls for service and pleasing their team sergeants by addressing long-term quality-of-life issues. In many instances, fulfilling temporal responsibilities to assist the shift sergeant, who granted requests for vacation and personal days, was given a higher priority. This tendency was exacerbated by the immediacy of emergency calls for service and the need to provide sufficient backup for officers responding to high-risk calls.

Lesson 7: Best Practices. Despite problems reviewed in this chapter, the MCPD did experience some gratifying successes through the team system. Neighborhood problems were addressed, community groups became empowered, and bridges were built between the police and citizens. Unfortunately, these successes often did not receive sufficient attention and did not become models for best practices. If the department had worked harder to record successful problem-solving efforts, these successful efforts might have served as a starting point for other teams confronting similar problems. By creating and effectively disseminating a catalog of resources and strategies, the department could have increased the efficiency of subsequent problem-solving efforts, compounding their overall success with community-policing efforts in Motor City.

Lesson 8: Interagency Cooperation. For nearly a decade, the MCPD had been struggling to improve the services it provides to the community. Unfortunately, they have found that other governmental and social service providers were not always interested in collaborating to improve the quality of life in the community. Often, other government agencies were not prepared to act as partners in proactive problem-solving efforts. MCPD officers indicated that broader problem-solving success might have been realized if the employees of these other agencies had been willing and able to assist in problem-solving endeavors. Some officers raised the fundamental question of whether the police are properly trained and equipped to spearhead community transformation.

Lesson 9: Unions.   In police organizations with strong unions, managers must be constantly cognizant of the support (or lack there of) that their proposed change may receive from labor representatives. Without such support, planned change may fail. The MCPD was able to secure union support in letter, but not in spirit. The union consented to the reorganization on the condition that the department converted to 10-hour shifts (i.e., to a 4-day workweek). Department leaders never worked with union leaders in an effort to demonstrate why the reorganization was good for the agency and its employees. In a sense, though the union did not resist the change efforts (in order to secure a perceived benefit for its members), it also did not endorse generalized community policing. By enlisting union support for their plans, top leaders might have been able to secure more support from members of the rank and file. The implementation and acceptance of the change might have been more successful if the union had been a vocal advocate of the reorganization.

Lesson 10: Communication.   Despite the use of voice-mail technology, communication was still a crucial problem in the MCPD. Employees felt there was a lack of communication between and within the teams. Even with overlapping shifts, officers still felt disconnected from personnel working other shifts. With the two-precinct system, dispatching was divided into two separate radio frequencies. As a result, officers complained that they found out about major crimes in the other precinct by watching the evening news. The communication problem was also acute for patrol sergeants. Sergeants were expected to provide effective supervision over the problem-solving efforts of personnel with whom they usually had infrequent contact. Although technology was introduced to facilitate communication, the organization's culture did not embrace this technology as an innovation that might improve communication within the agency.

CONCLUSION

It must be emphasized that, although the MCPD encountered many internal problems in attempting to generalize community-policing operations, their efforts to bring about change were somewhat successful. Quality-of-life issues were identified and addressed, neighborhood ties were strengthened, and many citizens saw that their police department cared. From the perspective of the public, the adoption of generalized community policing improved many neighborhoods in Motor City. The public was largely unaware of the internal problems and conflicts generated by the reorganization of the department. Although department leaders were not satisfied with the level of community policing and problem solving within the organization, members of the community appeared to be content.

Organizational development is a complex endeavor. Bringing about change in an organization requires more than simply reallocating personnel and changing written policies and procedures. Other portions of this book have described strategies that leaders may use to overcome resistance to change within their organizations (see Chapters 7 and 8). This chapter has addressed these issues within the context of implementing community policing using the experiences of a specific police organization. When police planners and leaders are contemplating ways in which they might transform their organizations, they must be cognizant of the fact that such change is difficult to realize. Valuable lessons may be learned from the experiences of other organizations that have attempted various forms of large- and small-scale change. More recently, the Internet has allowed police agencies to share their experiences in attempting to implement various forms of community policing.[3]

When organizations seek to bring about change, there are basic issues that must be addressed and resolved if such efforts are to be successful. This chapter, and others in this book, presented a myriad of issues that must be addressed by leaders if they wish to enhance the possibility of successfully changing their organization's structure and/or culture. The range of issues discussed is not comprehensive; however, these issues are common considerations that leaders must confront in the process of initiating change. At times, trying to resolve one of these issues might first require the resolution of several other issues; such is the nature of organizational change and development.

The key lesson learned from the MCPD experience is that achieving organizational change is a feasible goal; however, it requires planning, forethought, flexibility, assessment, and constant fine-tuning.

NOTES

1. Motor City is a medium-size Midwestern community that is a part of a larger metropolitan area consisting of approximately 300,000 residents. Its economic base is a mix of blue-collar production positions (primarily in the auto industry) and white-collar business, education, and government positions. The police department employs over 200 sworn officers.

2. Despite the use of the term *team* and the combination of patrol and investigative personnel, the MCPD plan should not be confused with team policing. The department's plan was designed to maximize communication and enhance community service through *proactive* policing techniques.

3. For example, the Regional Community Policing Institutes at Michigan State University and Wichita State University both have Web sites that allow users to post their experiences and best practices. The Community Policing Consortium Web site (www.comunitypolicing.org) links users to a database cataloging problem-solving resources and experiences.

REFERENCES

Barkdoll, G. L. (1998, August 15). Individual personality and organizational culture: Or let's change this place so I feel more comfortable. *Public Administration and Management: An Interactive Journal, 3* [Online]. Retrieved August 30, 2001, from www.hbg.psu.edu/Faculty/jxr11/barkdoll. html.

Eck, J. E. (1992, June). Helpful hints for the tradition-bound chief. *Fresh Perspectives,* pp. 1–8.

Eck, J. E., & Spelman, W. (with Hill, D., Stephens, D. W., Stedman, J. R., & Murphy, G. R.). (1987). *Problem-solving: Problem-oriented policing in Newport News.* Washington, DC: Police Executive Research Forum.

Gaines, L. (1994). Community-oriented policing: Management issues, concerns, and problems. *Journal of Contemporary Criminal Justice, 10*(1), 17–35.

Greene, J. R., & Mastrofski, S. D. (Eds.). (1988). *Community policing: Rhetoric or reality.* New York: Praeger.

Guyot, D. (1991). *Policing as though people matter.* Philadelphia: Temple University Press.

Hewitt, W. H., Sr. (1978). Current issues in police collective bargaining. In A. W. Cohn (Ed.), *The future of policing* (pp. 205–223). Beverly Hills, CA: Sage.

Kennedy, D. M. (1993). *Perspectives on policing (no. 14): The strategic management of police resources* (NCJ 139565). Washington, DC: U.S. Department of Justice.

Lipsky, M. (1980). *Street-level bureaucracy: Dilemmas of the individual in public services.* New York: Russell Sage.

Moore, M. H., & Stephens, D. W. (1991). *Beyond command and control: The strategic management of police departments.* Washington, DC: Police Executive Research Forum.

Moorhead, G., & Griffin, R. W. (1998). *Organizational behavior: Managing people and organizations* (5th ed.). Boston: Houghton Mifflin.

More, H. W. (1998). *Special topics in policing* (2nd ed.). Cincinnati, OH: Anderson.

Polzin, M. J. (1998, October 12). *A labor-management approach to community policing* [Online]. Retrieved August 30, 2001, from www.cj.msu.edu/~outreach/cp/labman.html.

Reuss-Ianni, E., & Ianni, F. A. J. (1983). Street cops and management cops: The two cultures of policing. In M. Punch (Ed.), *Control in the Police Organization* (pp. 251–274). Cambridge, MA: MIT Press.

Rosenbaum, D. P. (Ed.). (1994). *The challenge of community policing: Testing the promises*. Thousand Oaks, CA: Sage.

Sadd, S., & Grinc, R. (1994). Innovative neighborhood oriented policing: An evaluation of community policing in eight communities. In D. P. Rosenbaum (Ed.), *The challenge of community policing: Testing the promises* (pp. 27–52). Thousand Oaks, CA: Sage.

Schafer, J. A. (2000). *The challenges of implementing successful organization change: A study of community policing.* Unpublished doctoral dissertation, Michigan State University.

Skogan, W. G., & Hartnett, S. M. (1997). *Community policing, Chicago style.* New York: Oxford University Press.

Skolnick, J. H., & Bayley, D. H. (1986). *The new blue line: Police innovation in six American cities.* New York: Macmillan.

Sparrow, M. K., Moore, M. H., & Kennedy, D. M. (1990). *Beyond 911: A new era for policing.* New York: Basic Books.

Swanson, C. R., Territo, L., & Taylor, R. W. (1998). *Police administration: Structures, processes, and behavior* (4th ed.). Upper Saddle River, NJ: Prentice Hall.

Trojanowicz, R. C., Kappeler, V. E., Gaines, L. K., Bucqueroux, B. (1998). *Community policing: A contemporary perspective* (2nd ed.). Cincinnati, OH: Anderson.

Walker, S. (1977). *A critical history of police reform.* Lexington, MA: D. C. Heath.

Walker, S. (1993). Does anyone remember team policing? Lessons of the team policing experience for community policing. *American Journal of Police, 12*(1), 33–55.

Weisel, D. L., & Eck, J. E. (1994). Toward a practical approach to organizational change: Community policing initiatives in six cities. In D. P. Rosenbaum (Ed.), *The challenge of community policing: Testing the promises* (pp. 53–72). Thousand Oaks, CA: Sage.

Wilkinson, D. L., & Rosenbaum, D. P. (1994). The effects of organizational structure on community policing: A comparison of two cities. In D. P. Rosenbaum (Ed.), *The challenge of community policing: Testing the promises* (pp. 110–126). Thousand Oaks, CA: Sage.

Wycoff, M. A., & Skogan, W. G. (1994). Community policing in Madison: An analysis of implementation and impact. In D. P. Rosenbaum (Ed.), *The challenge of community policing: Testing the promises* (pp. 75–91). Thousand Oaks, CA: Sage.

CHAPTER 13

Reflections on the Move to Community Policing

David L. Carter

*T*his chapter considers bits and pieces of history, theory, and practice that are either superficially addressed or ignored in the debate about the community-policing strategy. Essentially, the discussion has two roots. First, the discussion centers on a combination of my collective observations over the last 20-plus years in policing and academe. Second, I revisit some milestones of policing practice that have somehow "fallen through the cracks" of the legacy that led to community policing.

DEVELOPING A PERSPECTIVE

By pure serendipity, I had the fortune of being associated with policing during some critical junctures. Starting my career in Kansas City, Missouri, I was a police officer while the Police Foundation Task Forces were experimenting with alternate patrol models. Under the leadership of the late Clarence Kelly, the Kansas City Police Department (KCPD) was aggressively conducting experimental research. Together, researchers from the Police Foundation and KCPD officers worked in developing concepts, taking the best ideas and translating them to operational plans, implementing the plans as independent variables in patrol operations, and then evaluating the results.

The process alone was instructional. First, contrary to conventional wisdom in the early 1970s, police officers and researchers produced a creative team approach in developing and testing concepts that were nontraditional. Second, it became apparent that experimental research could be effectively performed in a police agency without posing undue threats to public safety or compromising the integrity of the research design. Third, some ineffective approaches were identified, but it was difficult, without a preexisting conceptualization of information as useful feedback, to dismantle or change the programs. The importance of building informational feedback into the process of change has been highlighted throughout this book, and it is underscored by the early experimentation in Kansas City.

Despite shortcomings of the experiment in Kansas, much of the subsequent experimentation in community policing has methodological and substantive roots in the groundbreaking efforts started in Kansas City. Chief Kelley showed both persistence and leadership by challenging conventional wisdom and opening himself to ridicule in an organization where peer support is obsessive. Following the turbulence of the 1960s, the organizational culture in policing was cloistered, suspicious, and cynical. Thus, the process experienced in Kansas City was important for starting an important legacy of research in policing.

No less important were the findings of the Kansas City Patrol Task Forces (Kelling, Pate, Dieckman, & Brown, 1974). The well-known outcome that officers could free up time from patrol and use that time more efficiently through problem solving is critical to the community-oriented policing model. High-visibility patrol, low-visibility patrol, directed patrol, patrol technicians, and crisis intervention were among the other diverse projects tested in Kansas City during the same years as the Preventive Patrol Study. The findings of these lesser-known projects were similar: Essentially, the results demonstrated that these strategies provided no lasting, cost-beneficial effects as alternate models for managing a patrol force.[1]

An important lesson from these projects was that not every idea translates to useful policy. Indeed, many ideas were simply ineffective. The lone productive experiment, testing preventive patrol, which produced a watershed of debate and stimulated the general application of scientific research to policing, was the exception, not the rule. It is important to recognize that police managers and researchers alike need the freedom to experiment without the obligation to succeed, because failed ideas and rejected hypotheses can help an organization learn.

Following debate of the Preventive Patrol findings, and spurred on by both the leadership of the Police Foundation and funding from the

National Institute of Law Enforcement and Criminal Justice (NILECJ), there was a plethora of creative research conducted in police departments across the country. Response time (Kansas City, Missouri, Police Department, 1977; Spelman & Brown, 1981), differential police response (McEwen, Connors, & Cohen, 1986), patrol deployment (Levine & McEwen, 1985), split force patrol (Cahn & Tien, 1980), police productivity measures (Whitaker, 1982), staffing allocation models (Levine & McEwen, 1985), patrol staffing (Boydstun, Sherry, & Moelter, 1977) and patrol force management (Larson & Cahn, 1985) are samples of the higher profile projects. With each project, we learned more about what works in policing. Perhaps more important, these projects offered new questions to answer:

- What do the police actually do?

- How well do they do it?

- Are there alternate models of police deployment and service delivery that may be more efficacious?

- Are any of the "self-evident truths" of police practice valid?

- What is the relationship between police practice and other government service delivery?

- What could that relationship be?

Despite the ever expanding body of research on community policing (see, e.g., Carter, 2001), the concept remains experimental. Very little of the community-policing research has been replicated; thus, the reliability of the results are unknown. Instead of replication, new research is searching for new hypotheses to test. Replication, reliability, and consistency are important benchmarks in verifying a theory. We must not conclude that we have been successful until the body of evidence supports that conclusion. The caveat, therefore, is to pursue continued research, particularly that which can replicate important findings.

THE PAST AS FUTURE

One frequently hears critics argue that community policing is nothing new. From my perspective, these individuals have not completely grasped the subtle, but significant, differences from past practice and the concepts underlying community policing. It is not simply the tasks the officer does on the street—for example, foot patrol, meeting with citizens, and dealing with quality of life issues; rather it is the organizational and community infrastructure supporting community policing that is radically different, that is the transformation in the police department, in its connections to the community, and in the community itself.

In the past, proponents of reform-era policing postulated that the police role was simply that of crime fighter. Though police responded to domestic disturbances, landlord-tenant disputes, ambulance calls, missing persons, and so forth, such calls were ancillary, not really part of the police role. However, the public called the police to handle these problems because no one else would. Reform policing viewed these calls as interruptions in crime-fighting duties (including preventive patrol).

Community policing takes a pragmatic view of these calls for service: If the public, who finance the police and from whom the police derive their authority, regularly call the police department to handle these incidents, then handling such incidents is implicitly part of the police role. As such, taking proactive measures (i.e., prevention and problem solving) is the most efficient and effective way to deal with the issues. Reform policing self-defines the police role, whereas community policing recognizes that the public defines the police role.

Building on this premise, community policing endeavors to develop operating policies and procedures that emphasize problem solving as a primary activity, supporting officers' creativity, and developing performance measures recognizing community-policing skills. Call prioritization also gives parity to handling order-maintenance and quality-of-life issues along with crime issues (with the exception, of course, being life-threatening emergencies). In essence, the community-policing movement provides organizational support and rewards that simply were not present in reform-era policing. Although most police agencies are still attempting a transition to this new approach, it remains significantly different from the traditional model.

Changes in the traditional model were tried earlier, but the spirit of the times and the available technology were apparently not right. Two examples of this exploratory legacy are rarely mentioned, but provide interesting insights: Project STAR (Systems and Training Analysis Requirements) and the Integrated Criminal Apprehension Program.

Project STAR

In the early 1970s, a group of criminal justice professionals, educators, and social scientists developed a comprehensive policy research initiative called Project STAR. Funded by the Law Enforcement Assistance Administration, the California Council on Criminal Justice, the Michigan Office of Criminal Justice Programs, the New Jersey Law Enforcement Planning Agency, and the Texas Criminal Justice Council, Project STAR developed forecasts related to future criminal justice system requirements. Specifically, using sociodemographic and economic indicators, this complex project identified changing system requirements and roles, tasks, and performance objectives for criminal justice personnel to meet these future conditions.

Key points and recommendations in the report were that

- the majority of police work is not law enforcement, but a unique form of social service;

- standard police organizational structure and operating practices, particularly in urban regions, diminish the opportunities for the police and public to have face-to-face relationships,

- police departments should demilitarize their role and emphasize nonauthoritarian, cooperative relationships with the public;

- the police role should be professionalized, with wider criteria for selecting officers and a minimum requirement of a baccalaureate degree; and

- police officers should broaden their specialties to handle more diverse problems beyond crime control more efficiently and effectively. (Project STAR, 1976)

Many of the forecasts from Project STAR in 1976 were surprisingly accurate, as evidenced throughout the next two decades. Moreover, these recommendations to change the role of police officers bear important similarities to the community-policing model. Despite the comprehensive nature of Project STAR and the wide array of policy-directed and user-friendly publications released by the project, most of the recommendations slowly disappeared, and little was heard of the project after the 1970s. Yet, moving into the late 1980s and 1990s, many changes occurring in policing reflected the findings from STAR.

Integrated Criminal Apprehension Program (ICAP)

Influenced by systems theory, ICAP sought to take the best knowledge learned from research on policing and integrate it to develop a police management and delivery system that would efficiently and effectively fight crime. A foundation to ICAP was effective crime analysis that, unfortunately, experienced some limitations. With the technology of the time, the output of computerized crime analysis (usually batch processing) was always comparatively slow and, consequently, its decision-making impact was hindered. Crime analysis was performed via hand calculations, and the analytic capability was not particularly robust.

The idea of ICAP was comprehensively and regularly to analyze crime patterns (and in some cases the calls for service) to more accurately deploy personnel (including alternate deployment models by time, day, and location) and respond to special crises. Deployment was also based on the best knowledge of "what worked" in policing according to research. Because the ability to do timely analysis was limited, the application of ICAP was also limited. Deployment of personnel relying on contemporary research findings was also difficult to accomplish, because many of the managers and decision makers were "old school" and did not understand, or perhaps believe, the research. They essentially became obstacles to change. Although ICAP was used, it never really gained widespread acceptance. Like Project STAR, it was somewhat ahead of its time.

PROBLEM-ORIENTED AND COMMUNITY POLICING: DEVELOPMENT AND INTEGRATION

Although many police professionals and academics were questioning the fundamental processes of policing, two catalysts spurred the current movement beginning in the late 1970s. Professor Herman Goldstein of the University of Wisconsin, building on both his research and experience working with O. W. Wilson at the Chicago Police Department, offered the concept of Problem-Oriented Policing (POP) as a fundamental police strategy. Believing that the police could be more effective in crime control and order maintenance by being proactive, Goldstein (1990) discussed POP as a fundamental shift in the way police officers approached their job. POP asked officers to identify problems within their communities (*Scanning*) and then determine critical causal factors that permitted the problem to exist (*Analysis*). Next, officers were to develop a strategy to change the variables and remedy the problem (*Response*), and, finally, to keep an eye on the problem to determine if the desired change occurred (Assessment). Thus, the SARA (Scanning, Analysis, Response, and Assessment) model became an intellectual tool for street-level policing (Spelman & Eck, 1987).

Importantly, POP was an application of the scientific method to policing. The SARA protocol is a policy-based approach to research that Goldstein suggested officers could use as a fundamental part of their daily duties (Spelman & Eck, 1987). Changing an organization's philosophy, and hence culture, is difficult. However, the short yet intense legacy of research in policing, coupled with the rapidly increasing educational level of officers and more enlightened police management, paved the way for an easier transition to a more analytic patrol officer.

A second prominent figure in this movement was the late Professor Robert Trojanowicz of Michigan State University. Trojanowicz's initial experimentation in the "new policing" was called Neighborhood Foot Patrol, which he extensively tested in Flint, Michigan, beginning in the late 1970s (Trojanowicz, 1982). He shared Goldstein's view that the police needed to be more aggressive in identifying and solving community problems. The approach was somewhat different, however, owing to the influence of his father, who had been a police officer. Rather than predominantly relying on the patrol officer proactively to identify community problems, Neighborhood Foot Patrol sought to get officers out of their cars talking with citizens to learn what specific issues in the community were diminishing their quality of life. The police would then seek to remedy those problems or, in the case of more endemic issues, the officer would work as a community organizer to facilitate the community helping itself. Thus, it would be the citizens, not the police, who determined police priorities. Similarly, the role of police managers changed from an authoritarian one to that of a facilitator linking people to resources that could be used to solve problems (Kelling & Moore, 1988).

A second priority of Neighborhood Foot Patrol was to arrest serious and repeat offenders. One of the ideas of Neighborhood Foot Patrol was that, as citizens got to know officers and their presence, talking to citizens was accepted as routine and people would be more likely to provide information to the police about crimes and criminals. Essentially, good community contacts meant the collection of good intelligence. Ironically, this was intended to be an aggressive approach toward crime; however, the label *Neighborhood Foot Patrol* portrayed the image of "soft policing," which was interpreted as being little more than social work (Trojanowicz & Bucqueroux, 1990).

In both POP and Neighborhood Foot Patrol, patrol officers were asked to perform tasks for which they were unaccustomed: They were to

- think creatively,

- overtly interact with the law-abiding community,

- get out of their cars rather than reactively patrolling waiting for calls,

- conduct research,

- view quality-of-life issues and order-maintenance responsibilities on a par equal to crime, and

- be responsible for overt activity, not just "bean counting" work such as taking reports, issuing traffic citations, checking buildings, towing cars, and so forth.

As the concepts have evolved and been placed into practice, both POP and Neighborhood Foot Patrol have largely become integrated under the rubric of community policing.

Breaking the Bonds of Tradition

In the early 1980s, some people viewed community policing as a new, radical, social-work approach to policing that did little more than add to the mound of responsibilities the police already faced. During this time, law enforcement touted its crime-fighting role and lamented how busy it was doing such things as conducting investigations, profiling serial killers, doing buy-and-bust dope deals, and refining street survival skills. Though these issues certainly faced the police, the reality was (and generally remains) that police officers spend more time answering calls for service than fighting crime on the streets. Taking offense reports, responding to disturbances, answering prowler calls, dealing with juvenile pranks and noise complaints, and checking out suspicious persons are the types of calls that remain the major time consumer of uniformed law enforcement officers.

The change to community policing is not simple. For example, a police officer is typically socialized in the academy and during field training to believe that, when not handling calls, the most important activity is to patrol one's beat area. Implicitly, the officer learns that while patrolling one should also seek performance measures, such as buildings to check, cars to tow, and tickets to write. The socialization continues as the officer learns that, when dispatched to a call, the problem should be handled quickly so he or she may "get back in service" as soon as possible to await the next call.

Interestingly, patrol sergeants historically do not seem to be as concerned with patrolling as a way to prevent crime, but as a way to occupy an officer's time. It does not "look good" to have an officer simply parked somewhere or, worse, sitting in a restaurant for a prolonged period. Thus, the patrol officer has learned that to receive good performance evaluations and keep the sergeant happy, he or she must simply handle calls quickly, keep moving, and look busy. When a police department adopts the community-policing philosophy, this same officer is told to change the way he or she does the job. For example, police are told, "Stay out of service longer to handle the problem," "You may leave your patrol area if it facilitates your problem solving," and, "Instead of patrolling, you should spend more time out of your car talking to people getting to know them."

Based on the officer's socialization, these changes "don't feel right." The officer wonders if this is legitimate policy or whether the organization is fickle, and some officers opt for the latter explanation. It is difficult to adjust to the new model, because it opposes everything the officer has learned. Coupled with the cynicism and conservative personality common to police officers is a distrust of the commitment to change and concern about whether the change will be lasting. Moreover, firstline supervisors must go through a similar change process. Although they typically pass along the directives of change, they must also change the way they supervise and evaluate officers on a daily basis. It is a difficult mental adjustment when, for years, a sergeant has told officers to stay in service as much as possible and patrol, and then suddenly must tell them the opposite. These are substantial obstacles to overcome—simply instructing that the change will occur and issuing organizational proclamations is insufficient. Personnel must be engaged in a substantial change process of the type that has been described by several earlier chapters in this book.

Quality Management and Change to Community Policing

An important concept was becoming the conventional wisdom for American business at about the same time that community policing was emerging. Total quality management (TQM), or the Deming method, sought to be customer driven and provide the best product or service to the customer while at the same time giving the worker ownership in the product or service (Couper & Sabine, 1991). Moreover, TQM sought to be proactive by ensuring that the product was manufactured correctly "the first time" rather than being manufactured, then inspected, then repaired. This element of TQM is similar to the community-policing principle of proactivity in dealing with crime and order-maintenance problems (see Hoover, 1996). TQM, followed by value-added service, continuous quality improvement, and benchmark management, all produced philosophical changes in management practices directed toward customers that have positive implications for policing. Perhaps the greatest proponent of TQM in policing was David Couper, the former chief in Madison, Wisconsin, who, when adopting the community-policing philosophy, referred to it as quality policing. The timing of TQM's popularity helped drive the popularity of community policing.

The application of TQM to community policing leads police leadership to see community policing as a new management style (a form of TQM) as opposed to a new approach to policing has been effective in gaining the support of police leadership. The vision of community policing as social work immediately turns off most officers: They see the new philosophy as a *substantive* change in the work they do as police officers. However, when told that the management style has changed, officers are more receptive, because they see this as a *procedural* change. Thus, they are still doing police work, only in a different way. Furthermore, when presented with the comparatively concrete principles of TQM, the concept appears to make more sense to officers.

FINAL THOUGHTS

What's next? Beyond continued experimentation and full implementation of community policing, three factors are likely to emerge as complementary initiatives. The first is comprehensive, real-time crime analysis. Problem identification and solving, personnel deployment, and resource allocation can all be most effectively achieved with timely, accurate information. Crime analysis, including analysis of broad-based order-maintenance issues, remains a key element in this regard. With the growth of technological capabilities, ranging from high-performance laptop computers connected via an Intranet with simple-to-use yet powerful complaint-reporting software to simple, reliable telecommunications, the ability to capture the data we need and analyze it quickly is within our grasp. As these systems become more affordable, the value of crime analysis will increase dramatically. Ideally, such systems would include information and data sharing to permit regional crime analysis across jurisdictions, not just within a jurisdiction. Coupled with management accountability, a key ingredient in the computerized statistical analysis process, crime analysis becomes an important ingredient to the most effective problem-solving activities.

A second issue will be the growth and integration of crime-specific policing. A number of people argue that crime-specific policing is the antithesis of community policing, because it seeks tactical suppression of certain crimes and is little more than a short-term solution. Moreover, it is argued that crime-specific policing uses loosely created criminal profiles—such as for gang members—as a tool to stop or harass citizens, whereas community policing seeks a more cooperative approach to law enforcement. In reality, crime-specific policing is an emerging strategy that is still being conceptually developed. It serves a legitimate need, and can complement community policing when there are unique crime trends or problems that need to be addressed in a community. For example, in metropolitan areas where there is a burglary ring operating, the burglars are very likely to be from a different jurisdiction than their targets. Though community policing may help by adding eyes and ears to the street, community policing alone will be limited in its ability to identify the nonresident burglars. If using crime analysis and intelligence profiles can be developed to help forecast burglaries and probable suspects, then arrests are more likely. If the burglaries are stopped using the crime-specific approach, the community members will be better protected, their fear of crime will go down, and their quality of life will increase. Crime-specific policing should not be viewed as a "competitive" or "anti–community policing" strategy. Instead, it should be viewed in a cooperative light that can provide citizens better safety and security.

The third factor is regional initiatives in community policing. At first blush, the ideas of "regional" and "community-based" initiatives may seem incongruent. However, many crime and quality-of-life issues are systemic, transcending jurisdictional boundaries. Too frequently, one community's problems are largely influenced by a neighboring community. This problematic characteristic of crime is addressed by regional drug task forces and regional major case squads. Community policing should be no different. With regional crime analysis and regional problem investigations, officers can develop more holistic pictures of problems to solve. Being given the ability to work cooperatively with other agencies in the region can enhance the effectiveness of community-based problem-solving activities.

The rapid expansion of community policing can be traced to a number of variables, not the least of which is money. The Office of Community Oriented Policing Services (COPS) has provided millions of dollars to communities across the country to hire police officers. The COPS office has also funded research and is involved in a massive training initiative. The significant question is what will happen to community policing when the concept has lost its luster, lost its national stage, and lost its federal funding. That is when the true commitment and its conceptual viability will be tested, and when research can have a critical impact.

NOTE

1. This information is based on a series of meetings and unpublished reports that I had access to during my tenure in Kansas City.

REFERENCES

Boydstun, J. E., Sherry, M. E., & Moelter, P. (1977). *Patrol staffing in San Diego.* Washington, DC: Police Foundation.

Cahn, M., & Tien, J. M. (1980). *An evaluation report of an alternative approach in police response: The Wilmington management of demand program.* Cambridge, MA: Public Systems Evaluation.

Carter, D. L. (2001). The police and the community (7th ed.). New York: Prentice Hall.

Couper, D., & Sabine, S. H. (1991). *Quality policing: The Madison experience.* Washington, DC: Police Executive Research Forum.

Goldstein, H. (1990). *Problem oriented policing.* New York: McGraw-Hill.

Hoover, L. (1996). Quantifying quality in policing. Washington, DC: Police Executive Research Forum.

Kansas City, Missouri, Police Department. (1977). *Response time analysis: Executive summary.* Kansas City, MO: Board of Police Commissioners.

Kelling, G. L., & Moore, M. H. (1988). The evolving strategy of policing. *National Institute of Justice/Harvard University Perspectives on Policing.* Washington, DC: U.S. Department of Justice, Office of Justice Programs, National Institute of Justice.

Kelling, G. L., Pate, T., Dieckman, D., & Brown, C. E. (1974). *The Kansas City preventive patrol experiment* [Technical Report]. Washington, DC: Police Foundation.

Larson, R. C., & Cahn, M. F. (1985). *Synthesizing and extending the results of police patrol studies.* Washington, DC: U.S. Department of Justice, Office of Justice Programs, National Institute of Justice.

Levine, M., & McEwen, J. T. (1985). *Patrol deployment.* Washington, DC: U.S. Department of Justice, Office of Justice Programs, National Institute of Justice.

McEwen, J. T., Connors, E. F., & Cohen, M. I. (1986). *Evaluation of the differential police response field test.* Washington, DC: U.S. Department of Justice, Office of Justice Programs, National Institute of Justice.

Project STAR. (1976). *The impact of social trends on crime and criminal justice.* Cincinnati, OH: Anderson.

Spelman, W., & Brown, D. K. (1981). *Calling the police: Citizen reporting of serious crime.* Washington, DC: Police Executive Research Forum.

Spelman, W., & Eck, J. (1987). *Problem-oriented policing: The Newport News experiment.* Washington, DC: Police Executive Research Forum.

Trojanowicz, R. C. (1982). *Neighborhood foot patrol in Flint, Michigan.* East Lansing, MI: Michigan State University, National Neighborhood Foot Patrol Center.

Trojanowicz, R. C., & Bucqueroux, B. (1990). *Community policing: A contemporary perspective.* Cincinnati, OH: Anderson.

Whitaker, G. (1982). *Basic issues in police performance.* Washington, DC: U.S. Department of Justice, Office of Justice Programs, National Institute of Justice.

CHAPTER **14**

Directing the Future of Community-Policing Initiatives

Merry Morash
J. Kevin Ford
Jane P. White
Jerome G. Boles III

What currently dominates police agencies across the country is the overriding theme of adopting the community-policing philosophy. The majority of the literature on community policing has focused on the implementation of a few successful programs or the fallacy of such efforts altogether.

The chapters in this book have focused instead on identifying the necessary processes that will assist in actual changing the delivery of police services. They show the commitment of a variety of experts to developing the processes and content necessary to assist police administrators in identifying the various obstacles, making the critical decisions, and implementing the change to community policing. These efforts are intended to make policing services more effective, efficient, and equitable. Although each chapter has focused on a particular set of issues relevant to community policing, the overall theme of the book is the importance of taking a continuous improvement approach and focusing on "getting better." This type of perspective represents a change in the philosophy of policing rather than the adoption of a program with elements of community policing embedded in it. A program ends with the implementation of one or more "changes" in police services. An adoption of a philosophical shift, in contrast, is characterized by the choices people must make to institute continuous improvement in a variety of related organizational processes.

The purpose of this final chapter is to revisit the core principles of the community-policing philosophy. Based on that review, key challenges identified throughout the book are described and discussed. Finally, the series of choices or decision points that must be considered in any attempt to adopt a community-policing philosophy are presented to guide future research and practice in the field.

THE CORE ELEMENTS OF COMMUNITY POLICING

Community policing is the delivery of police services through a customer-focused approach, utilizing partnerships to maximize community resources in a problem-solving format to prevent crime, reduce the fear of crime, apprehend those involved in criminal activity, and improve a community's quality of life. As shown in this book, a customer-based approach requires a transformation in the police organization itself to improve police services. Input from both internal customers (i.e., police employees at all levels) and external customers (e.g., residents, businesses, and visitors) is stressed to strike a balance between legally mandated services and the delivery of police services deemed important for all stakeholders in maintaining or improving a community's quality of life.

To maximize a community's resources in dealing with identified problems, partnerships must be developed that can routinely bring the key stakeholders to the table on any particular problem of concern to both the police and the public. Partnerships must be developed and maintained for maximum efficiency and effectiveness in the problem-solving process. These partnerships include the residential community, the business community, public and private social service delivery agencies, and all other local governmental services in addition to the police. Partnerships also develop trust and allow for customer input on a regular basis, and a network of partnerships focused on crime control and quality-of-life improvement increases the social capital available to address problems within a community.

An informational-based, unified effort to solve problems highlights the need for a collective identification of problems through customer input and a strong partnership base. This collaborative effort allows for the prioritization of police services from both a police and a community perspective. A problem-solving process is uniformly utilized (e.g., the SARA [Scanning, Analysis, Response, and Assessment] model) to identify, analyze, respond to, and assess the response to such problems. The goal of problem solving is to identify the underlying causes of a problem and then to address those underlying causes rather then continuing to react to the same problem repeatedly. By addressing the underlying causes, recurrent problems can be resolved to the satisfaction of the community and the police. Police resources can then be directed towards resolving other issues and problems. Information and data are key components in all phases of the problem-solving process.

Operationalizing the three components of a community-policing philosophy is intended to improve the efficiency, effectiveness, and equitability of police service delivery. Taken in their entirety, the chapters in this book highlight the importance of consistently emphasizing the customer-based approach, the building of partnerships, and the need to work jointly on problems. Only in this way can the police and community dramatically increase the mutual trust needed to improve the delivery of police services and improve the community's quality of life. The chapters have also highlighted the central challenges in translating philosophy into action. The next section provides a summary of key challenges that police organizations face in the move to community policing.

KEY CHALLENGES

Key challenges to the move to community policing can be examined in terms of the three core elements of community policing. The overview of challenges illustrates not only the practical issues, but also points the way to needed future research.

A Customer-Based Organizational Transformation

A customer-based approach to policing implies a major shift in the relationship between community members and the police agency. Traditionally, the customers—the community members—of police services have been forced to adapt to the police organization and the way the police agency is organized. The move to community policing implies that customers must be partners in shaping the priorities of the police department and must help realign the shape of the organization and its work. In addition, a customer-based approach needs to be taken within the police department walls. For example, detectives are customers of the information provided by officers; officers, in turn, are customers of crime analysis data summarized by administrators.

The traditional model focuses on community participation in policing from an informational perspective. For example, citizen complaints and community surveys provide information to the police agency that might be used to improve the delivery of police services. These approaches can lead to the community providing some input, but the police agency continues in its role as the powerful entity that decides what to do with this input. A transformational change in the relationship requires police agencies to view the community as consultants and, in some cases, even joint decision makers in the process of prioritizing work and shaping how the agency responds to community needs. This requires a firm commitment to community connection (involving the community more directly in the work of the police department), community promotion (expanding the ways in which the public gains a deeper understanding of the police department's efforts and the needs of the community), and resource allocation (working with the community stakeholders in the prioritization of services relevant to critical resource issues). For example, the community could become highly involved in developing with the police a more effective and efficient call management strategy. Such a move to a differential response system can generate more time for officers to dedicate to their assigned area or neighborhood. On the other hand, such a move can reduce rapid response to nonemergency calls for service that will be seen as a significant change for many community members. Thus, community members must be involved in the planning and decision making to understand the change and support it in terms of what they will receive in return. Similarly, partnerships with schools or domestic violence advocates require an ongoing commitment by the police to understanding and sharing expertise and shaping the community response, which will include the police response. Given the tensions endemic to the relationship between police and domestic violence advocates, the police cannot assume that they will be regarded as experts or that they will not have to achieve some shared understanding of the causes and consequences of domestic violence with people who look at the phenomena from a different standpoint.

This transformational approach to community building requires that police and community members come to trust each other, understand each other, and even empathize with each other in the process of participation. The focus on building relationships with these qualities requires the development of a long-term strategy of engagement between the community and police members and the constancy of purpose by police leaders to take actions that are consistent with the vision of a customer focus. For example, trust does not develop from infrequent community meetings or one-time community surveys. In addition, citizens are used to police coming in for a short period for special enforcement purposes, and then leaving for the next crisis. Therefore, community members will need to see constancy of purpose and longer-term police commitments to working on problems to develop the trust necessary for effective community policing. Actions must be taken that show the community not only that their input is valued, but also that they have a "seat at the table"—that community members are actively engaged with police on critical issues as identified by the community and police personnel. Thus, they are involved in the analysis of problems and root causes, and in the development of action plans for improvement, rather than simply providing input or information.

Community-oriented policing requires a change from shift work, which is driven by the clock, to teamwork, which is driven by ownership of and responsibility for a geographic area and the people in it. The focus of the move to geographic teams is to provide 24-hour ownership of an area. Most departments moving to a team approach use sergeants as team leaders or coordinators. This places the sergeant in the dual role of having a tactical or command role on a shift basis, and a 24-hour focus to a team area and the officers making up that team. The team leaders in the police department become critical in facilitating change by linking members of the team and making sure that they receive needed information from and have contact with each other. The idea of teamwork is often met with the question, at several different levels, "What's in it for me?" Group interactions and individual discussions, often with input from internal and external change agents, are important venues for identifying the benefits of teamwork for all parties involved, and are a key step in the process of developing community-oriented policing.

In a team context, the supervisor's role is complicated. The supervisor has tactical responsibilities for ensuring that police services (e.g., response to calls for service, investigations of criminal activity, and response to accidents) are provided during an eight-hour shift. An additional responsibility is to take ownership for a group anchored in geography rather than an eight-hour window of time. Supervisors working in the same area must meet on a regular basis, must have continuing conversation with their superiors, and must respond to both tactical and neighborhood concerns. Communication across functions and related to geography, rather than to time on duty, requires new approaches. For example, all officers and members of partnerships could be provided with e-mail access to each other, as well as be allocated time for team meetings. Some departments have tried to institute shift teams, rather than involving supervisors in geography-based oversight. The result is a misfit of new objectives with old structures.

The notion of the customer is also quite relevant for the internal workings of the police agency. The move to community policing requires a transformational change within the police department, where individuals begin to see each other from a customer perspective. The traditional approach is a continuation of the command-and-control orientation with little potential for participation in decisions that have an impact on the individual and his or her workgroup. In addition, such an approach focuses on each specialty (e.g., detectives, records, field sergeants) doing their job, rather than on viewing things from a systems perspective.

An internal customer perspective focuses on the fact that people within an organization receive many things from other people within that same organization in order to produce a product or service to the community. For example, the records department provides data to officers regarding a summary of the criminal activity in an area. In this case, the records person is the supplier, whereas the officer who must use that information to address a community issue is the customer. The timeliness and quality of that information will have an impact on what outcomes or products can be produced by the officer in the community. The move to an internal customer orientation requires a proactive commitment to continuous improvement in how the units of a department work together to produce the right products, services, and information for each internal customer. The goal is to increase efficiency by reducing friction, developing increasingly cooperative relationships, and enhancing mutual respect among all people within the police agency. Only in this way can police delivery of services become more effective.

The challenge, then, for police agencies is to discover how to make progress in building relationships with the external customer (i.e., the community) at the same time that progress is made on building stronger internal customer relationships within the police agency. Most attention in the literature has focused on the important aspect of community engagement with police departments. Most of the efforts to move to community policing have emphasized building better community relations. Building better community relations requires that police personnel view the community members as customers and that customers play a big part in how the department is structured and how it prioritizes action. In addition, it requires a commitment within the police department to improve the delivery of services within the department itself. As an example, once steps are taken to improve labor-management relations (see Chapter 8), or in departments that have positive labor-management relations, there is still a continuing need for labor and management to work cooperatively. Similarly, once a department's training design team has identified an internal need for training and that training has been delivered, the group must meet to assess the impact and identify continuing or new needs. Without this trust building within the department, ongoing learning and change in the organization is unlikely to progress, and the chances for trust building between the department and the community is limited.

Unlimited Partnerships

The literature on community policing clearly identifies the need to develop effective partnerships with a wide range of groups within a community, such as neighborhood watch groups, business entities, schools, victim advocates, churches, and social service groups. Officers are often empowered to cultivate, develop, and sustain partnerships in the field. They become the visible symbols of a new approach to linking police and community groups. Another visible symbol is the police chief. The community-policing literature is clear in pointing out the need for the chief to cultivate, develop, and sustain partnerships at the governmental level (e.g., with the city council or mayor) and broad community level to generate the support and resources needed to move to community policing.

A common mistake in planning to develop partnerships is limiting the effort to an officer working with a neighborhood association or in a geographic area. The formation of partnerships must be the responsibility of all personnel across all levels of the department. Police leadership can partner with other units of government and other agencies' leadership, while sergeants can partner with community groups that are city- or countywide in scope. For example, in Chicago, a set of supporting relationships have resulted in immediate response of city services to community police officer requests. When a police officer submits a request for a city service (e.g., to remove graffiti), it is honored within 24 hours. Another example is the neighborhood network centers in Lansing, Michigan, where state and county services are brought together in the same location as city services, including police and neighborhood group centers. Proximity and partnerships at a higher level facilitate identifying and solving both local and citywide problems quickly.

The organizational preparation for a police department's engaging the community has considerable affect on the progress of a successful transformation to community policing. If adequate organizational change does not occur before the community is engaged, officers are faced with unrealistic community expectations for partnerships and joint problem solving. In addition, the officers face the reality that they lack skills, organizational structure, and practices that make these activities possible. Before engaging the community, a police organization must be prepared to support a customer orientation—both externally and internally. Police leadership and others in the department often feel that they must defend their police officers and themselves when there is community criticism of police actions. At every level, officers and civilian staff must be prepared to receive input from community members, and to respond by asking for even more information on the nature of problem. There needs to be dialogue to develop a full description of problems and their causes. Only then can a community-police partnership develop a joint description of the problem and its cause, and work together to fashion a solution. In addition, police personnel must be better equipped to deal with these changing realities. Internal preparation of all police members relevant to the skills needed to deliver a customer focus, develop partnerships, and solve problems must become a priority.

Alternatively, there are points at which it becomes too late to engage a community. Community partners must be involved in time to have an influence on the shape of a plan and to participate in evaluation and revision of steps taken to implement it. At some point, they will have a part in driving change, either along with police leadership or separate from it. Police leadership needs to be prepared for the push that the community will make for change, which may be at a pace and in a direction that is unexpected. In some communities, at some points, it is the partners who jump-start the change process, resulting in pressure for the organizational preparation to occur very quickly.

Not only are community partners unpredictable, but communities vary considerably in their interest and capacity to form partnerships that address crime and quality-of-life problems. Correia's essay (Chapter 11) described this variation within community types. If a community has limited social capital, and is faced with serious crime and quality-of-life problems, the police department, other resources, and outside change agents must be committed to working with the community for a lengthy period. Short-term efforts at problem solving followed by a quick fix (e.g., removing graffiti, constructing a fence or gate) have a very limited impact in comparison to a law enforcement commitment to staying involved with the community long enough to actually change the quality of life within a specific area. Outside technical assistance may be needed to promote and support partnerships, for instance, by helping residents supportive of dealing with community problems in concrete ways (e.g., by providing childcare or safe passage to and from meetings).

Relationships relevant to a particular type of crime or a specific quality-of-life issue are often not easy to form. Responses to domestic violence and to people affected by mental illness are time-consuming for police. As Morash and Robinson (Chapter 9) explained, it is not easy to partner to address domestic violence, because special strategies are necessary. Similarly, advocates for the mentally ill, the police, and neighbors and businesses often have dramatically differing understandings of the role that police should play when a person with mental illness (who may be homeless) affects perceptions of the local quality of life.

Despite the difficulty of partnering to address such common issues as community disruption related to mental illness and domestic violence, there are some important examples of successful efforts. In Lansing, Michigan, a program called CARE (Capital Area Response Effort) has shared responsibilities with police for response to domestic violence incidents. CARE staff work in the police department, and receive information about domestic violence calls, so that, in addition to police response, there is an immediate follow-up response by community volunteers trained to support victims with safety planning and referrals for themselves and others in the household.

The focus of police work cannot be simply on developing partnerships as an end in itself. Oftentimes we have seen agencies that are happy to have better relationships with key constituency groups. Yet this end is not the focus of the move to community policing, but must instead be seen as a means to more efficient, effective, and equitable delivery of police services.

Thus, the challenge for police agencies is not to fall into the trap that partnering is something done by only a few individuals within the department. In addition, partnering is not just about creating better relationships, but also about developing a firm and continuing commitment to finding better ways of policing through the involvement of the various partners.

Unified Effort to Solve Problems

A common shortfall of problem-solving efforts is that they are too driven by police. Tactical problems related to crimes of particular concern to the police are the focus rather than the quality-of-life issues that citizens are most troubled about. In some cases, police focus on high profile crimes and not other criminal activity of more concern to citizens. The lack of fit between police emphasis and citizen concerns results when stakeholders are not at the table to engage in a thorough process of defining local problems and identifying possible solutions. For instance, if the problem is loitering and disruptive behavior by individuals suffering from mental illness, advocacy groups for the mentally ill, as well as business leaders, residents, and professionals who work with the mentally ill, must be present to describe the root causes of problems and to bring knowledge needed to address them. The gathered and analyzed data must then be fed back to officers and the community in formats that make sense to all groups.

Problem solving requires timely collection, organization, and presentation of information pertinent to a problem that has become the focus of a police-community partnership. Police typically collect a great deal of data as they fill out paperwork, but this may or may not be relevant to the problem at hand. San Diego, California, has been able to engage police in the generation of data on immediate problems, for instance homeless individuals or abandoned cars. Data are gathered for one or more areas of the city, and results fed back to concerned citizens. Because of the emphasis on citizens as customers, quality-of-life information is considered within the realm of police responsibility.

A particularly unique example of problem solving occurred on a citywide basis in Holland, Michigan. A Holland Police Department study committee's initial concern with gang violence and the reassignment of community police officers to other areas within the city led to a careful examination of community concerns and priorities as they related to policing. In a fairly short four-month period, through four five-hour meetings with various stakeholders, recommendations shifted from the citizen demand for reallocation of community police to a broader plan to restructure the police department so it could address citizen needs as they existed and changed over time. Major changes included the inclusion of all personnel in area teams, an emphasis on technology to improve communication among police and with the community, and the use of volunteers to handle some police responsibilities , freeing police for work with community teams. The problem-solving approach enabled the police department and the community to set the stage for structural changes that would support community-oriented policing, and that went far beyond reallocating personnel to selected neighborhoods to address gang problems.

DECISION POINTS

Our discussion of the dynamic quality of responding to both internal and external customers, forming partnerships, and problem solving has highlighted the key challenges that must be addressed in the move to community policing. Though the list of issues might seem daunting, the default of maintaining the *status quo* of traditional policing has a number of well-documented dysfunctional consequences for officer health, interdepartmental cooperation, and citizen satisfaction. Instead, this book has provided a reality-based approach to the change to community policing—anything worth doing is worth doing well.

In particular, a reality-based approach to change recognizes that there are critical decision points that are pivotal events in the move to community policing. The choices of how to prepare, plan, implement, and monitor steps consistent with the move to community policing pose dilemmas to police administrators, because there are alternative courses of action (e.g., to decentralize or to maintain centralized control) that have both advantages and disadvantages. For many of the choices relevant to moving to community policing, there is no clearly superior alternative method. There are trade-offs associated with many alternatives, and the choices made can have significant consequences for people within and outside the department. Underlying these choice points, then, are dual realities—uncertainty and opportunity. There is uncertainty about what to do and how to make change happen in a systematic and effective way. There is also opportunity in the choices, such that truly new and innovative strategies can be implemented to lead to more efficient and effective delivery of police services and support the development of a continuous learning organization.

Reality-based organizational change processes lie between superficially implementing a single-faceted "add-on" community officer or bike patrol program and the seeming impossibility of changing the de-livery of police services. Realistically looking at what needs to happen within a variety of policing processes, and planning accordingly, will significantly aid the change agent in his or her endeavors. Technical as-sistance by an expert in organizational change is often a critical input into the change process. Just as the police organization's longevity of commitment and involvement with the community is crucial to bring-ing about transformational change, so is the longevity of commitment and involvement by one or more organizational change experts to sup-porting an organizations' transformation crucial. Because of the com-plexity of organizational change and the variation in community inter-est and capacity to form partnerships, the Michigan Regional Community Policing Institute model has been to work with depart-ments and communities for a period of years, extending at this point to up to five years.

This book has focused on the strategies that police agencies should consider in the move to community policing. The strategies are levers for change in police organizations. They have been derived from work-ing with police administrators, supervisors, officers, and community members who are actively engaged in attempts to enhance the effi-ciency, effectiveness, and the equality in the delivery of police services and for improving the quality of life for its citizens. In addition, the chapters have provided avenues for new research directions. Only by linking the practical realities facing police agencies with research needs in the community-policing literature can be hope to drive improved po-lice services.

Index

About the Editors

Merry Morash is Professor of Criminal Justice at the Michigan State University School of Criminal Justice, where she served as director from 1991 to 2001. She also is founder, director, and faculty instructor of the Michigan Victim Assistance Academy, which provides education for individuals who work with crime victims; director of the Michigan Regional Community Policing Institute; and secretary of the Michigan DARE Advisory Board. Her primary research emphasis is on gender and crime, and current research is on domestic violence among Asian Americans and gender-responsive programming for women offenders. She has also done extensive research on women in policing and is currently engaged in research to follow up on women who participated in a study nearly a decade ago. She recently served on the Domestic Violence Homicide Prevention Task Force and on the advisory board for the Michigan Judicial Institute's bench book to assist judges in their work with crime victims. Dr. Morash is a coauthor of the textbook *Juvenile Delinquency: Concepts and Control,* and she has written and published extensively on women as offenders, police, and crime victims. Additional publications focus on assessment and implementation of criminal justice policy and juvenile delinquency programming and causation.

J. Kevin Ford is Professor of Psychology at Michigan State University. His major research interests involve improving training effectiveness by advancing our understanding of training needs assessment, design, evaluation, and transfer. He also concentrates on building continuous learning and improvement orientations within organizations. He has published over 50 articles, chapters, and technical reports, and serves on the editorial board of *Human Performance*. He was the lead editor of the book *Improving Training Effectiveness in Work Organizations* and is co-author, with Dr. Irwin Goldstein, of *Training in Organizations* (4th ed.). He is an active consultant with private industry and the public sector on training, leadership, and organizational development issues. Over the past 3 years, to facilitate the institutionalization of the community-policing philosophy, Dr. Ford has worked on issues of transformational change with the Michigan Regional Community Policing Institute. He is a Fellow of the American Psychological Association and the Society of Industrial and Organizational Psychology. He received his PhD in psychology from Ohio State University. Further information about Dr. Ford and his research and consulting activities can be found at www. io.psy.msu.edu.

About the Contributors

Mark E. Alley is Chief of Police in the Lansing, Michigan, Police Department, where, beginning in 1986, he has been promoted through the ranks. His experience includes the design and implementation of numerous innovative programs and initiatives to improve the quality of life for city residents and visitors. He teaches courses at the Michigan State University School of Criminal Justice and is a trainer in Human Diversity and the Incident Command System.

Jerome G. Boles III is Associate Director of the Michigan Regional Community Policing Institute at Michigan State University. He is the former Chief of Police in the Lansing, Michigan, Police Department, where he served as a police officer for over 30 years, the last 6 as chief. As chief in Lansing, he began the process of implementing community policing on a department-wide basis. His experience includes transforming the department by involving members from all work groups, the community, and political leadership. He was able to institute changes that have been lasting and that continue to be enhanced.

Elizabeth M. Bonello is a detective at the Lansing, Michigan, Police Department and holds a Master of Science degree from Michigan State University. She is conducting research on the socialization of firstline supervisors in police organizations for her doctoral dissertation, which she anticipates completing in 2003. The Criminal Justice Women of Michigan have recognized Officer Bonello as the 2000 Clarissa Young Officer of the Year for outstanding performance.

Julie L Brockman is a PhD student in the College of Education at Michigan State University and a consultant for PIERS (Project for Innovative Employee Relations) in the university's School of Labor and Industrial Relations. Her publications include "What Do Police Unions Want?" and (with Michael J. Polzin) "A Labor-Management Approach to Community Policing," both of which appeared in the 1999 volume of the *Journal of Community Policing.*

David L. Carter is Professor of Criminal Justice in the School of Criminal Justice at Michigan State University. A former Kansas City, Missouri, police officer, he has worked with police agencies and command colleges throughout the United States and in several foreign countries. He also served at the Federal Bureau of Investigation Academy's Behavioral Science Unit in the first academic faculty exchange with the bureau. He is the author or coauthor of five books and numerous articles on policing issues, and is a member of the editorial boards of various professional publications. His most recent book is *The Police and Community* (7th ed.).

Mark E. Correia is Assistant Professor of Criminal Justice at the University of Nevada, Reno. His primary research interests include the influence that social norms and networks have on crime, innovative policing, and citizen-government collaborative initiatives. He is the author of *Citizen Involvement: How Community Factors Affect Progressive Policing* and coeditor of *Policing Communities: Understanding Crime and Solving Problems.*

Cori A. Davis is a PhD student in the Industrial/Organizational Psychology program at Michigan State University. Her areas of interest include reactions to performance feedback, training, and organizational development. She works with the Michigan Regional Community Policing Institute analyzing organizational survey data, developing training, and assisting local departments with the move to community policing.

Monique Fields is a PhD student in Criminal Justice at Michigan State University. In addition to police data analysis, she has expertise in the area of race and crime. Her research includes juvenile antisocial behavior and juvenile justice. She has worked extensively with Michigan State Police Crime Data Program.

Andrew L. Giacomazzi is Assistant Professor of Criminal Justice Administration at Boise State University. He received his PhD in political science at Washington State University in 1995. He is coauthor of *Community Policing in a Community Era: An Introduction and Exploration* and recent articles have appeared in such journals as *Justice Research and Policy, Crime and Delinquency, Police Quarterly,* and *Justice Quarterly.* His research interests include community policing, organizational change, and family violence. Giacomazzi is principal investigator of an evaluation to determine the effects of organizational and community assessments on change toward community policing in five western states

Stephen D. Mastrofski is Professor of Public and International Affairs and Director of the Administration of Justice Program at George Mason University. His research interests include testing theories of police behavior, applying organization theory to police reform, and measuring the performance of police organizations. He and several colleagues recently conducted the Project on Policing Neighborhoods, a study for the U.S. Department of Justice on community policing at the street level. In 2000, the Academy of Criminal Justice Sciences gave him the O. W. Wilson Award for outstanding contributions to police education, research, and practice.

Audrey Z. Martini, MS, is Director of Outreach for the School of Criminal Justice, Michigan State University. She was instrumental in the organization and continued facilitation of the Michigan Safe Schools Initiative workgroup, and works closely with various key stakeholders in school safety to identify needs and maximize resources. Before joining the School of Criminal Justice, she was a special projects coordinator for the Lansing Community College Criminal Justice and Law Center. She retired with the rank of lieutenant from the Detroit Police Department in 1986.

Edmund F. McGarrell is Professor of Criminal Justice and Director of the Michigan State University School of Criminal Justice. He has served as Director of the Crime Control Policy Center at the Hudson Institute in Indianapolis. He is currently involved in an experiment on the use of restorative justice conferences as a response to juvenile crime, and is the research partner in the Indianapolis Violence Reduction Partnership, which is utilizing collaborative problem-solving strategies to reduce violence as part of the National Institute of Justice's Strategic Approaches to Community Safety Initiative.

Tracy Goss McGinley is a doctoral candidate at Michigan State University. Her main research interests are on policing and private security. She has experience working in various areas of the criminal justice system, including police departments, community correction programs, and private security. She is Assistant Director of the Identity Theft University-Business Partnership being developed at Michigan State University to help understand the crime of identity theft and develop policies to assist law enforcement become more reactive in their approach to this crime.

Michael J. Polzin is Director of and Senior Consultant for the Project for Innovative Employee Relations in the School of Labor and Industrial Relations, Michigan State University. His recent publications include "What Do Police Unions Want?" and (with Julie L. Brockman) "A Labor-Management Approach to Community Policing," both of which appeared in the 1999 volume of the *Journal of Community Policing*.

Michael D. Reisig is Assistant Professor of Criminal Justice at Michigan State University. His general interests include organizations, survey research, and applied statistical modeling. His research has been published in various journals, including *Criminology, Justice Quarterly*, and *Crime & Delinquency*.

Amanda L. Robinson is a Lecturer in Criminology and Criminal Justice in the School of Social Science at Cardiff University in Wales.. Her research interests include police and society; race, class, and gender in criminal justice; violence against women; trends in sentencing practices; social theory; and qualitative and quantitative methods. She has published articles in *Women and Criminal Justice, Crime and Delinquency, Policing: An International Journal of Police Strategies and Management, Journal of Criminal Justice*, and *Criminal Justice and Behavior*.

Joseph A. Schafer is Assistant Professor at the Center for the Study of Crime, Delinquency & Corrections at Southern Illinois University, Carbondale. His current research interests include police behavior, police organizations, community policing, perceptions of the police, fear of crime, criminal justice policy, and extremist organizations. He is the author of *Community Policing: The Challenges of Successful Organizational Change*, as well as numerous book chapters. His recent scholarly works have appeared in the *Justice System Journal* and the *Journal of Criminal Justice.*

Jeffrey B. Snipes is the Rockefeller Brothers Fellow in Nonprofit Law at New York University's School of Law and the Vera Institute of Justice in Manhattan. He is completing his JD at Stanford University and his PhD at the State University of New York at Albany. Previously, he was an analyst at the Office of Community Oriented Policing Services, U.S. Department of Justice, and Assistant Professor at Florida State University and Seattle University. His research interests include policing, theoretical criminology, and applied statistical models.

Jane P. White is Associate Director of the National Center for Community Policing for the School of Criminal Justice at Michigan State University. She has worked nationally as a consultant to numerous police agencies on reorganization as it relates to community policing. She was formerly Director of the Criminal Justice and Law Center at Lansing Community College, where she also headed the Mid-Michigan Police Academy,

James J. Willis is Assistant Professor of Sociology at the University of Massachusetts, Boston. His research interests are police behavior and policy, and the relationship between culture, punishment, and the state. Along with several colleagues, he is currently conducting research on computer-assisted statistical analysis. In addition, he continues to investigate the transportation of British convicts to America and Australia in the 18th and 19th centuries.